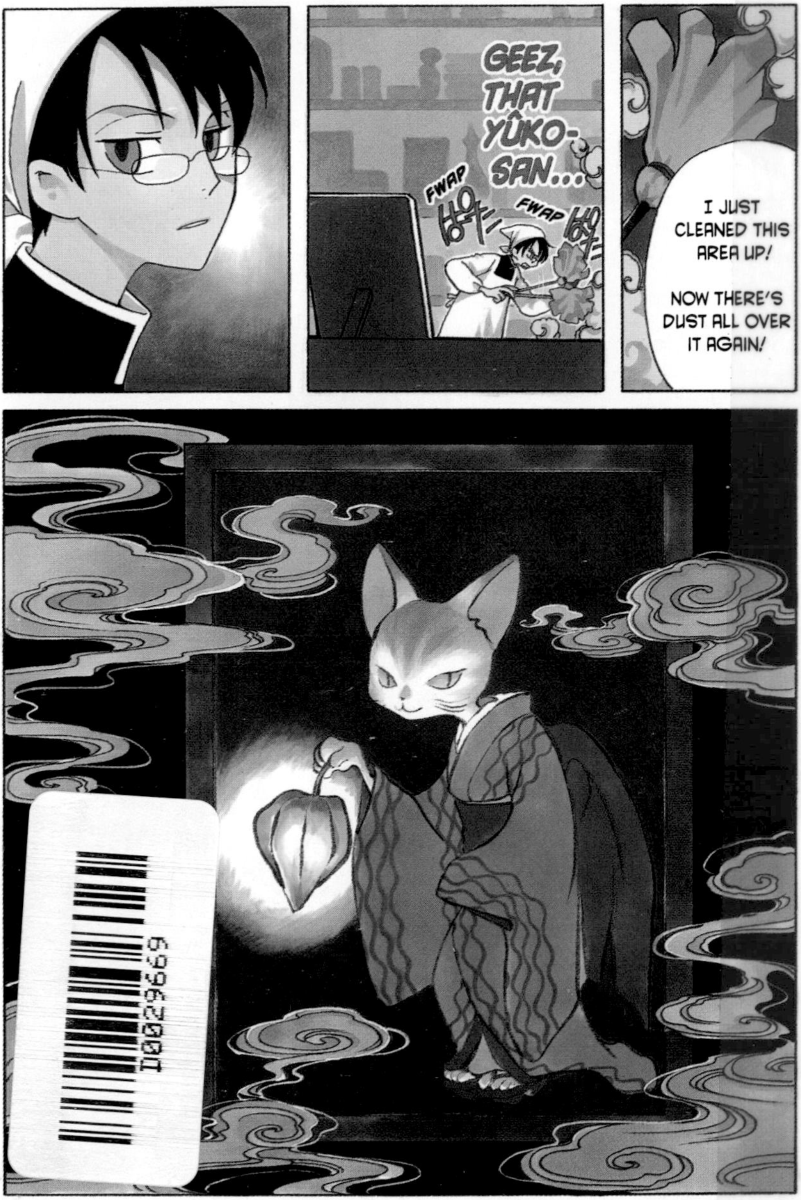
I JUST CLEANED THIS AREA UP!
NOW THERE'S DUST ALL OVER IT AGAIN!
GEEZ, THAT YÛKO-SAN...
FWAP
FWAP

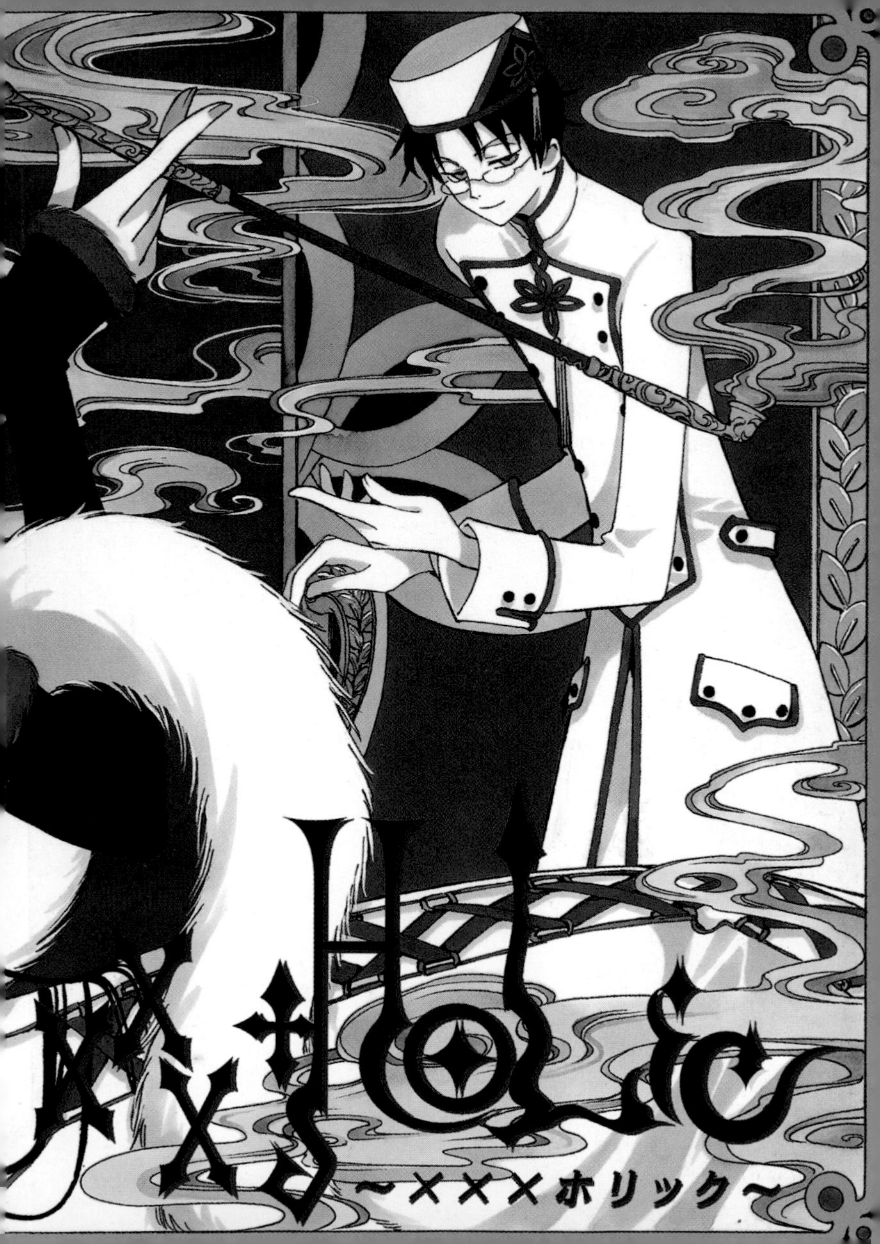
xxxHOLiC
~×××ホリック~

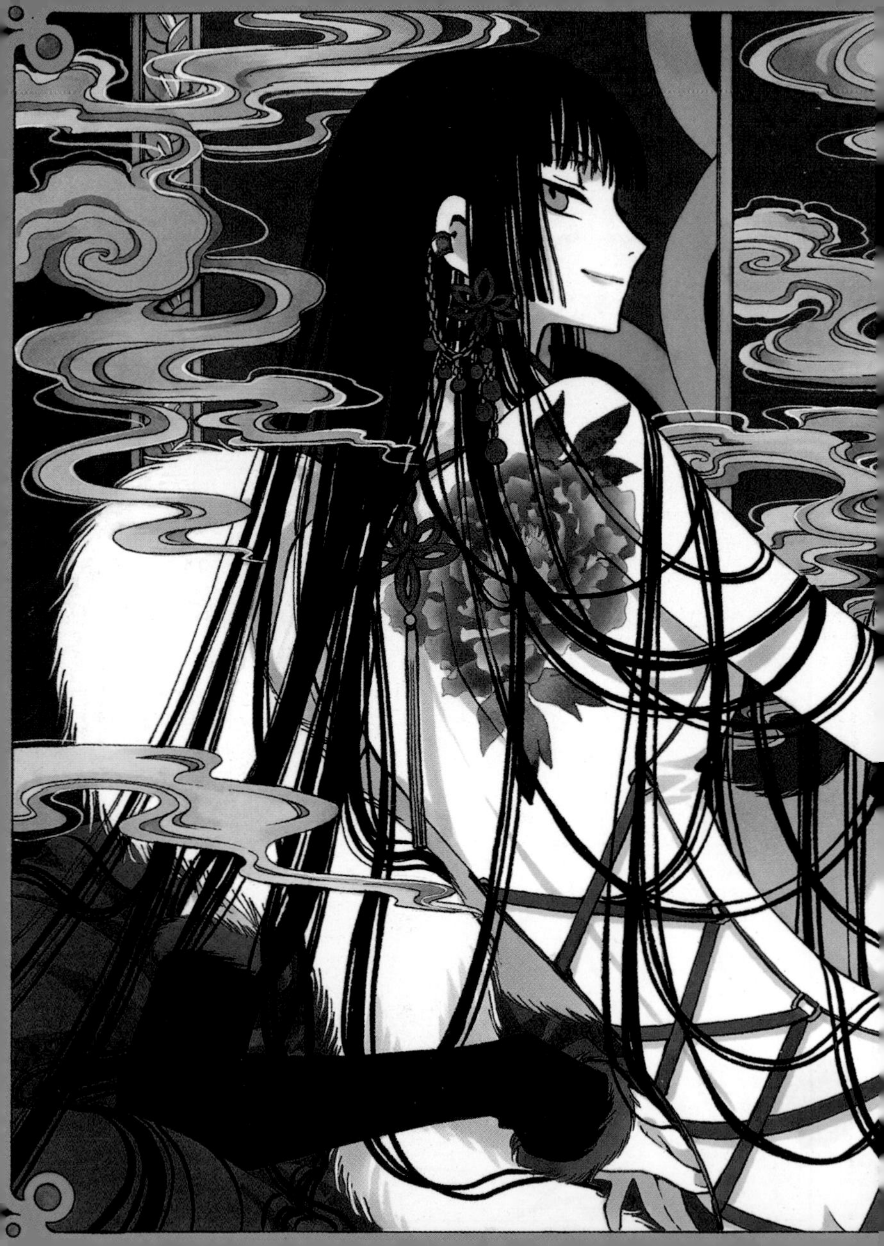

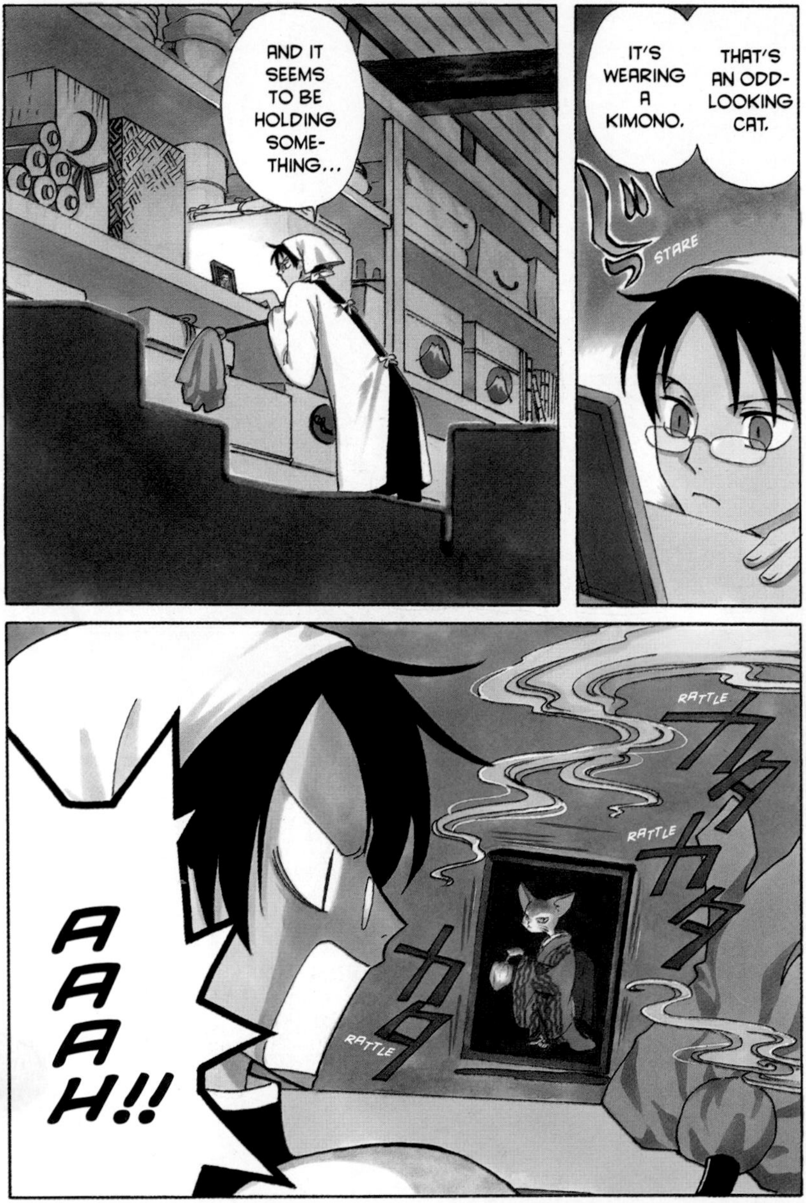
THAT'S AN ODD-LOOKING CAT.
IT'S WEARING A KIMONO.
STARE
AND IT SEEMS TO BE HOLDING SOME-THING...
RATTLE
RATTLE
RATTLE
カタカタカタ
AAAAH!!

6

CLAMP

TRANSLATED AND ADAPTED BY
William Flanagan

LETTERED BY
Dana Hayward

DEL
REY

BALLANTINE BOOKS • NEW YORK

xxxHOLiC, Volume 6 is a work of fiction. Names, characters, places, and incidents are the products of the author's imagination or are used fictitiously. Any resemblance to actual events, locales, or persons, living or dead, is entirely coincidental.

2005 Del Rey® Trade Paperback Edition

Published in the United States by Del Rey Books, an imprint of The Random House Publishing Group, a division of Random House, Inc., New York.

First published in serialization and subsequently published in book form by Kodansha Ltd., Tokyo in 2004, copyright © 2004 CLAMP.

ISBN 0-345-47790-1

Printed in the United States of America

www.delreymanga.com

9 8 7 6 5 4 3 2 1

Translator and Adaptor—William Flanagan
Lettering—Dana Hayward
Cover Design—David Stevenson

xxxHOLiC crosses over with *Tsubasa*. Although it isn't necessary to read *Tsubasa* to understand the events in *xxxHOLiC*, you'll get to see the same events from different perspectives if you read both series!

Contents

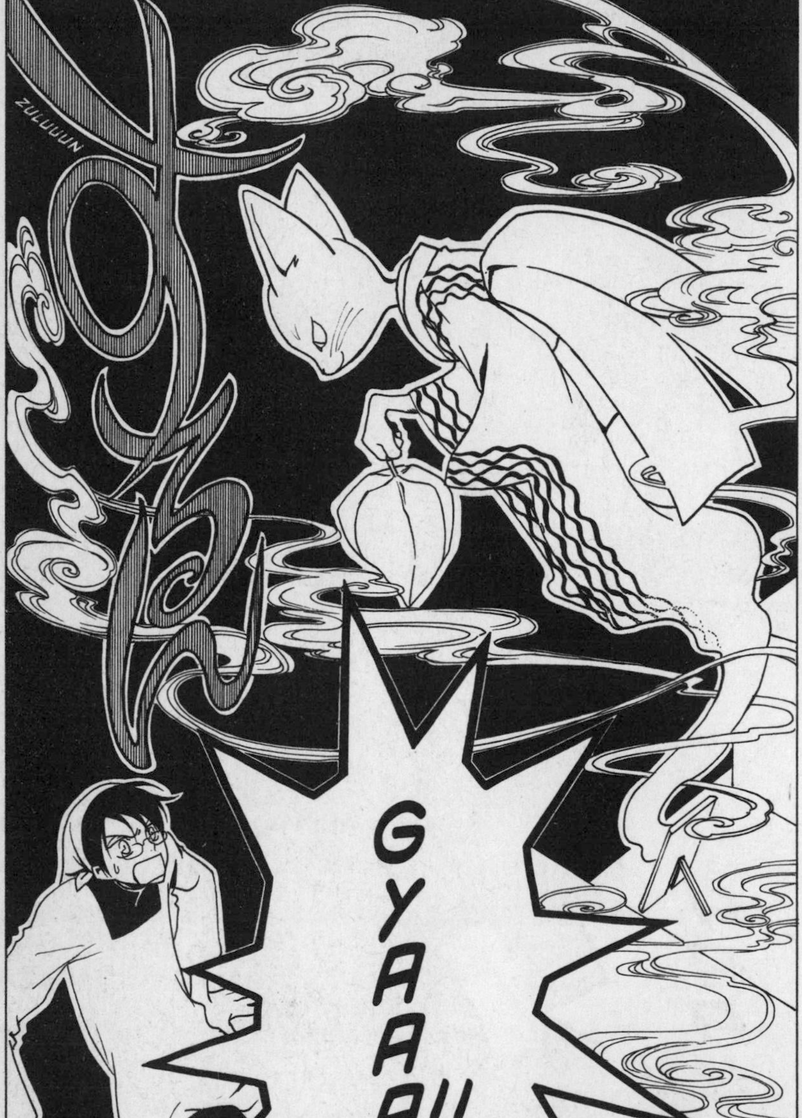
ZULUUUN
GYAAAA!!

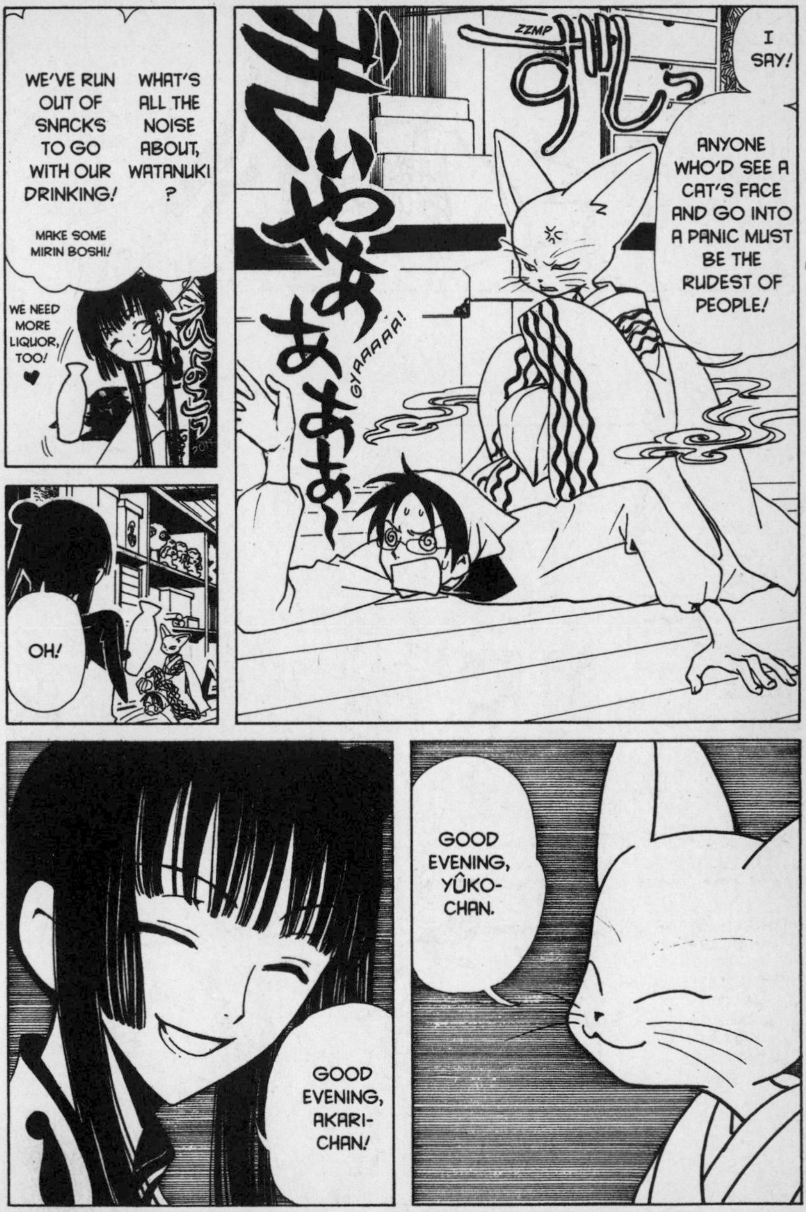
ZZMP
I SAY!
ANYONE WHO'D SEE A CAT'S FACE AND GO INTO A PANIC MUST BE THE RUDEST OF PEOPLE!
GYAAAAA!
WHAT'S ALL THE NOISE ABOUT, WATANUKI?
WE'VE RUN OUT OF SNACKS TO GO WITH OUR DRINKING!
MAKE SOME MIRIN BOSHI!
WE NEED MORE LIQUOR, TOO! ♥
OH!
GOOD EVENING, YÛKO-CHAN.
GOOD EVENING, AKARI-CHAN!

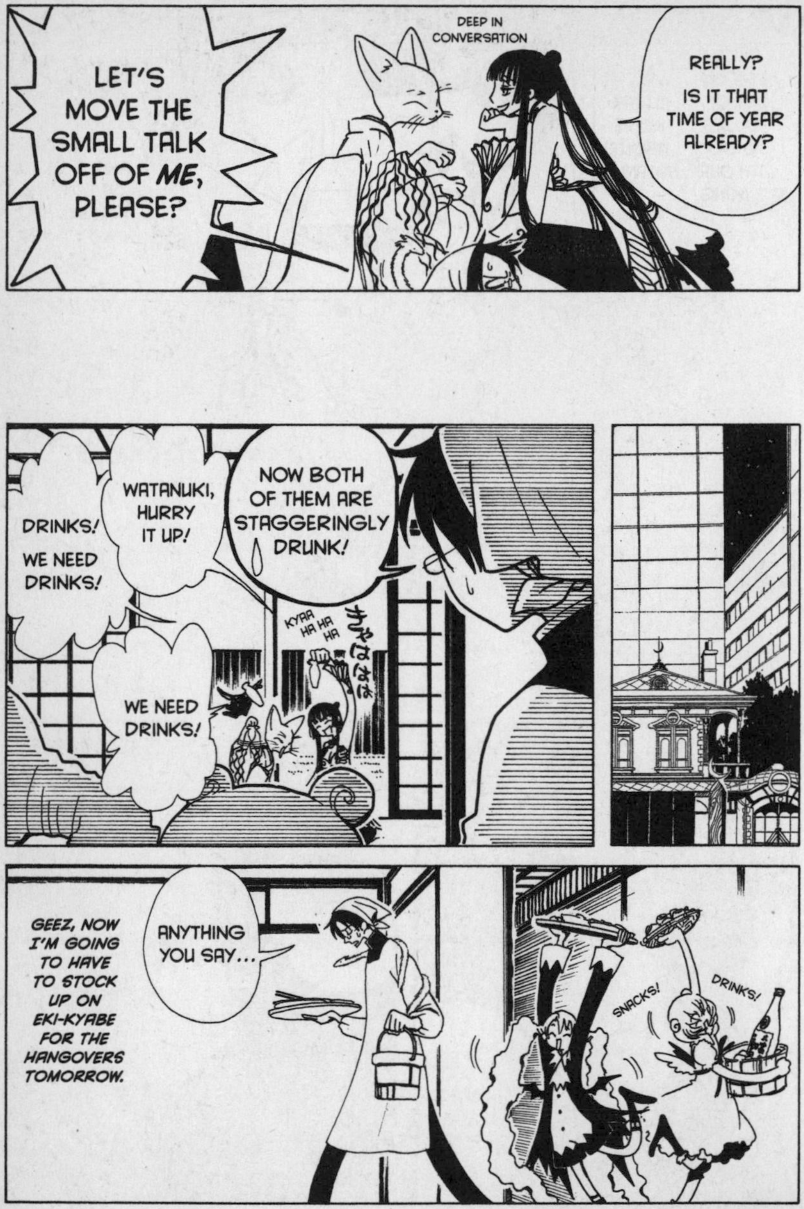
REALLY?
IS IT THAT TIME OF YEAR ALREADY?
DEEP IN CONVERSATION
LET'S MOVE THE SMALL TALK OFF OF *ME*, PLEASE?
NOW BOTH OF THEM ARE STAGGERINGLY DRUNK!
WATANUKI, HURRY IT UP!
DRINKS!
WE NEED DRINKS!
きゃははは
KYAA HA HA HA
WE NEED DRINKS!
DRINKS!
SNACKS!
ANYTHING YOU SAY...
GEEZ, NOW I'M GOING TO HAVE TO STOCK UP ON EKI-KYABE FOR THE HANGOVERS TOMORROW.

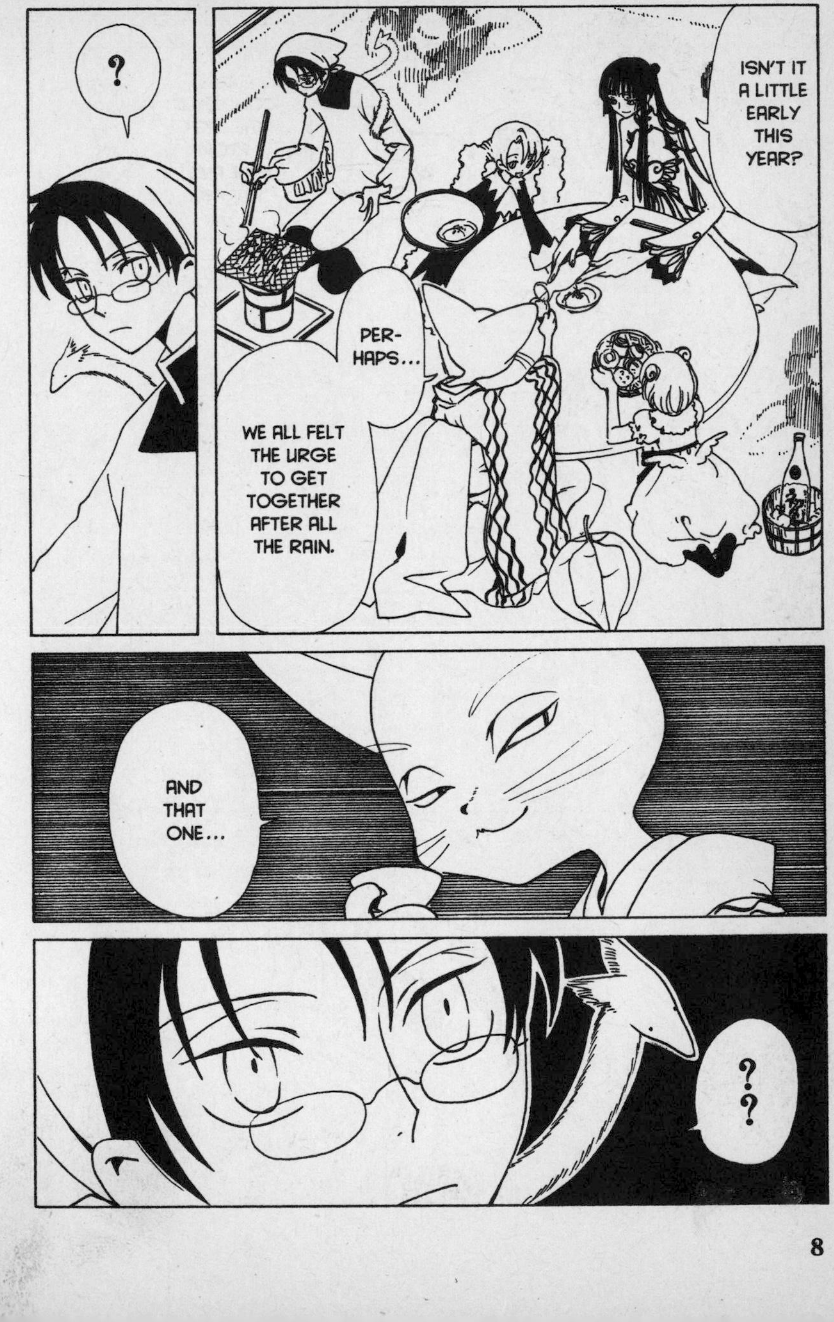
ISN'T IT A LITTLE EARLY THIS YEAR?
PER-HAPS...
WE ALL FELT THE URGE TO GET TOGETHER AFTER ALL THE RAIN.
?
AND THAT ONE...
??

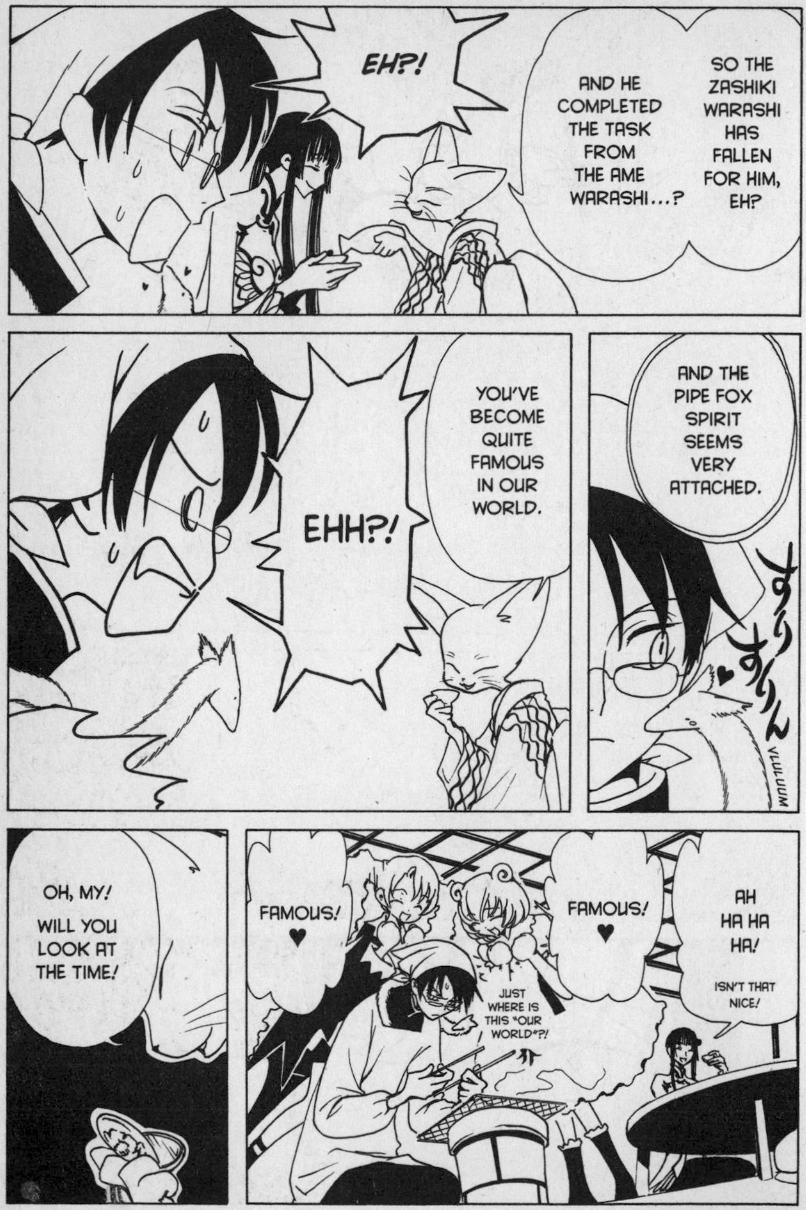
SO THE ZASHIKI WARASHI HAS FALLEN FOR HIM, EH?
AND HE COMPLETED THE TASK FROM THE AME WARASHI...?
EH?!
AND THE PIPE FOX SPIRIT SEEMS VERY ATTACHED.
すりすりん
VLULUUM
YOU'VE BECOME QUITE FAMOUS IN OUR WORLD.
EHH?!
AH HA HA HA!
ISN'T THAT NICE!
FAMOUS! ♥
FAMOUS! ♥
JUST WHERE IS THIS "OUR WORLD"?!
OH, MY! WILL YOU LOOK AT THE TIME!

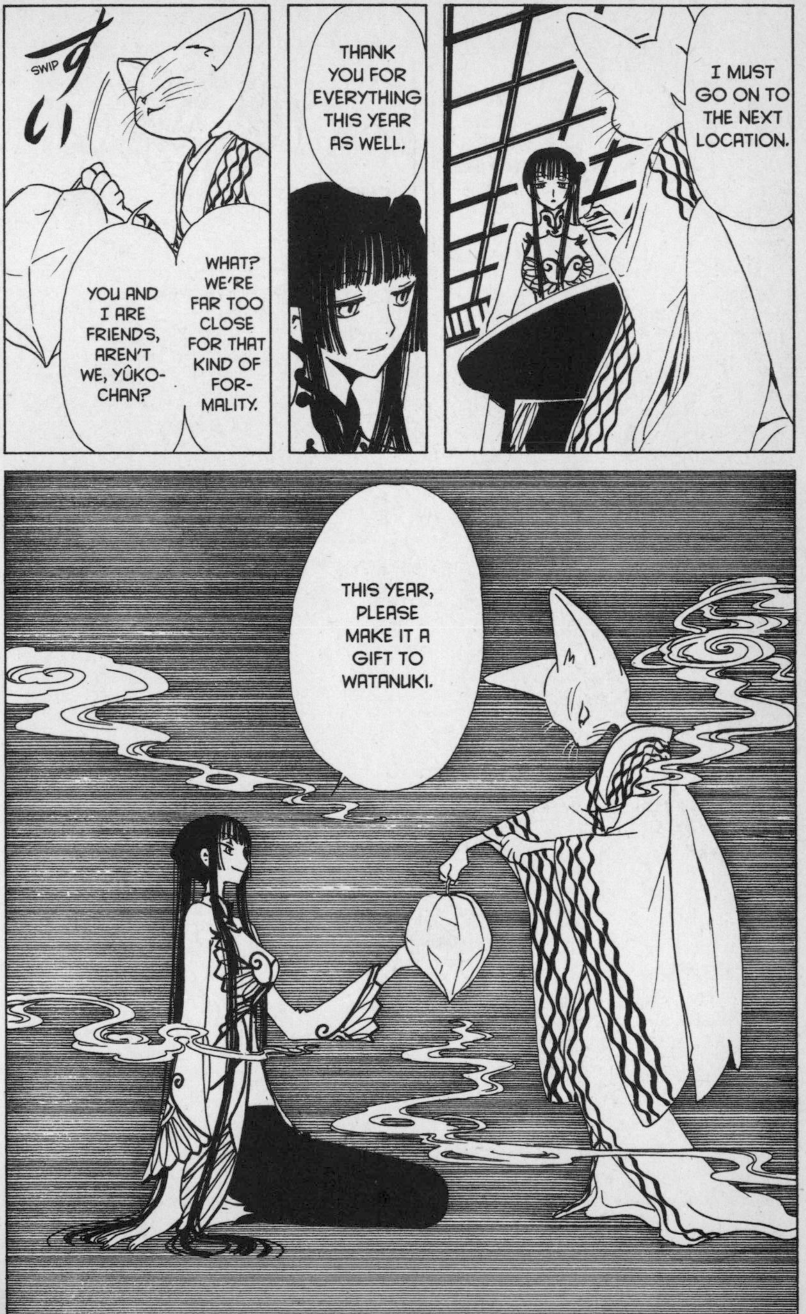
I MUST GO ON TO THE NEXT LOCATION.
THANK YOU FOR EVERYTHING THIS YEAR AS WELL.
すい
SWIP
WHAT? WE'RE FAR TOO CLOSE FOR THAT KIND OF FOR-MALITY.
YOU AND I ARE FRIENDS, AREN'T WE, YÛKO-CHAN?
THIS YEAR, PLEASE MAKE IT A GIFT TO WATANUKI.

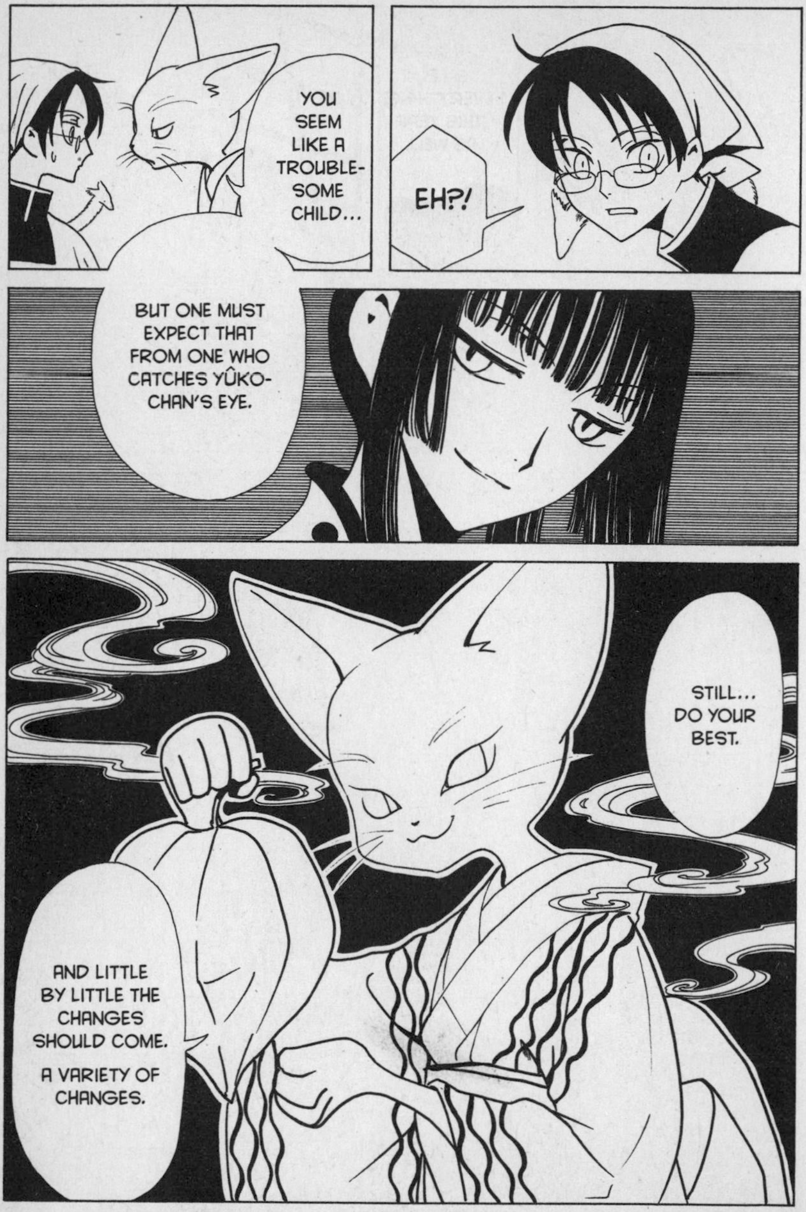
EH?!
YOU SEEM LIKE A TROUBLE-SOME CHILD...
BUT ONE MUST EXPECT THAT FROM ONE WHO CATCHES YÛKO-CHAN'S EYE.
STILL... DO YOUR BEST.
AND LITTLE BY LITTLE THE CHANGES SHOULD COME.
A VARIETY OF CHANGES.

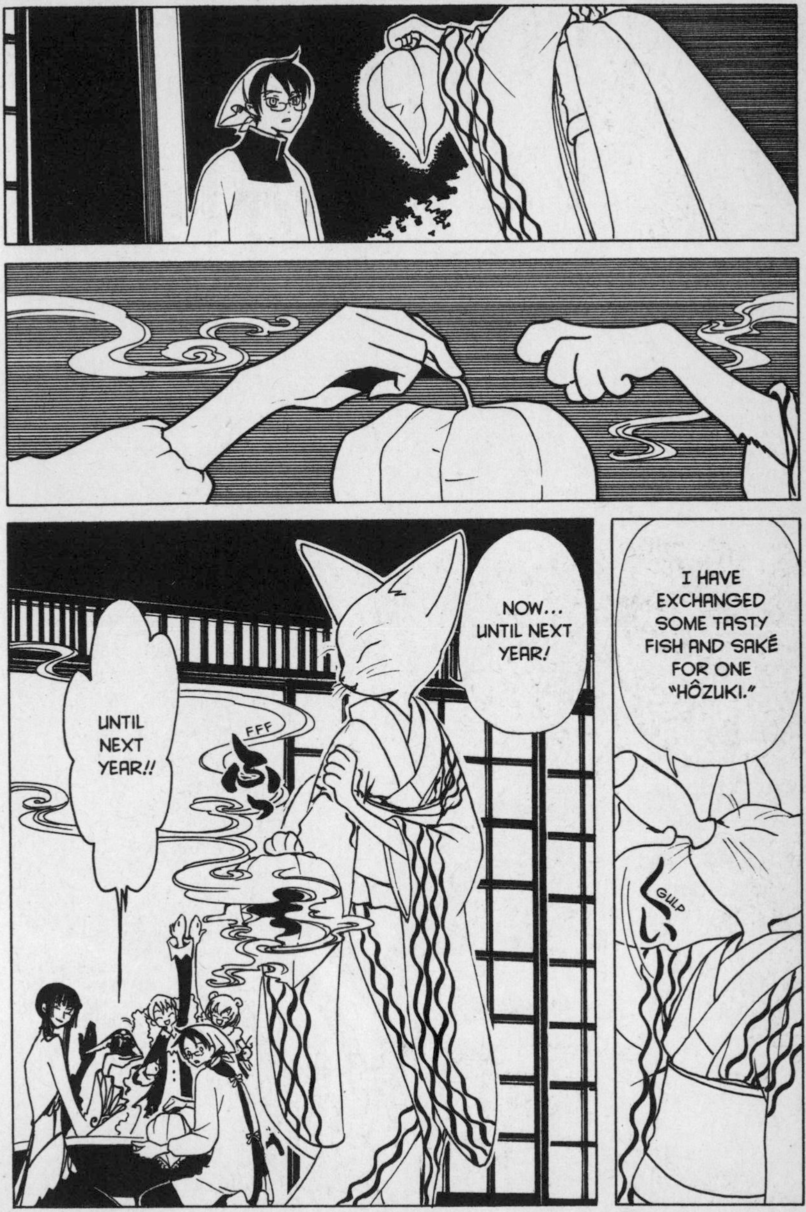
I HAVE EXCHANGED SOME TASTY FISH AND SAKÉ FOR ONE "HÔZUKI."
GULP
NOW... UNTIL NEXT YEAR!
FFF
UNTIL NEXT YEAR!!

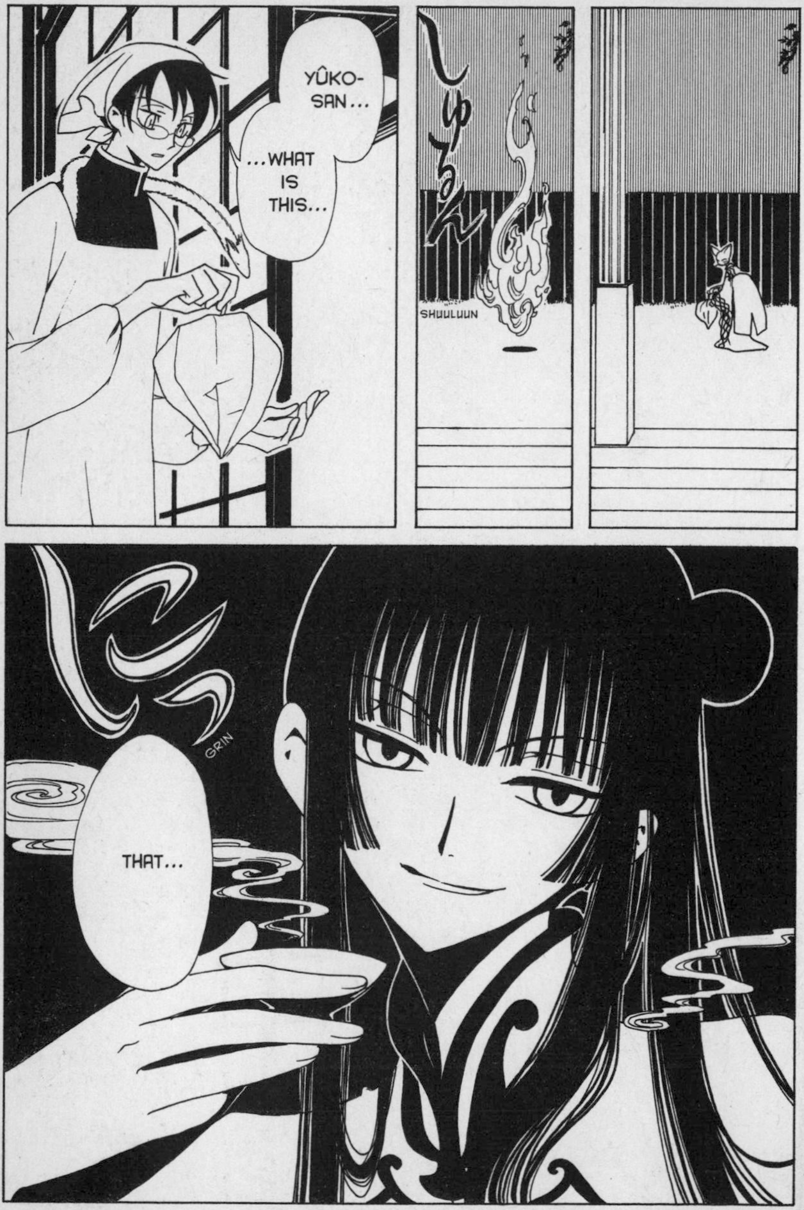
しゅるん
SHUULUUN
YÛKO-SAN...
...WHAT IS THIS...
GRIN
THAT...

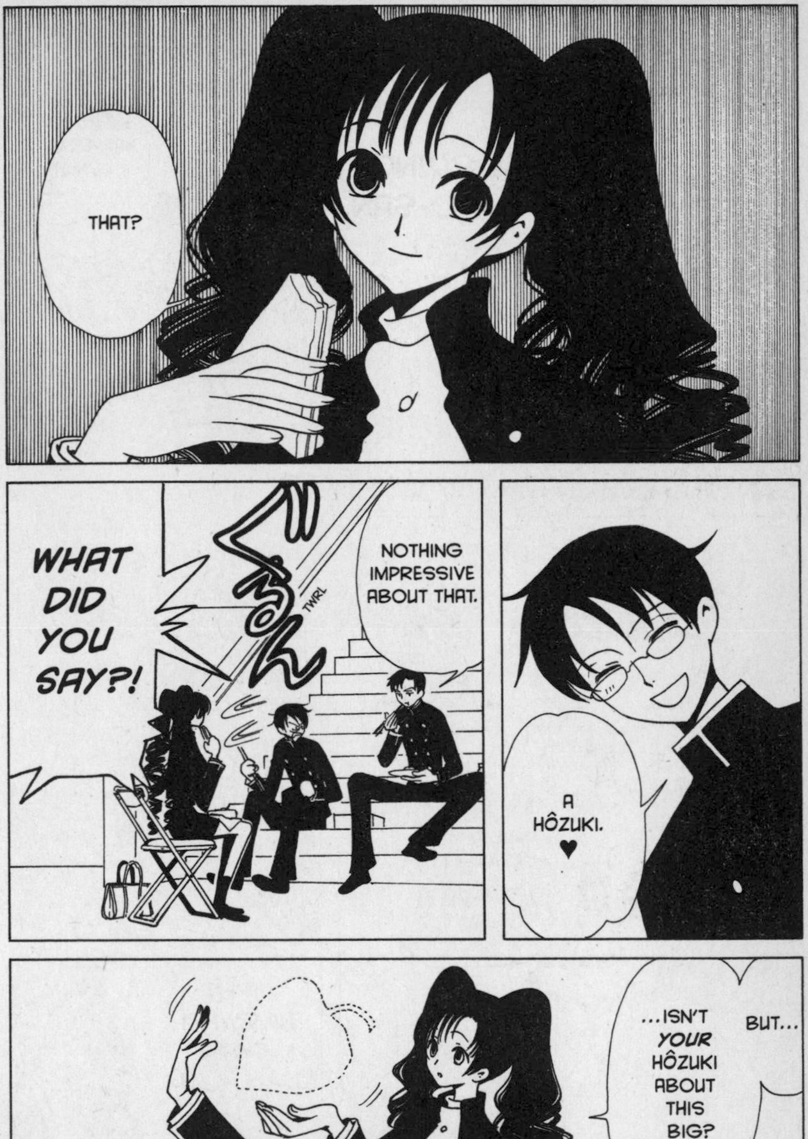
THAT?
A HÔZUKI. ♥
NOTHING IMPRESSIVE ABOUT THAT.
TWRL
WHAT DID YOU SAY?!
BUT...
...ISN'T YOUR HÔZUKI ABOUT THIS BIG?

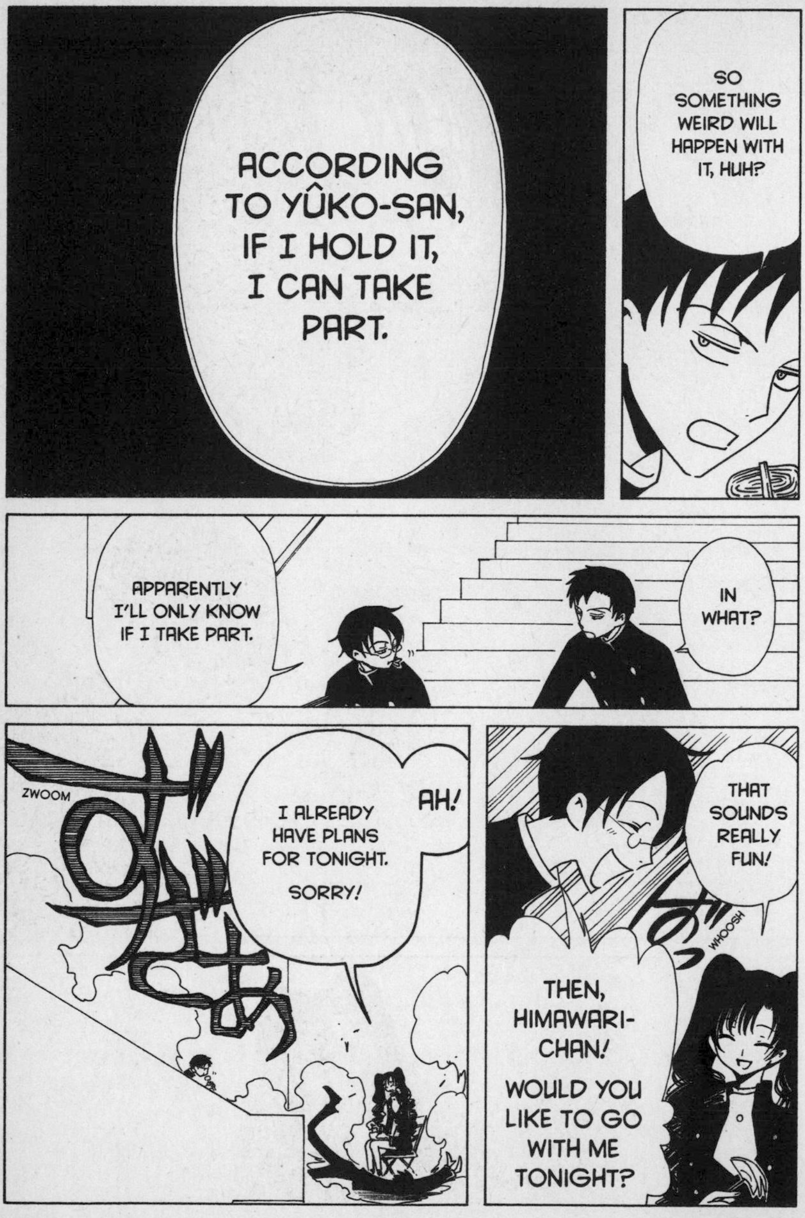
SO SOMETHING WEIRD WILL HAPPEN WITH IT, HUH?
ACCORDING TO YÛKO-SAN, IF I HOLD IT, I CAN TAKE PART.
IN WHAT?
APPARENTLY I'LL ONLY KNOW IF I TAKE PART.
THAT SOUNDS REALLY FUN!
WHOOSH
THEN, HIMAWARI-CHAN! WOULD YOU LIKE TO GO WITH ME TONIGHT?
AH!
I ALREADY HAVE PLANS FOR TONIGHT. SORRY!
ZWOOM

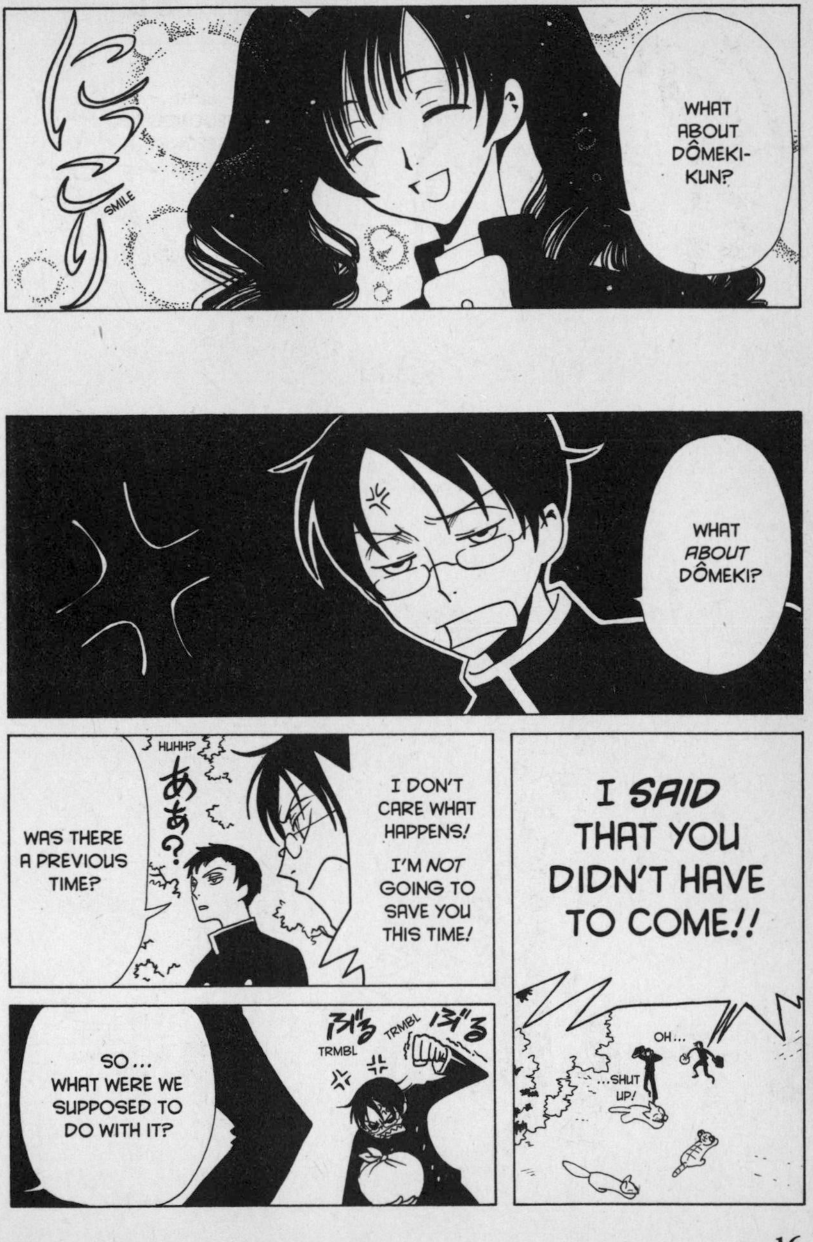
WHAT ABOUT DÔMEKI-KUN?
にっこり
SMILE
WHAT ABOUT DÔMEKI?
I SAID THAT YOU DIDN'T HAVE TO COME!!
OH...
...SHUT UP!
I DON'T CARE WHAT HAPPENS!
I'M NOT GOING TO SAVE YOU THIS TIME!
ああ?
HUHH?
WAS THERE A PREVIOUS TIME?
ぶる
TRMBL
ぶる
TRMBL
SO... WHAT WERE WE SUPPOSED TO DO WITH IT?

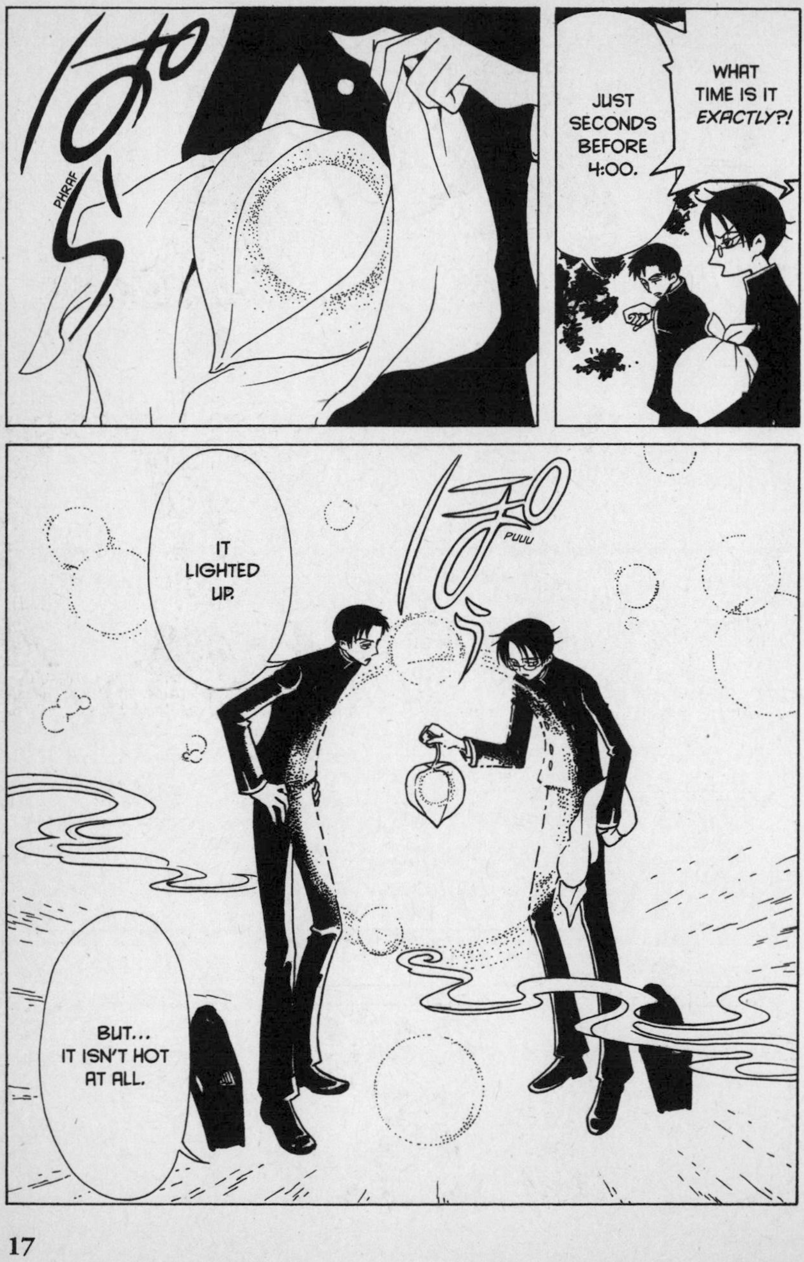
WHAT TIME IS IT *EXACTLY?!*
JUST SECONDS BEFORE 4:00.
PHRAF
PUUU
IT LIGHTED UP.
BUT... IT ISN'T HOT AT ALL.

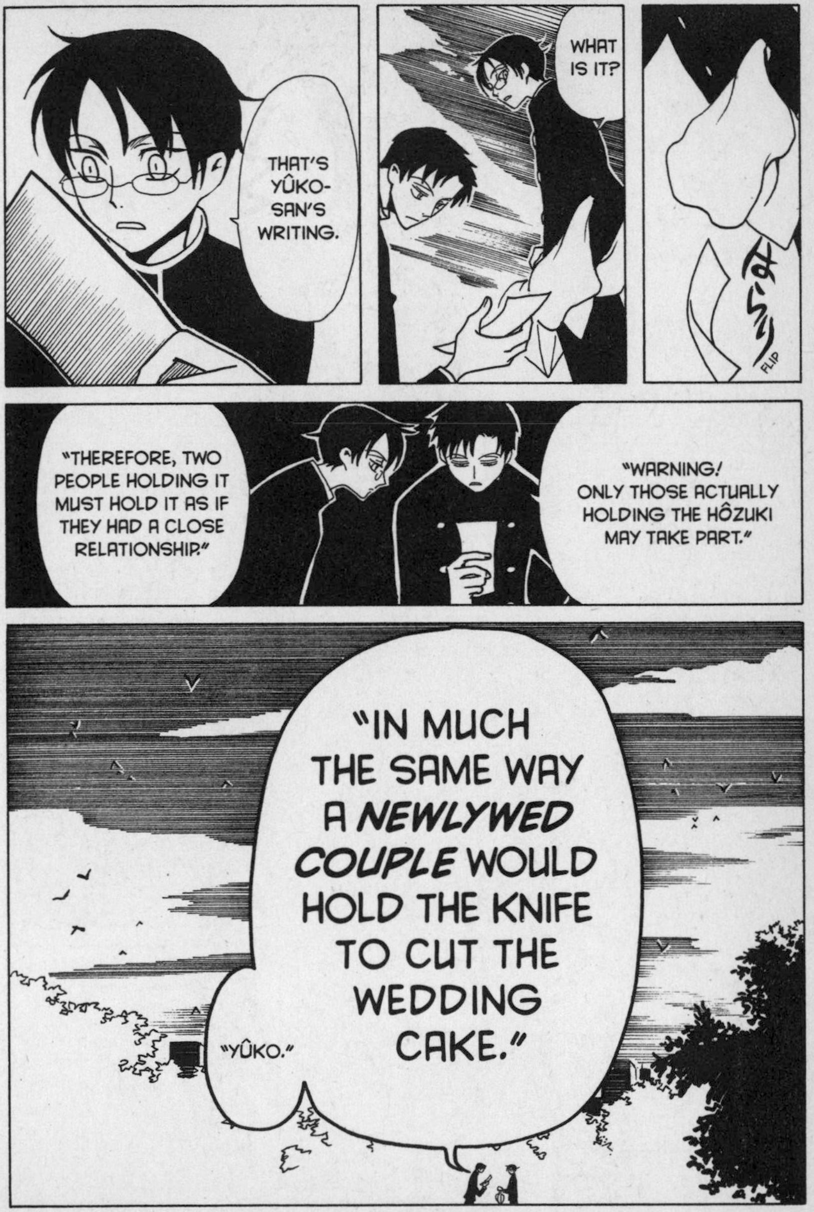
はらり
FLIP
WHAT IS IT?
THAT'S YÛKO-SAN'S WRITING.
"WARNING! ONLY THOSE ACTUALLY HOLDING THE HÔZUKI MAY TAKE PART."
"THEREFORE, TWO PEOPLE HOLDING IT MUST HOLD IT AS IF THEY HAD A CLOSE RELATIONSHIP."
"IN MUCH THE SAME WAY A NEWLYWED COUPLE WOULD HOLD THE KNIFE TO CUT THE WEDDING CAKE."
"YÛKO."

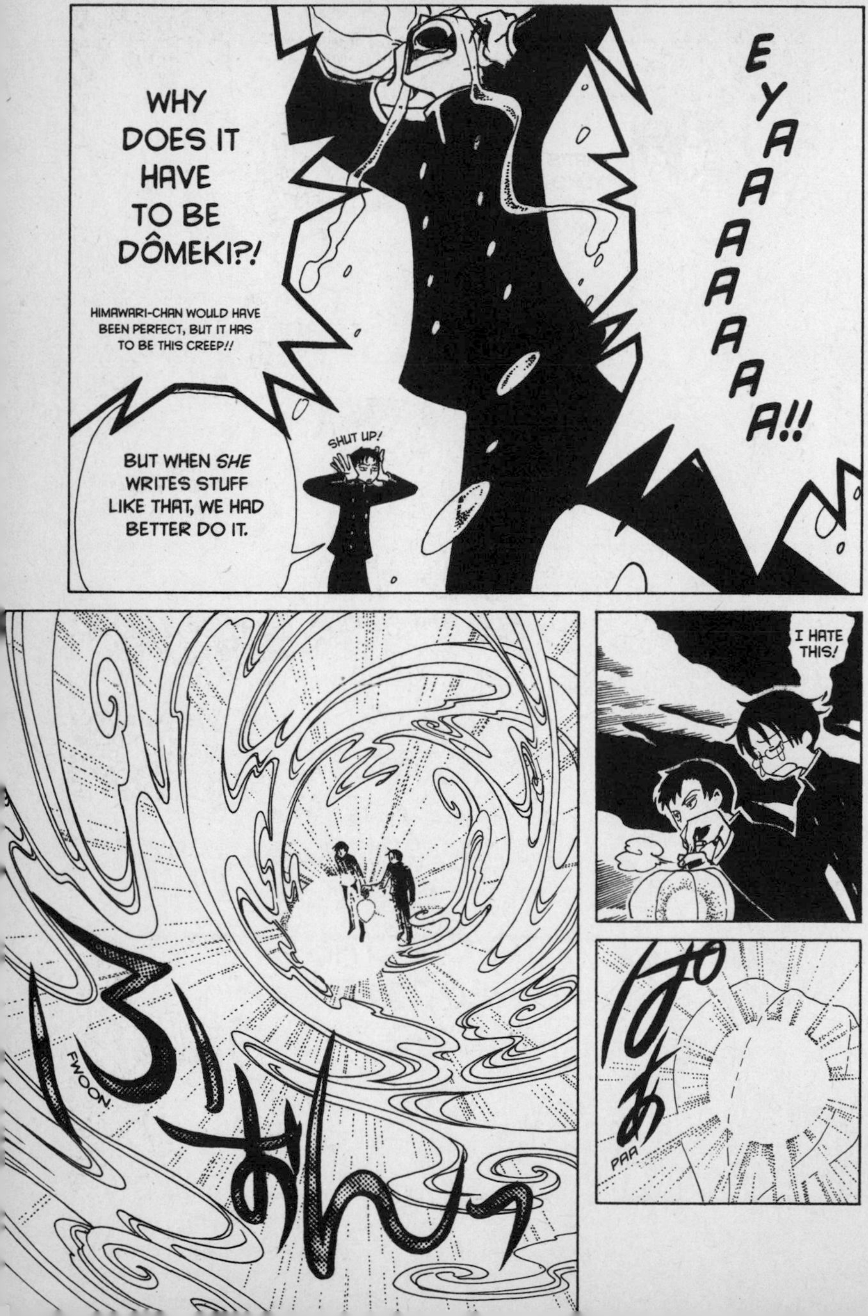
EYAAAAAAA!!
WHY DOES IT HAVE TO BE DÔMEKI?!
HIMAWARI-CHAN WOULD HAVE BEEN PERFECT, BUT IT HAS TO BE THIS CREEP!!
SHUT UP!
BUT WHEN SHE WRITES STUFF LIKE THAT, WE HAD BETTER DO IT.
I HATE THIS!
PAA
FWOON

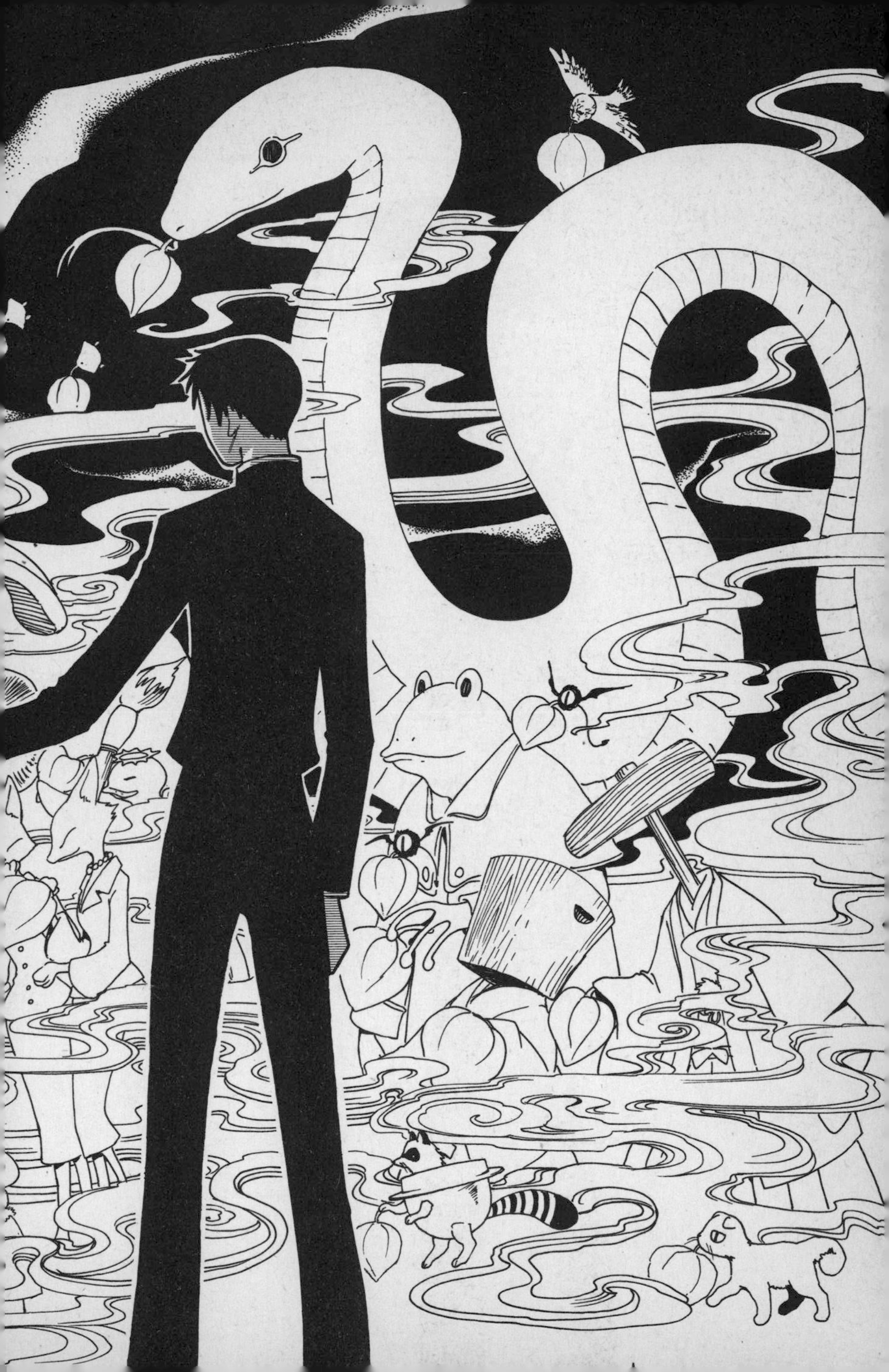

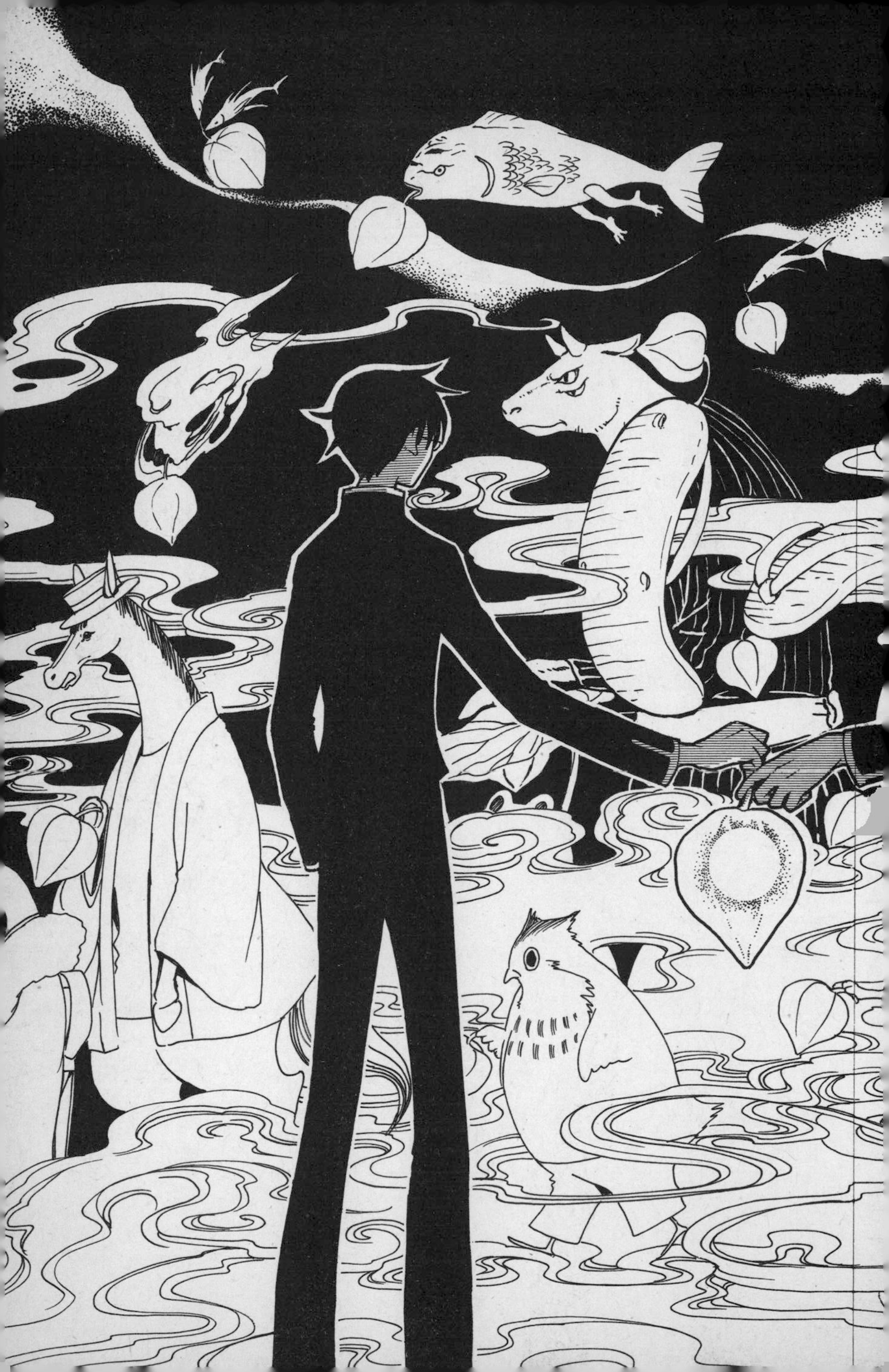

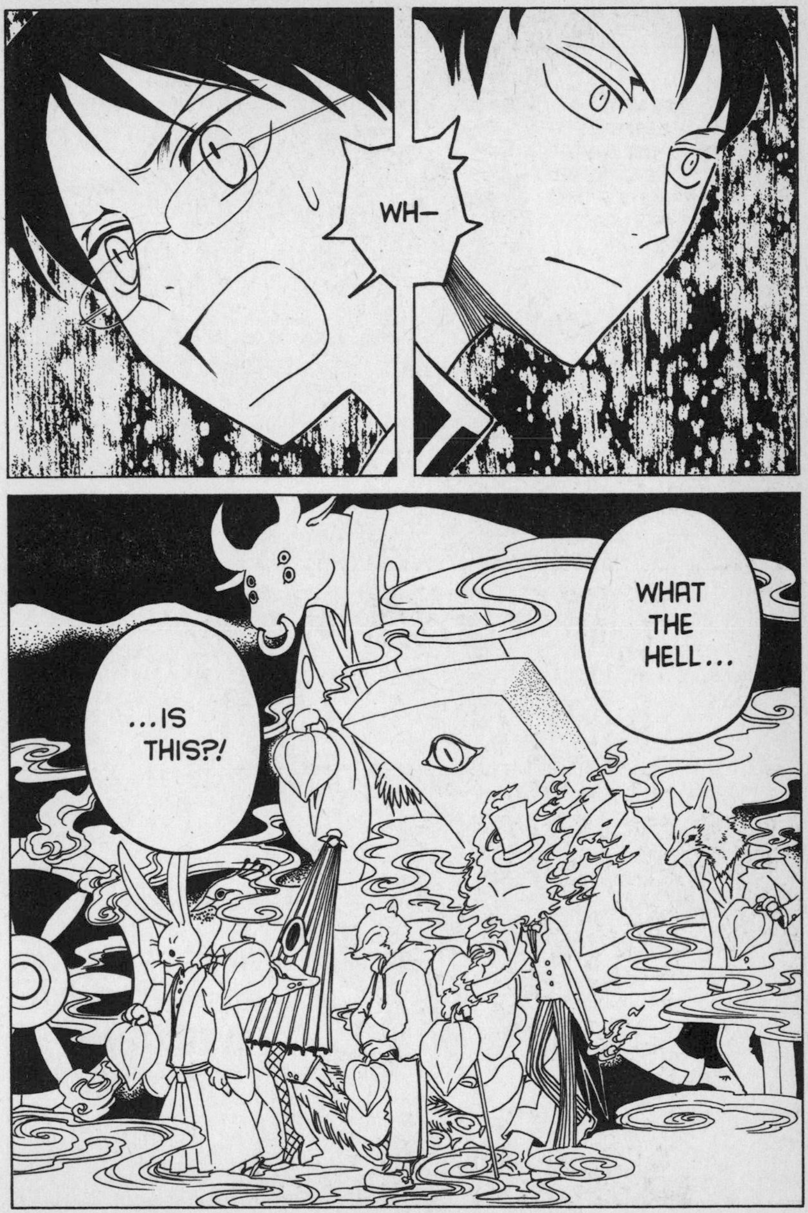
WH–
WHAT THE HELL...
...IS THIS?!

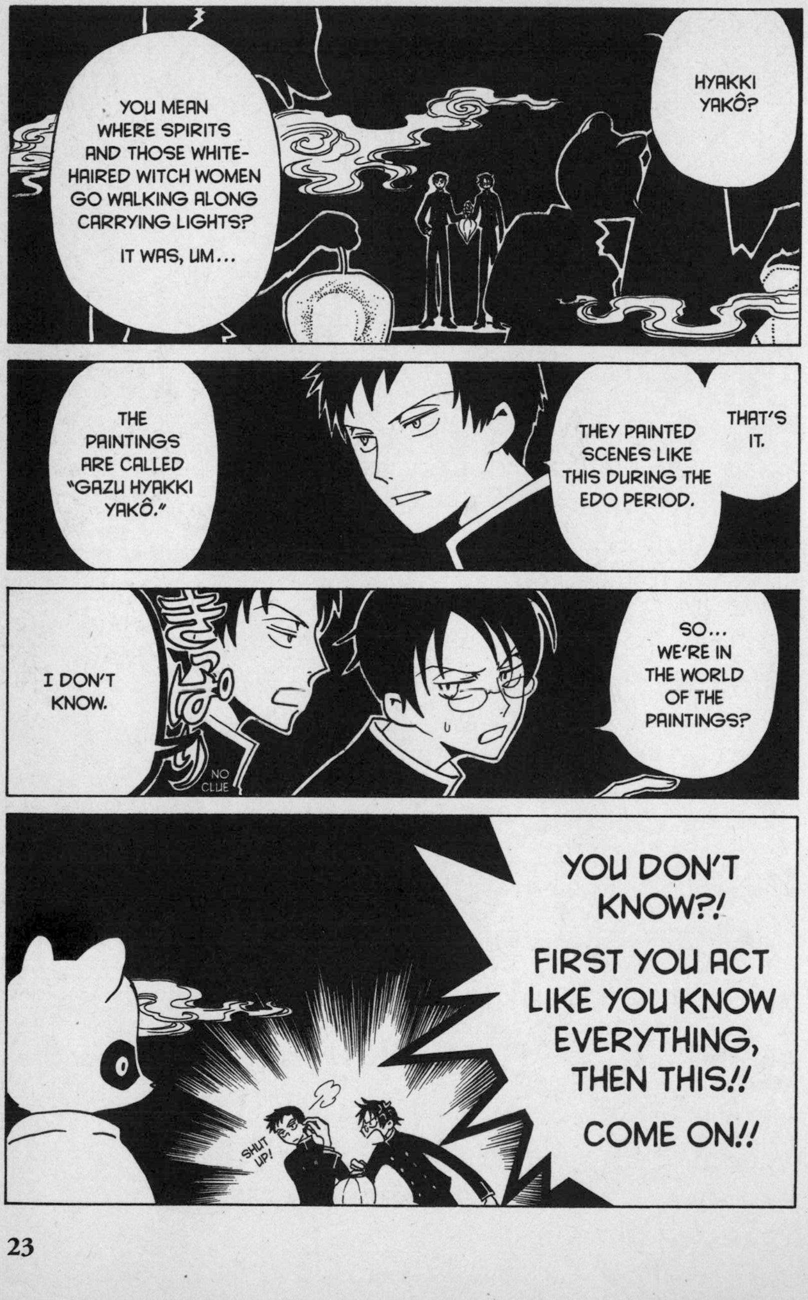
HYAKKI YAKÔ?
YOU MEAN WHERE SPIRITS AND THOSE WHITE-HAIRED WITCH WOMEN GO WALKING ALONG CARRYING LIGHTS?
IT WAS, UM...
THAT'S IT.
THEY PAINTED SCENES LIKE THIS DURING THE EDO PERIOD.
THE PAINTINGS ARE CALLED "GAZU HYAKKI YAKÔ."
SO... WE'RE IN THE WORLD OF THE PAINTINGS?
I DON'T KNOW.
NO CLUE
YOU DON'T KNOW?!
FIRST YOU ACT LIKE YOU KNOW EVERYTHING, THEN THIS!!
COME ON!!
SHUT UP!

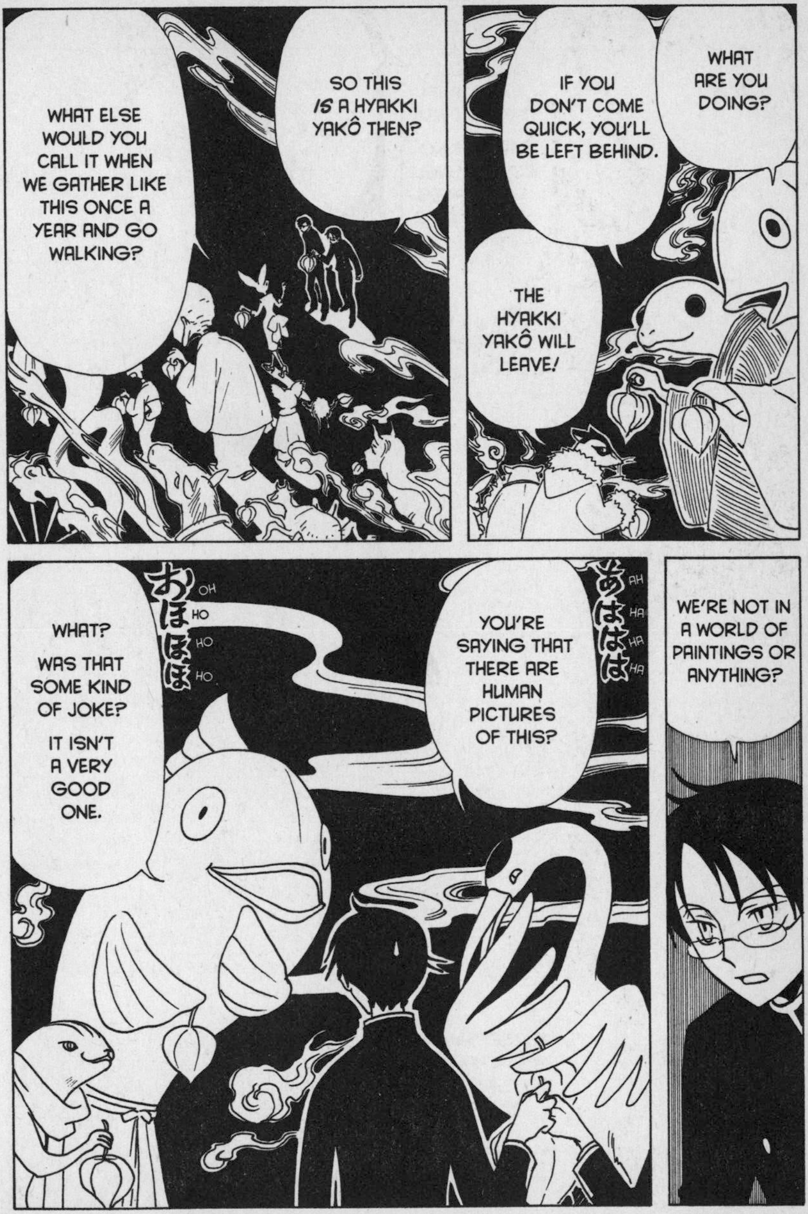
WHAT ARE YOU DOING?
IF YOU DON'T COME QUICK, YOU'LL BE LEFT BEHIND.
THE HYAKKI YAKÔ WILL LEAVE!
SO THIS *IS* A HYAKKI YAKÔ THEN?
WHAT ELSE WOULD YOU CALL IT WHEN WE GATHER LIKE THIS ONCE A YEAR AND GO WALKING?
WE'RE NOT IN A WORLD OF PAINTINGS OR ANYTHING?
あははは AH HA HA HA
YOU'RE SAYING THAT THERE ARE HUMAN PICTURES OF THIS?
おほほほ OH HO HO HO
WHAT?
WAS THAT SOME KIND OF JOKE?
IT ISN'T A VERY GOOD ONE.

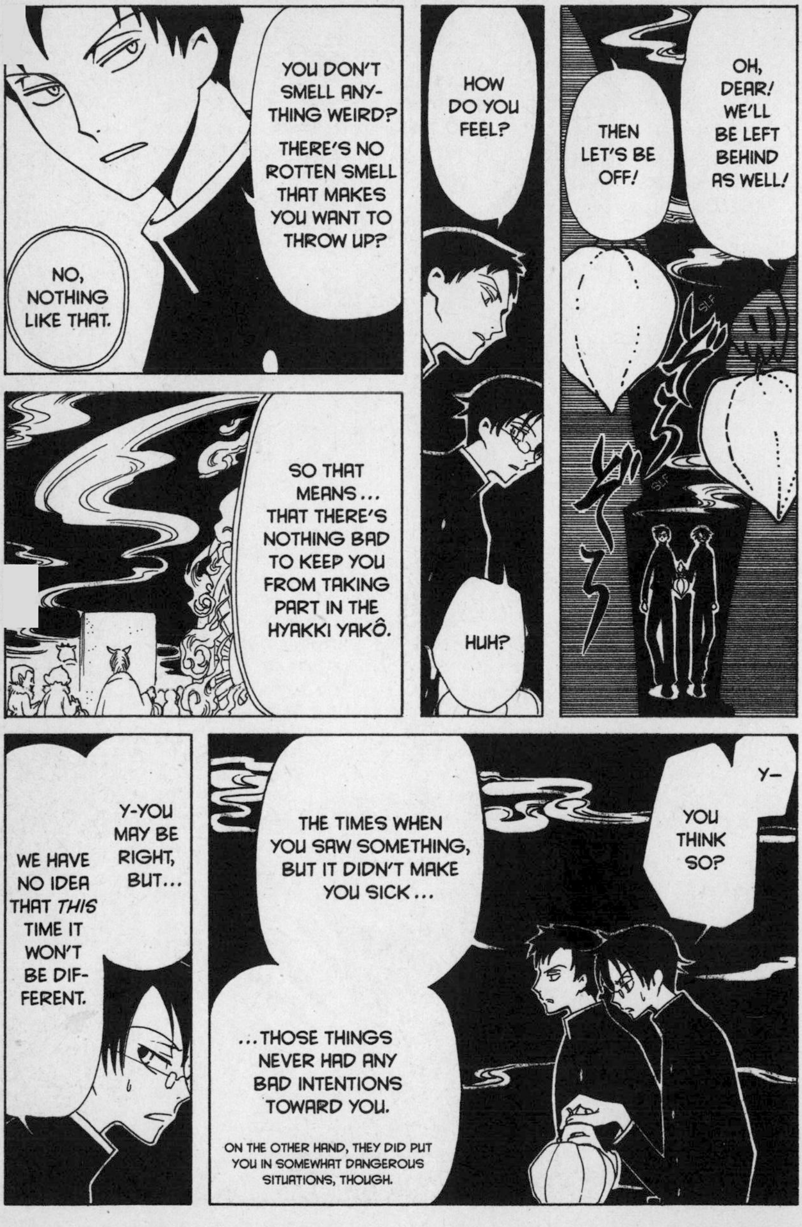
OH, DEAR! WE'LL BE LEFT BEHIND AS WELL!
THEN LET'S BE OFF!
SLF
SLF
HOW DO YOU FEEL?
HUH?
YOU DON'T SMELL ANYTHING WEIRD?
THERE'S NO ROTTEN SMELL THAT MAKES YOU WANT TO THROW UP?
NO, NOTHING LIKE THAT.
SO THAT MEANS... THAT THERE'S NOTHING BAD TO KEEP YOU FROM TAKING PART IN THE HYAKKI YAKÔ.
Y-
YOU THINK SO?
THE TIMES WHEN YOU SAW SOMETHING, BUT IT DIDN'T MAKE YOU SICK...
...THOSE THINGS NEVER HAD ANY BAD INTENTIONS TOWARD YOU.
ON THE OTHER HAND, THEY DID PUT YOU IN SOMEWHAT DANGEROUS SITUATIONS, THOUGH.
Y-YOU MAY BE RIGHT, BUT...
WE HAVE NO IDEA THAT *THIS* TIME IT WON'T BE DIFFERENT.

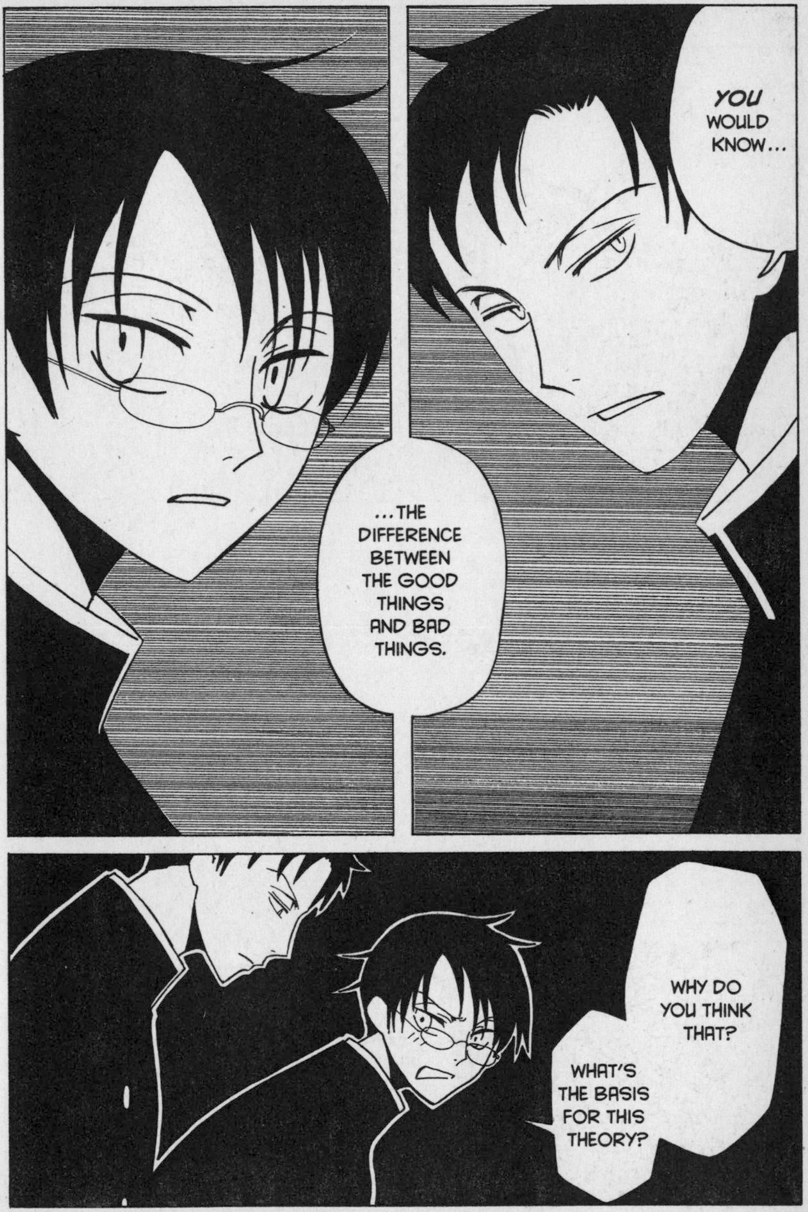
YOU WOULD KNOW...
...THE DIFFERENCE BETWEEN THE GOOD THINGS AND BAD THINGS.
WHY DO YOU THINK THAT?
WHAT'S THE BASIS FOR THIS THEORY?

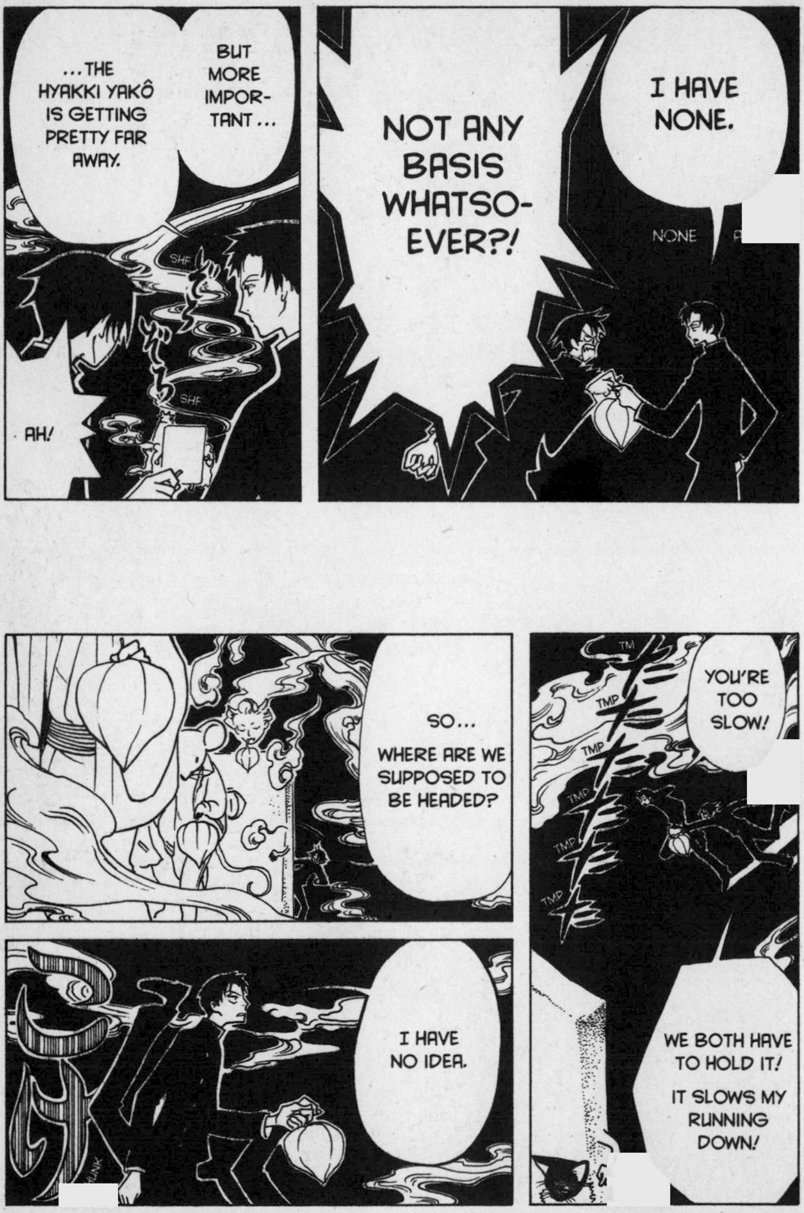
I HAVE NONE.
NOT ANY BASIS WHATSO- EVER?!
NONE
BUT MORE IMPOR- TANT...
...THE HYAKKI YAKÔ IS GETTING PRETTY FAR AWAY.
SHF
SHF
AH!
YOU'RE TOO SLOW!
TM
TMP
TMP
TMP
TMP
TMP
WE BOTH HAVE TO HOLD IT!
IT SLOWS MY RUNNING DOWN!
SO... WHERE ARE WE SUPPOSED TO BE HEADED?
I HAVE NO IDEA.

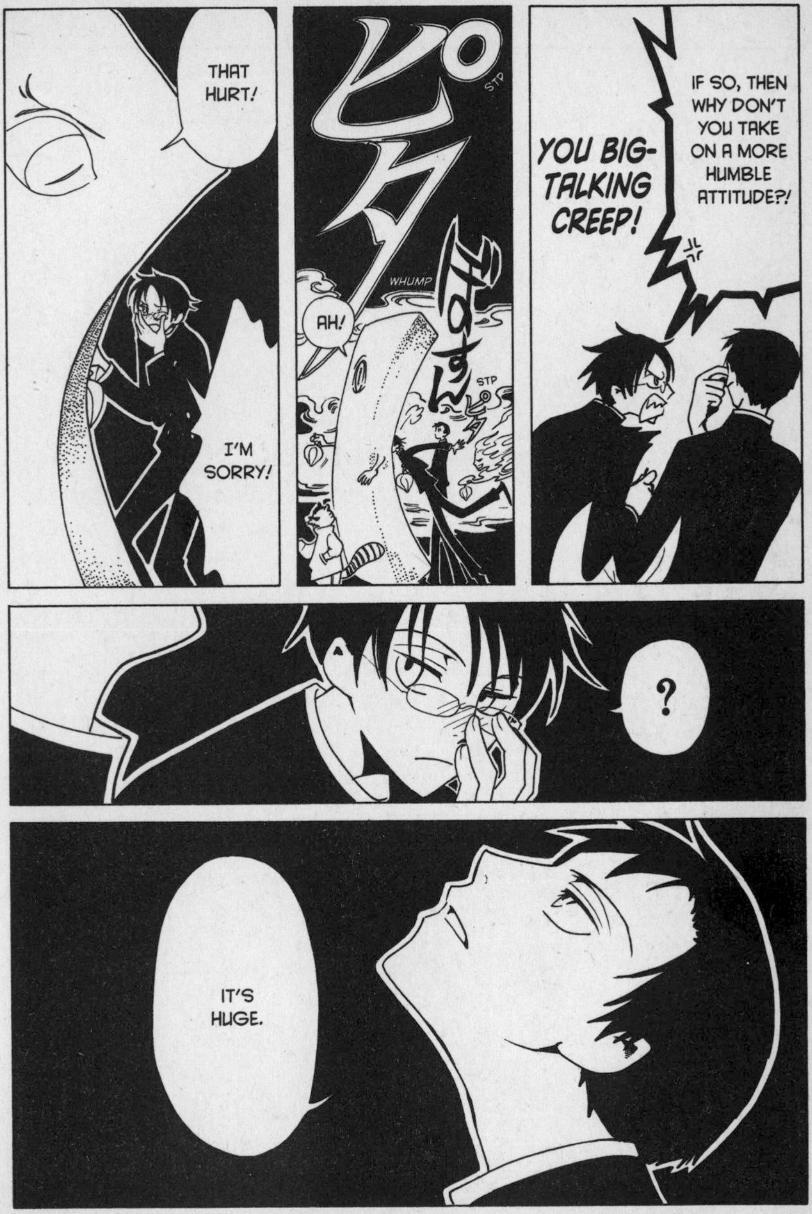
IF SO, THEN WHY DON'T YOU TAKE ON A MORE HUMBLE ATTITUDE?!
YOU BIG-TALKING CREEP!
ピタ
STP
WHUMP
AH!
STP
THAT HURT!
I'M SORRY!
?
IT'S HUGE.

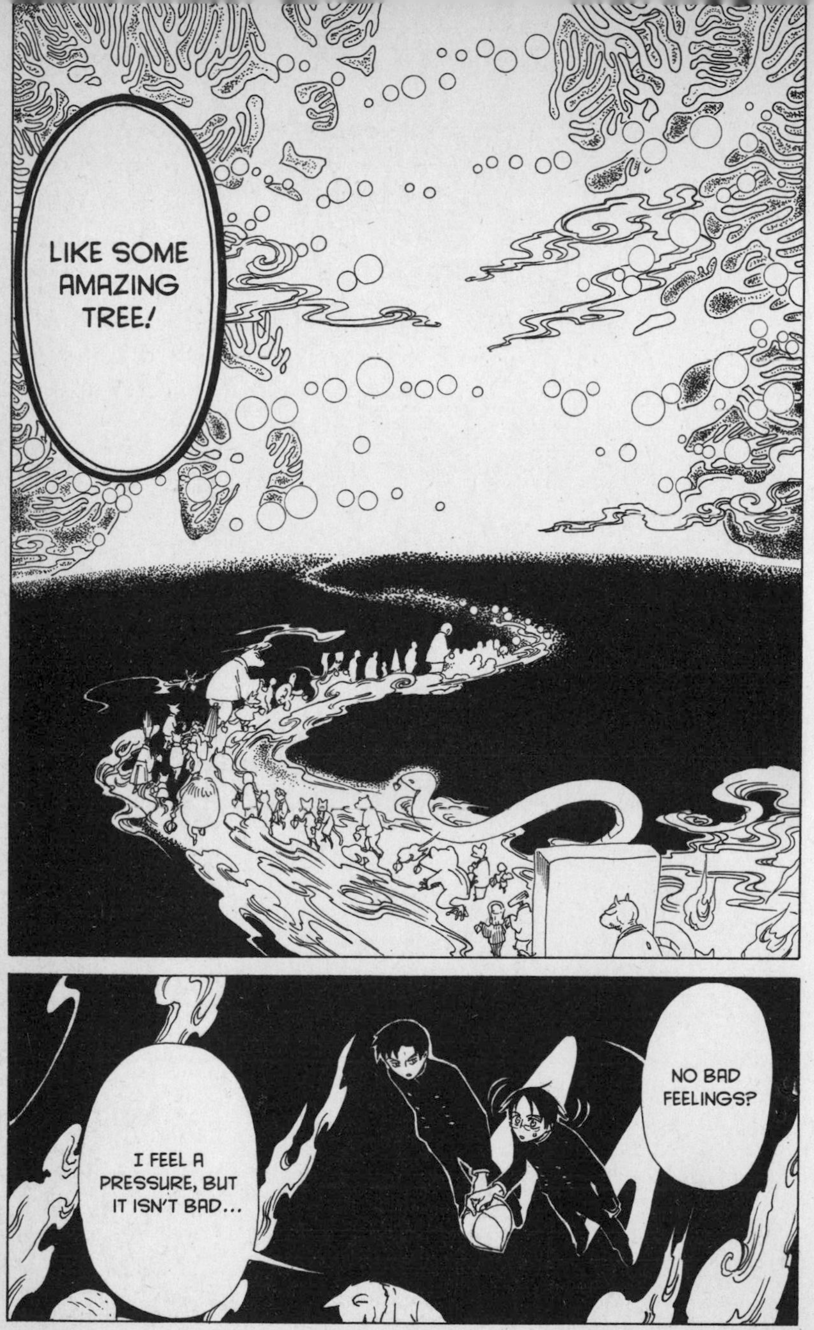
LIKE SOME AMAZING TREE!
NO BAD FEELINGS?
I FEEL A PRESSURE, BUT IT ISN'T BAD...

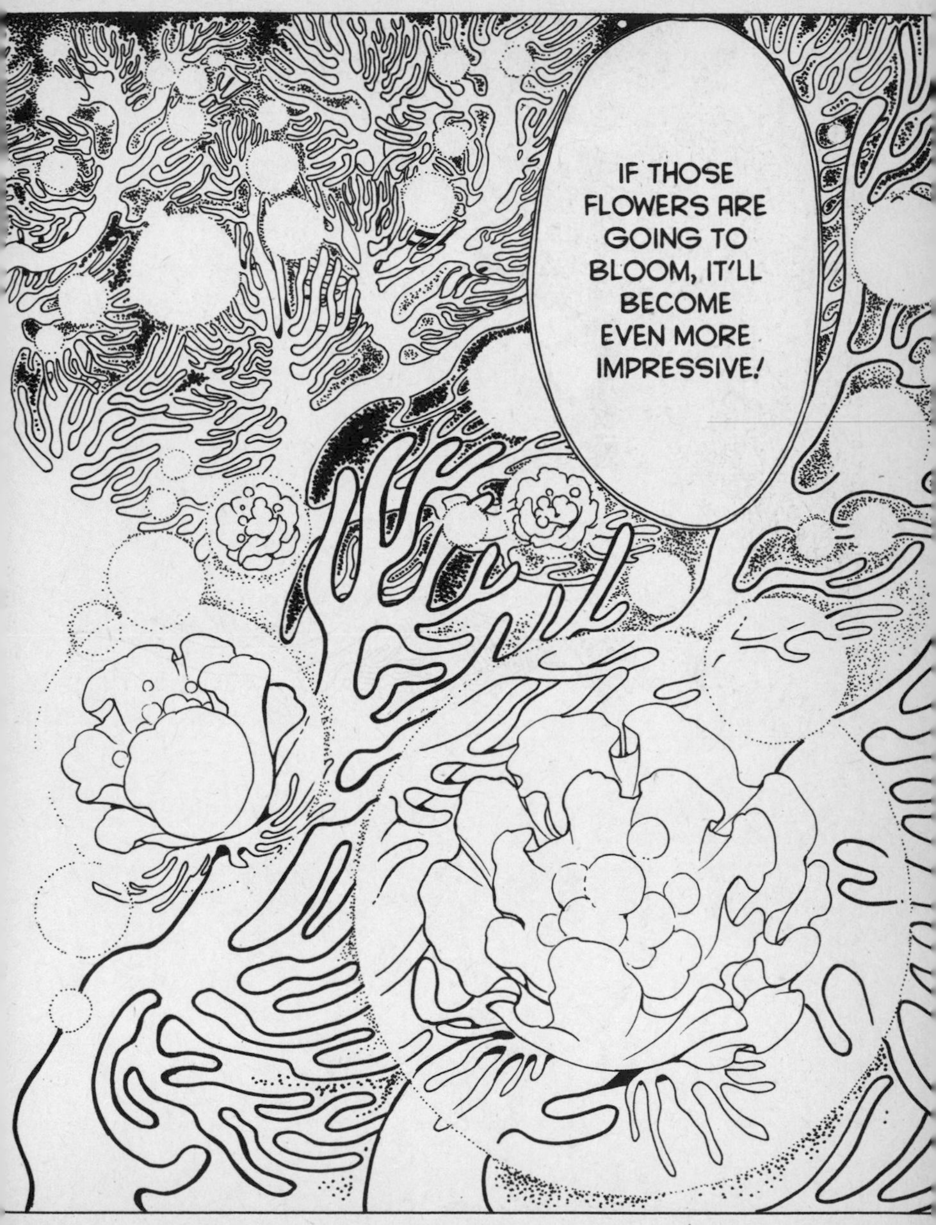
IF THOSE FLOWERS ARE GOING TO BLOOM, IT'LL BECOME EVEN MORE IMPRESSIVE!

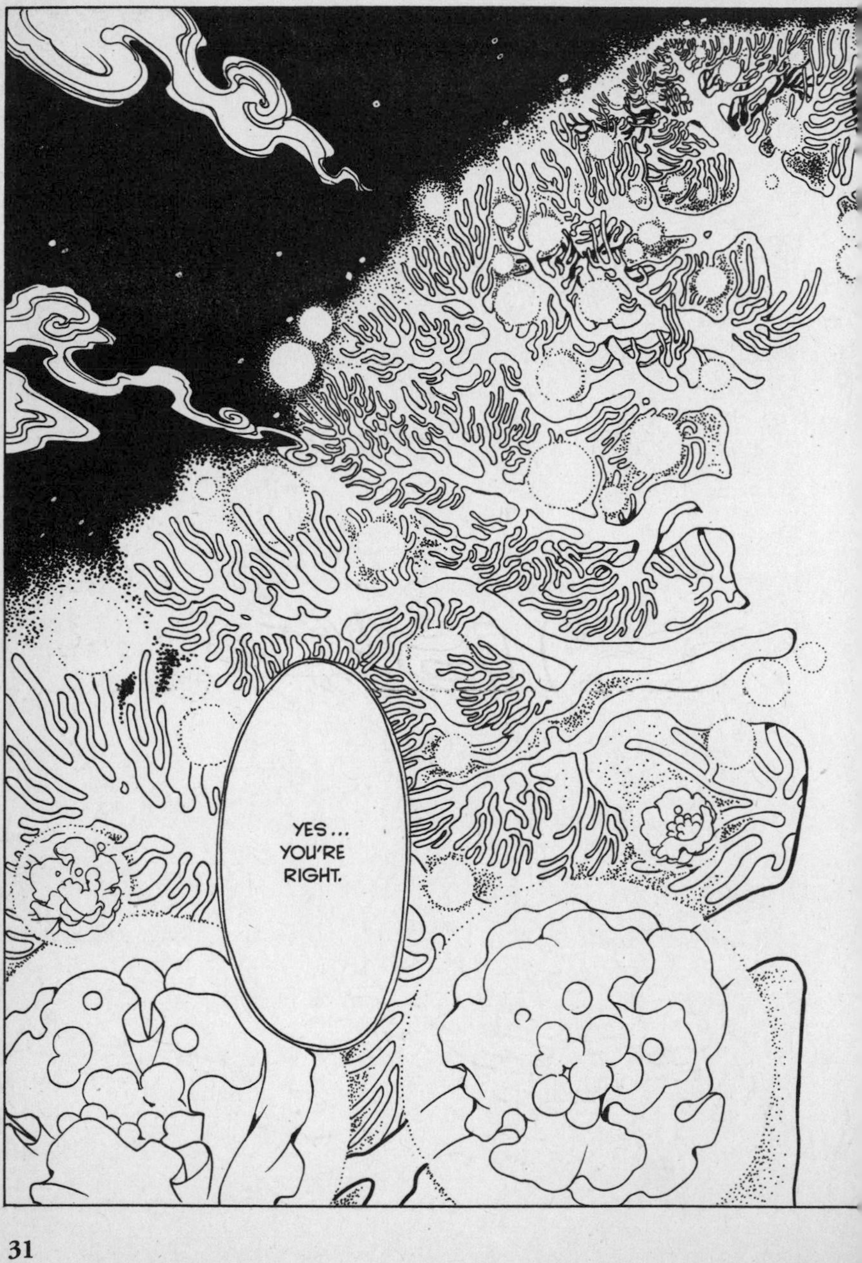
YES... YOU'RE RIGHT.

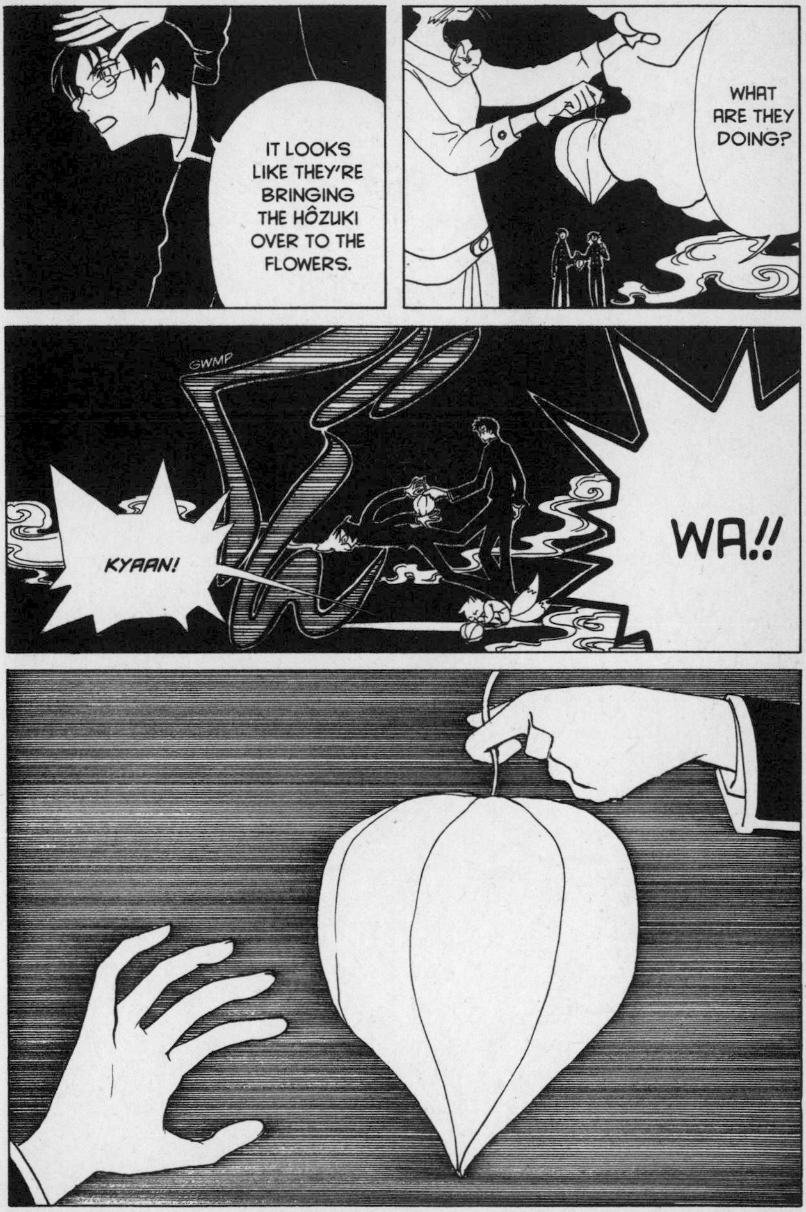
WHAT ARE THEY DOING?
IT LOOKS LIKE THEY'RE BRINGING THE HÔZUKI OVER TO THE FLOWERS.
WA!!
GWMP
KYAAN!

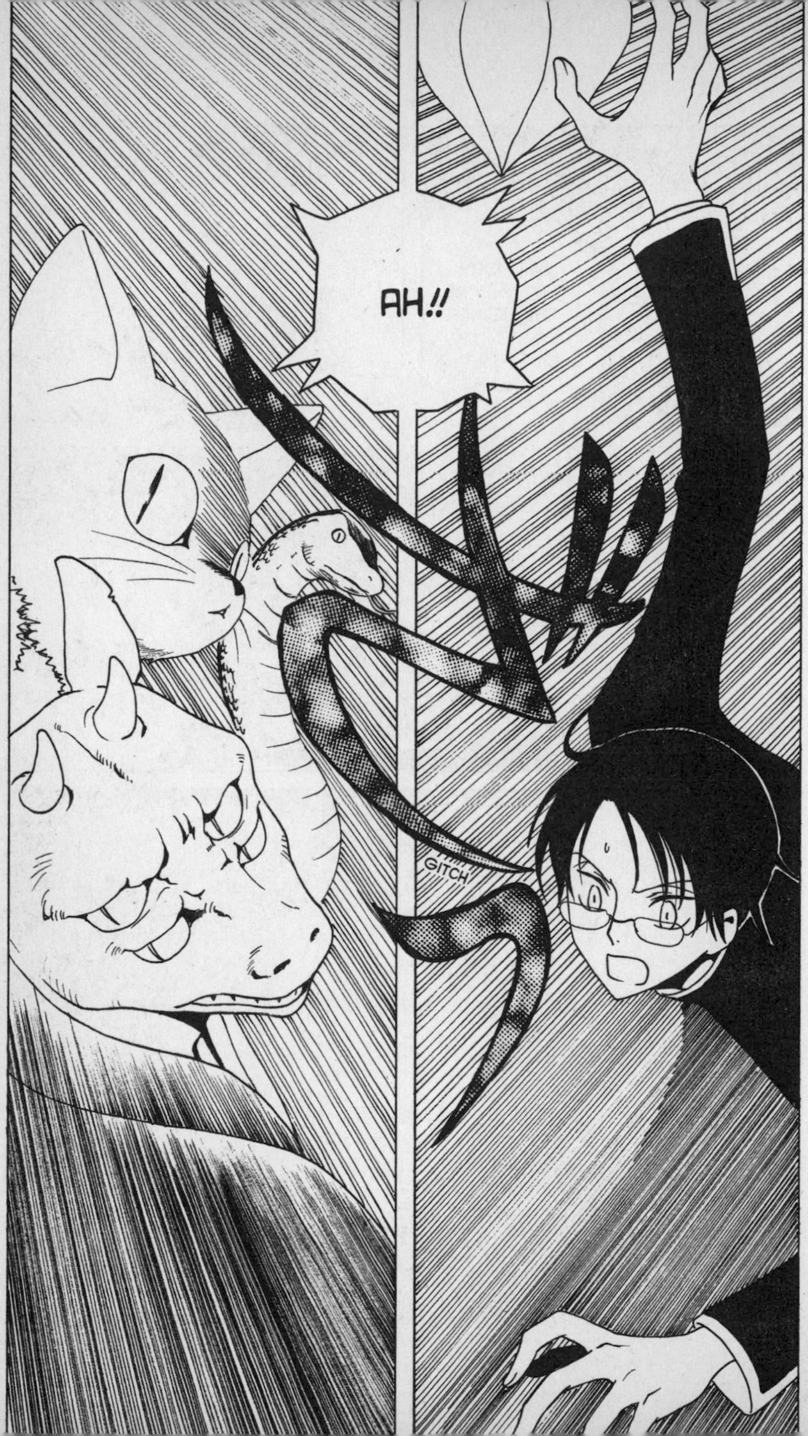
AH!!
GITCH

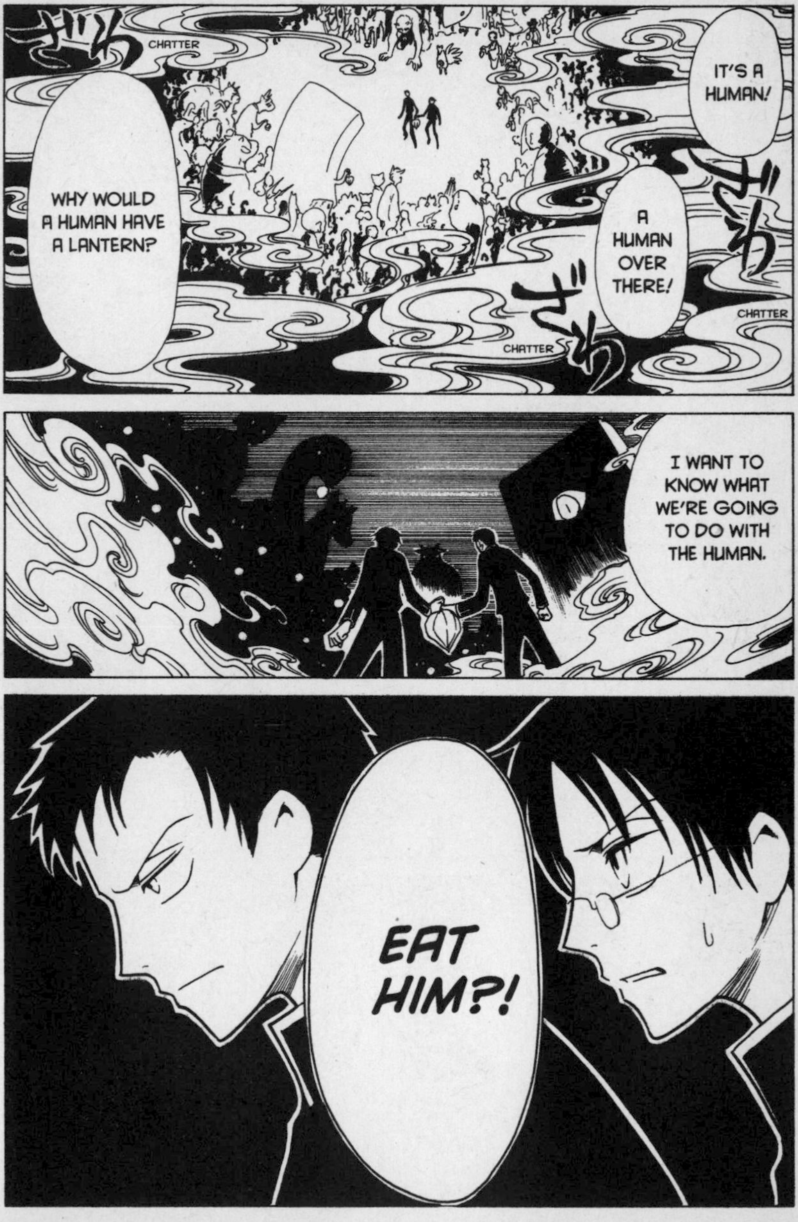

IT'S A HUMAN!
CHATTER
A HUMAN OVER THERE!
CHATTER
WHY WOULD A HUMAN HAVE A LANTERN?
CHATTER
I WANT TO KNOW WHAT WE'RE GOING TO DO WITH THE HUMAN.
EAT HIM?!

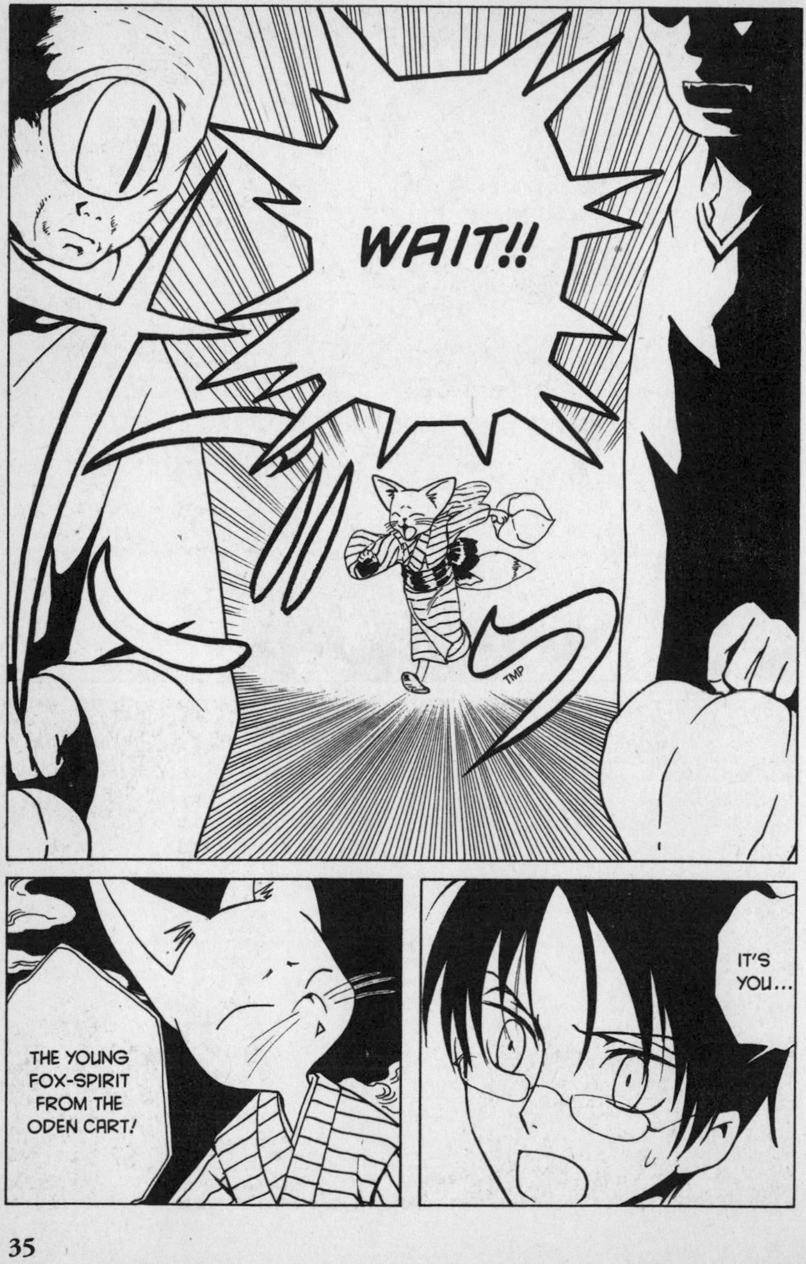
WAIT!!
TMP
IT'S YOU...
THE YOUNG FOX-SPIRIT FROM THE ODEN CART!

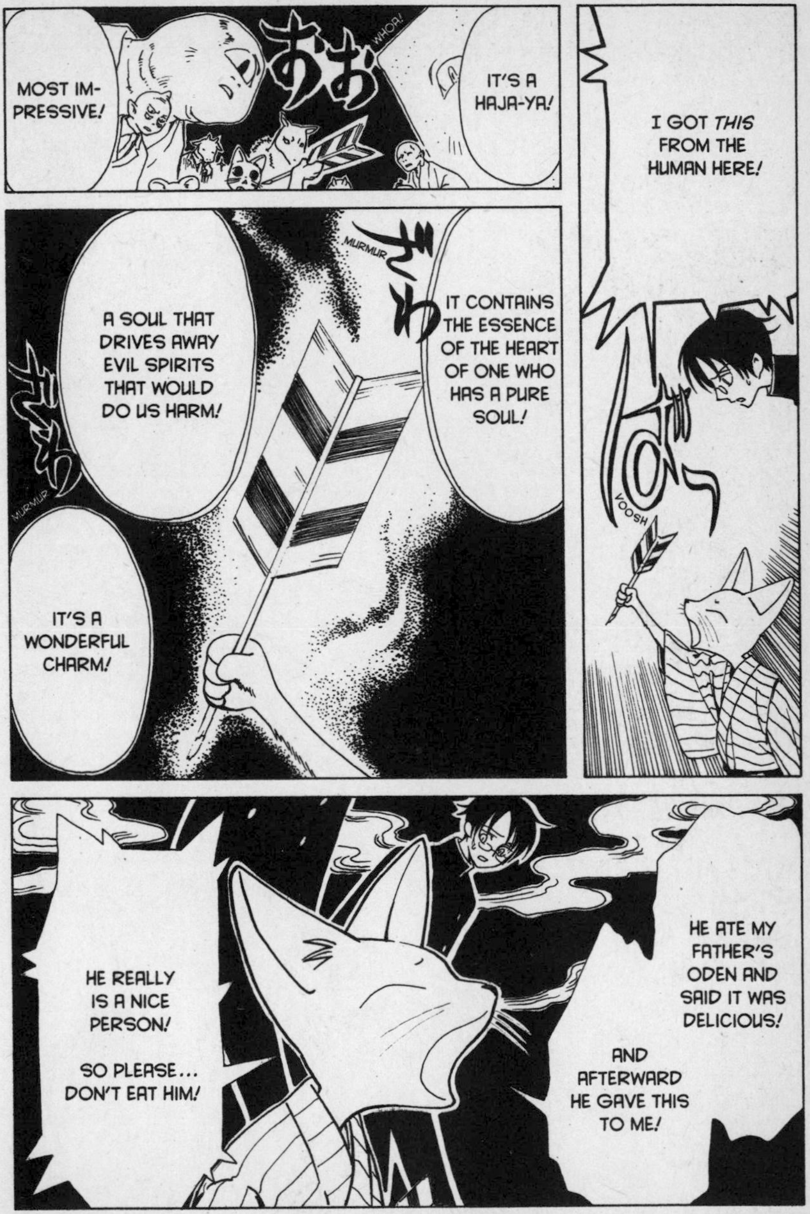
I GOT *THIS* FROM THE HUMAN HERE!
VOOSH
IT'S A HAJA-YA!
WHOA!
MOST IM-PRESSIVE!
IT CONTAINS THE ESSENCE OF THE HEART OF ONE WHO HAS A PURE SOUL!
MURMUR
A SOUL THAT DRIVES AWAY EVIL SPIRITS THAT WOULD DO US HARM!
MURMUR
IT'S A WONDERFUL CHARM!
HE ATE MY FATHER'S ODEN AND SAID IT WAS DELICIOUS!
AND AFTERWARD HE GAVE THIS TO ME!
HE REALLY IS A NICE PERSON!
SO PLEASE... DON'T EAT HIM!

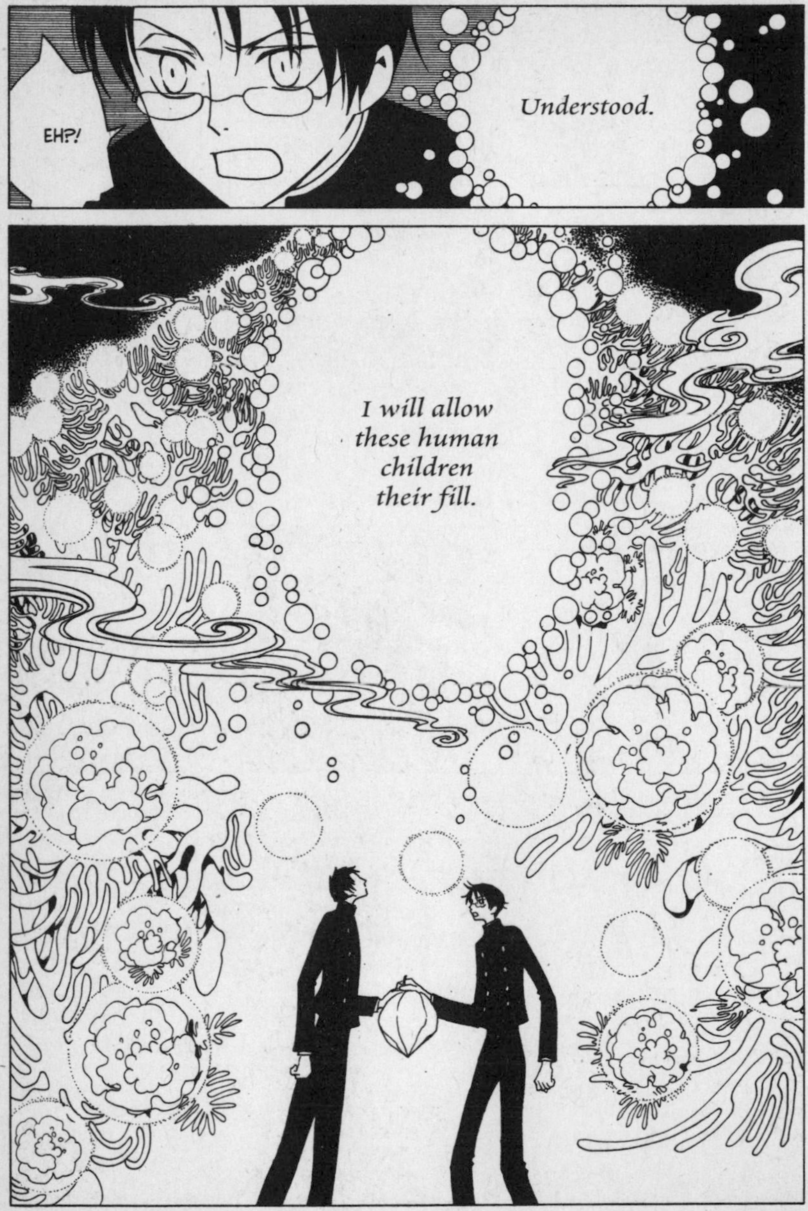
Understood.
EH?!
I will allow these human children their fill.

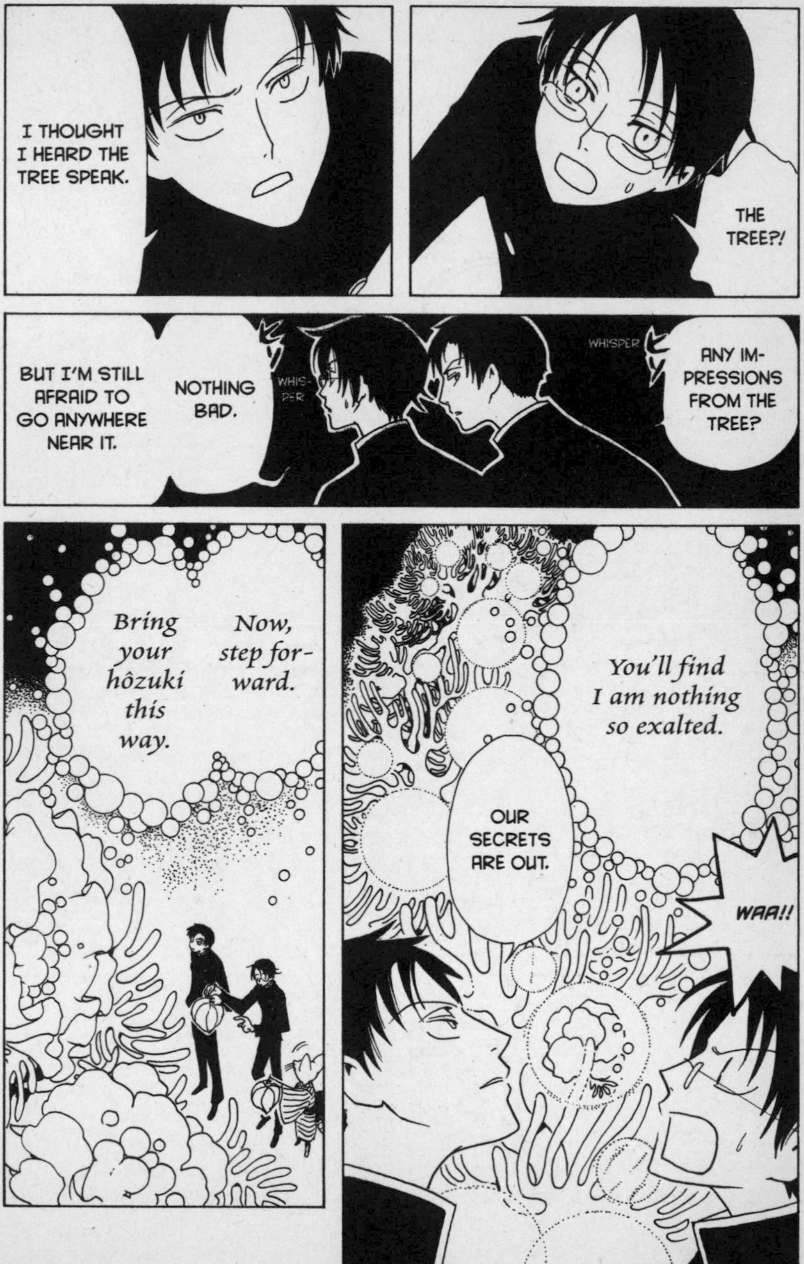
THE TREE?!
I THOUGHT I HEARD THE TREE SPEAK.
ANY IM-PRESSIONS FROM THE TREE?
WHISPER
WHIS-PER
NOTHING BAD.
BUT I'M STILL AFRAID TO GO ANYWHERE NEAR IT.
You'll find I am nothing so exalted.
OUR SECRETS ARE OUT.
WAA!!
Now, step for-ward.
Bring your hôzuki this way.

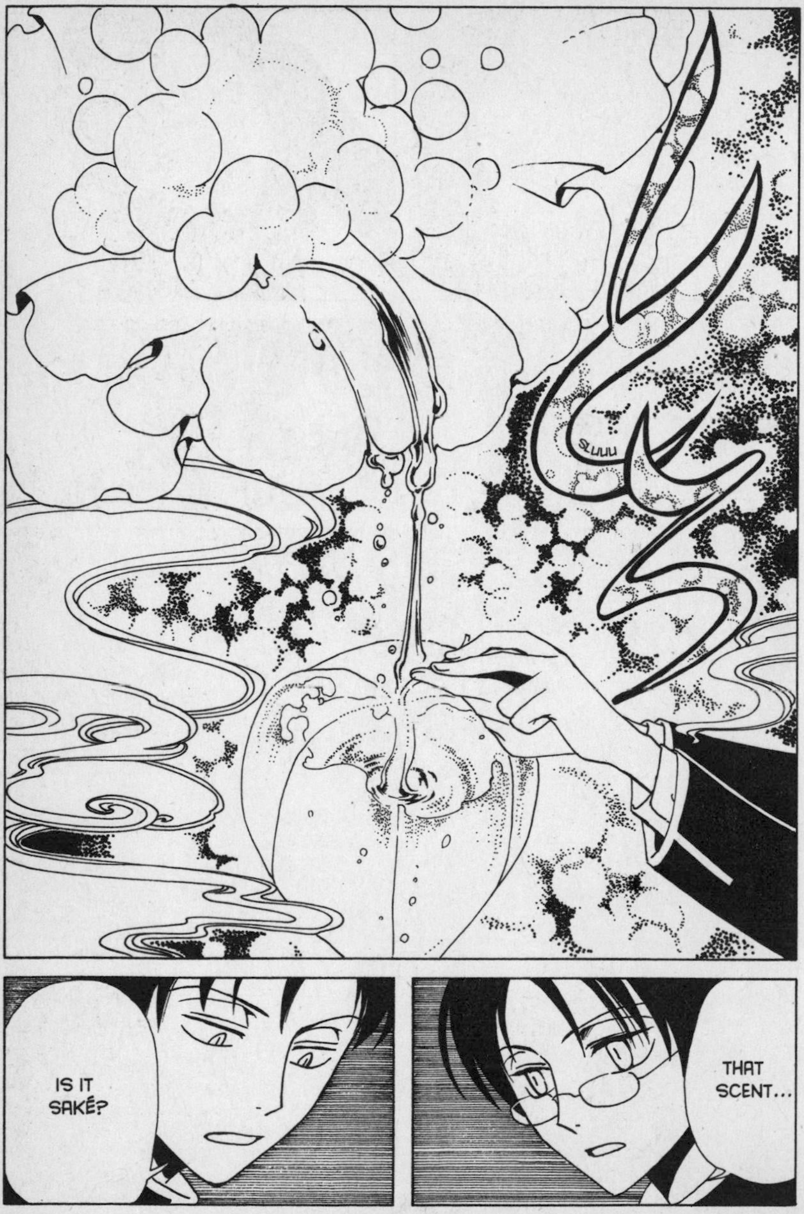
SLUUU
THAT SCENT...
IS IT SAKÉ?

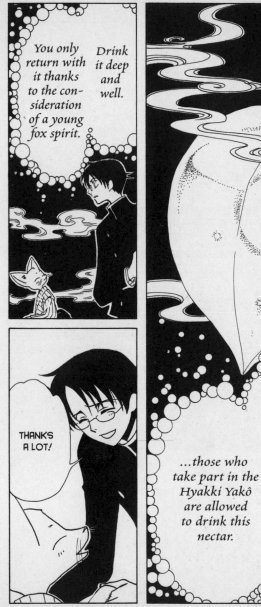

Yes.
Only once a year...
...those who take part in the Hyakki Yakô are allowed to drink this nectar.
Drink it deep and well.
You only return with it thanks to the consideration of a young fox spirit.
THANKS A LOT!

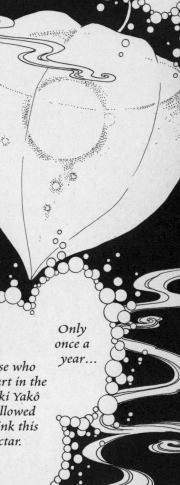

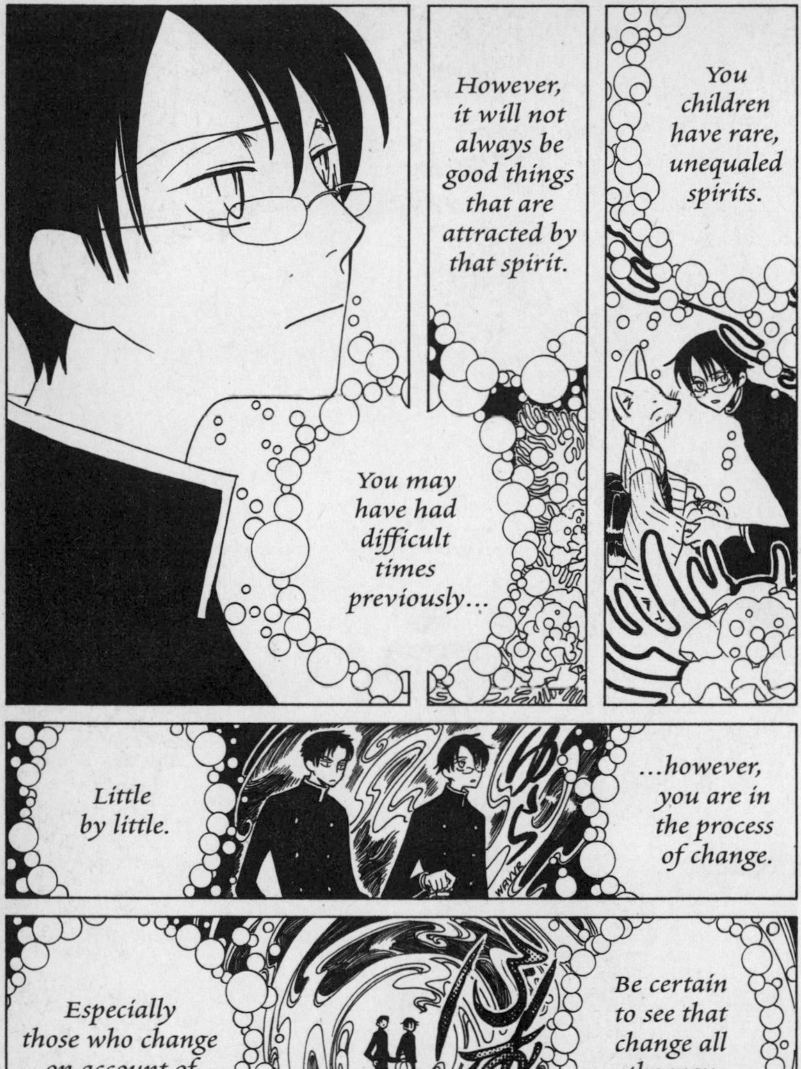
You children have rare, unequaled spirits.
However, it will not always be good things that are attracted by that spirit.
You may have had difficult times previously...
...however, you are in the process of change.
WAVVR
Little by little.
Be certain to see that change all the way through.
VLUUM
Especially those who change on account of meeting a certain someone.

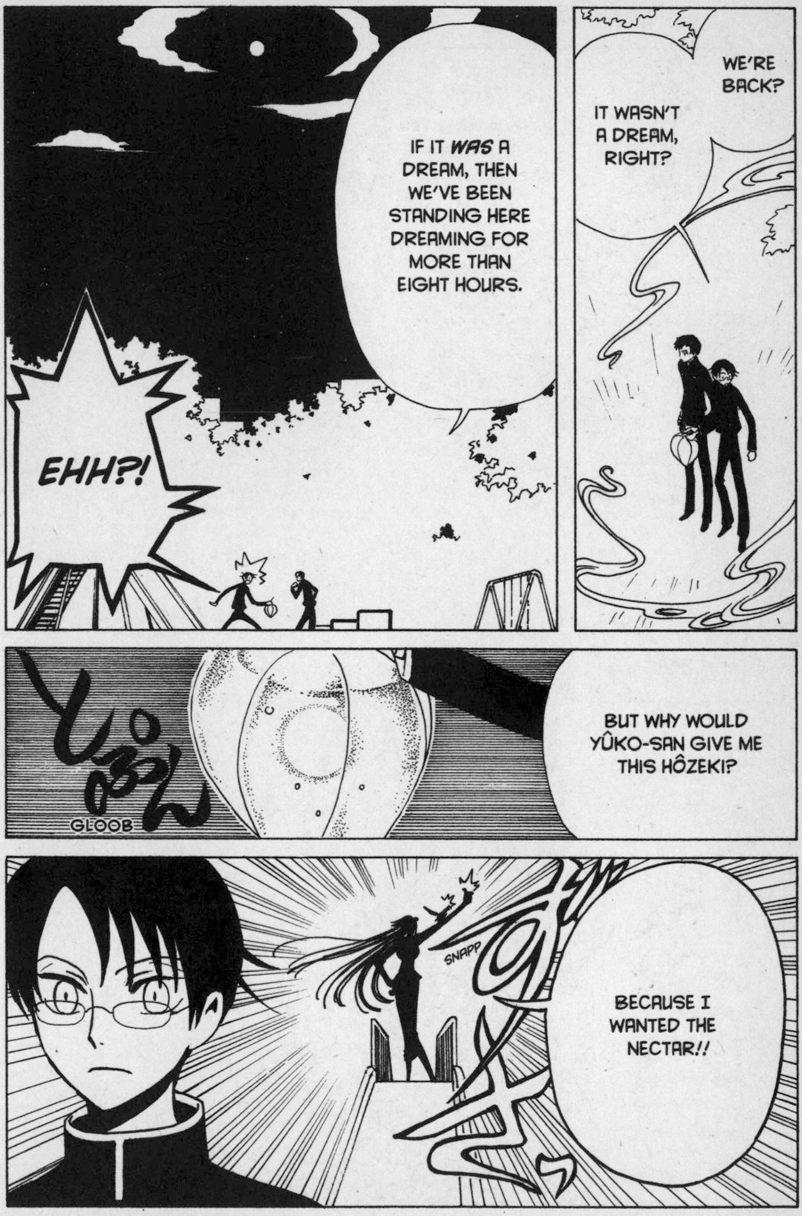
WE'RE BACK?
IT WASN'T A DREAM, RIGHT?
IF IT WAS A DREAM, THEN WE'VE BEEN STANDING HERE DREAMING FOR MORE THAN EIGHT HOURS.
EHH?!
BUT WHY WOULD YÛKO-SAN GIVE ME THIS HÔZEKI?
GLOOB
BECAUSE I WANTED THE NECTAR!!
SNAPP

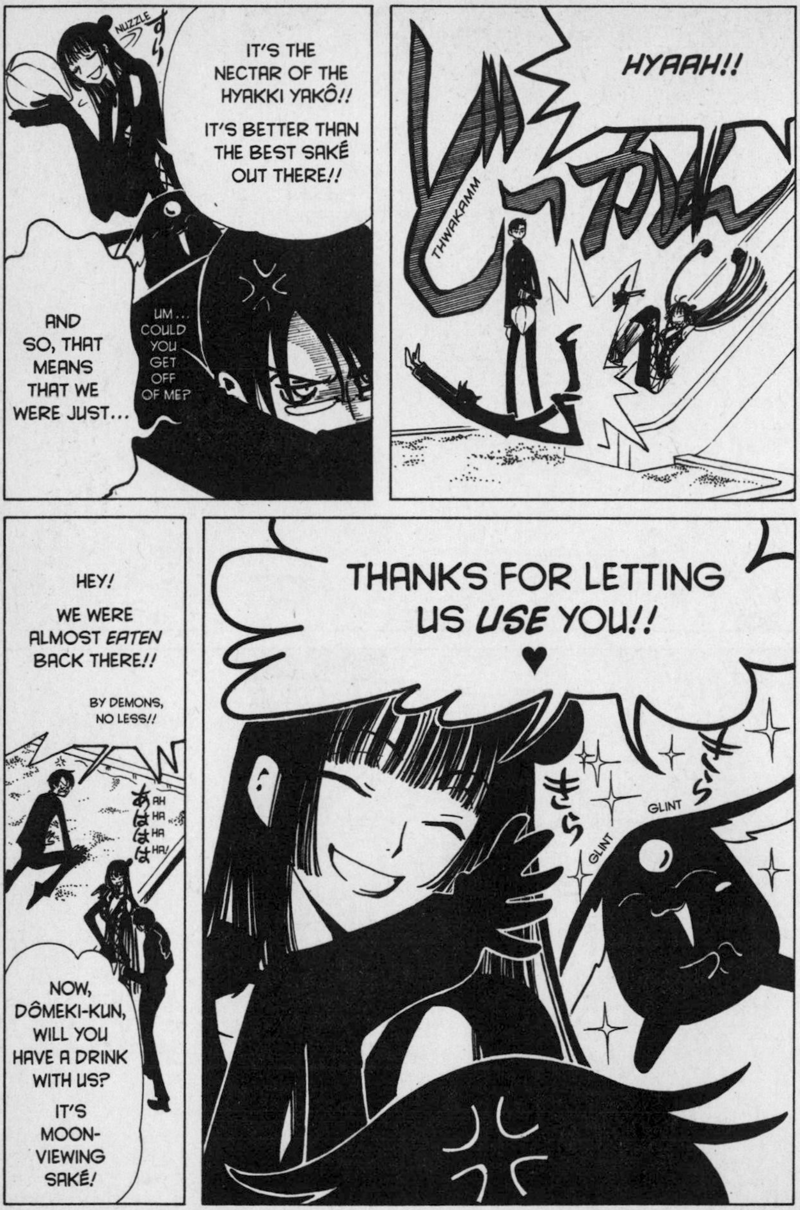
HYAAH!!
THWAKAMM
NUZZLE
すり
IT'S THE NECTAR OF THE HYAKKI YAKÔ!!
IT'S BETTER THAN THE BEST SAKÉ OUT THERE!!
UM... COULD YOU GET OFF OF ME?
AND SO, THAT MEANS THAT WE WERE JUST...
THANKS FOR LETTING US *USE* YOU!! ♥
きら
GLINT
きら
GLINT
HEY!
WE WERE ALMOST *EATEN* BACK THERE!!
BY DEMONS, NO LESS!!
あははは
AH HA HA HA!
NOW, DÔMEKI-KUN, WILL YOU HAVE A DRINK WITH US?
IT'S MOON-VIEWING SAKÉ!

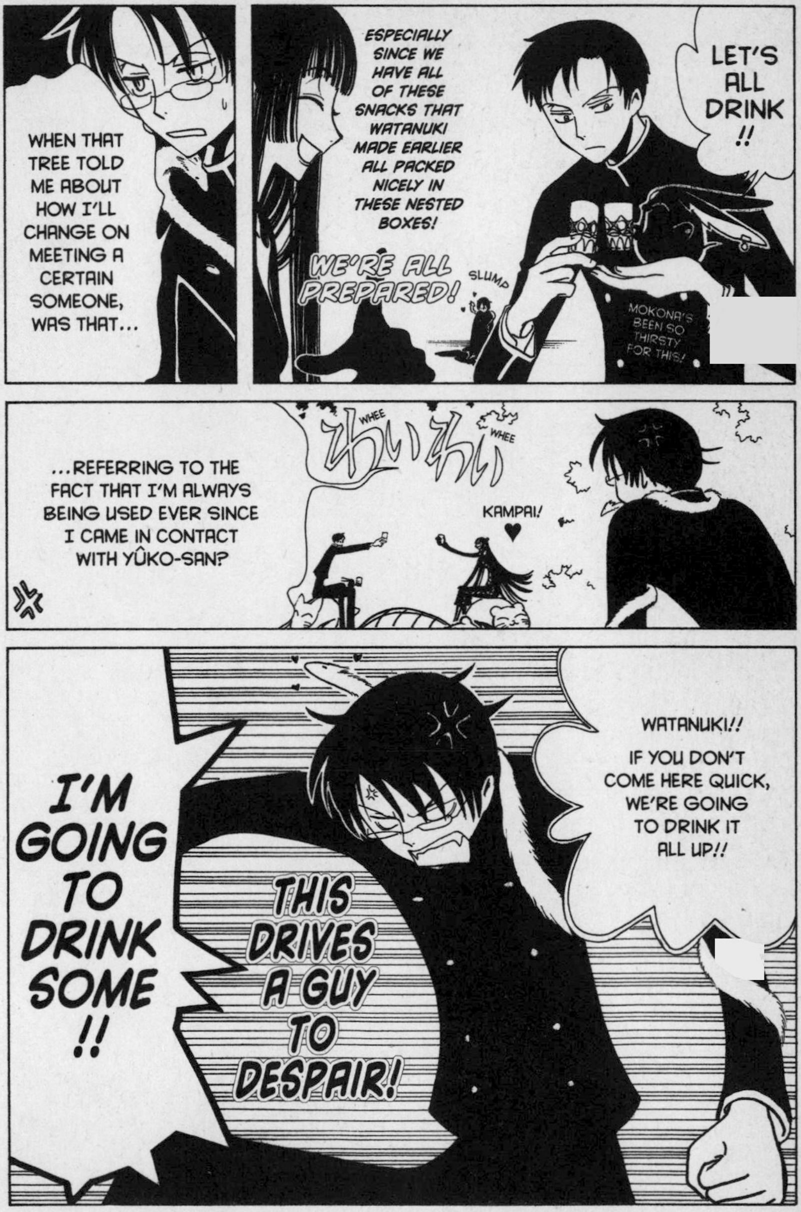
LET'S ALL DRINK!!
MOKONA'S BEEN SO THIRSTY FOR THIS!
ESPECIALLY SINCE WE HAVE ALL OF THESE SNACKS THAT WATANUKI MADE EARLIER ALL PACKED NICELY IN THESE NESTED BOXES!
WE'RE ALL PREPARED!
SLUMP
WHEN THAT TREE TOLD ME ABOUT HOW I'LL CHANGE ON MEETING A CERTAIN SOMEONE, WAS THAT...
WHEE
WHEE
KAMPAI!
...REFERRING TO THE FACT THAT I'M ALWAYS BEING USED EVER SINCE I CAME IN CONTACT WITH YÛKO-SAN?
WATANUKI!!
IF YOU DON'T COME HERE QUICK, WE'RE GOING TO DRINK IT ALL UP!!
THIS DRIVES A GUY TO DESPAIR!
I'M GOING TO DRINK SOME!!

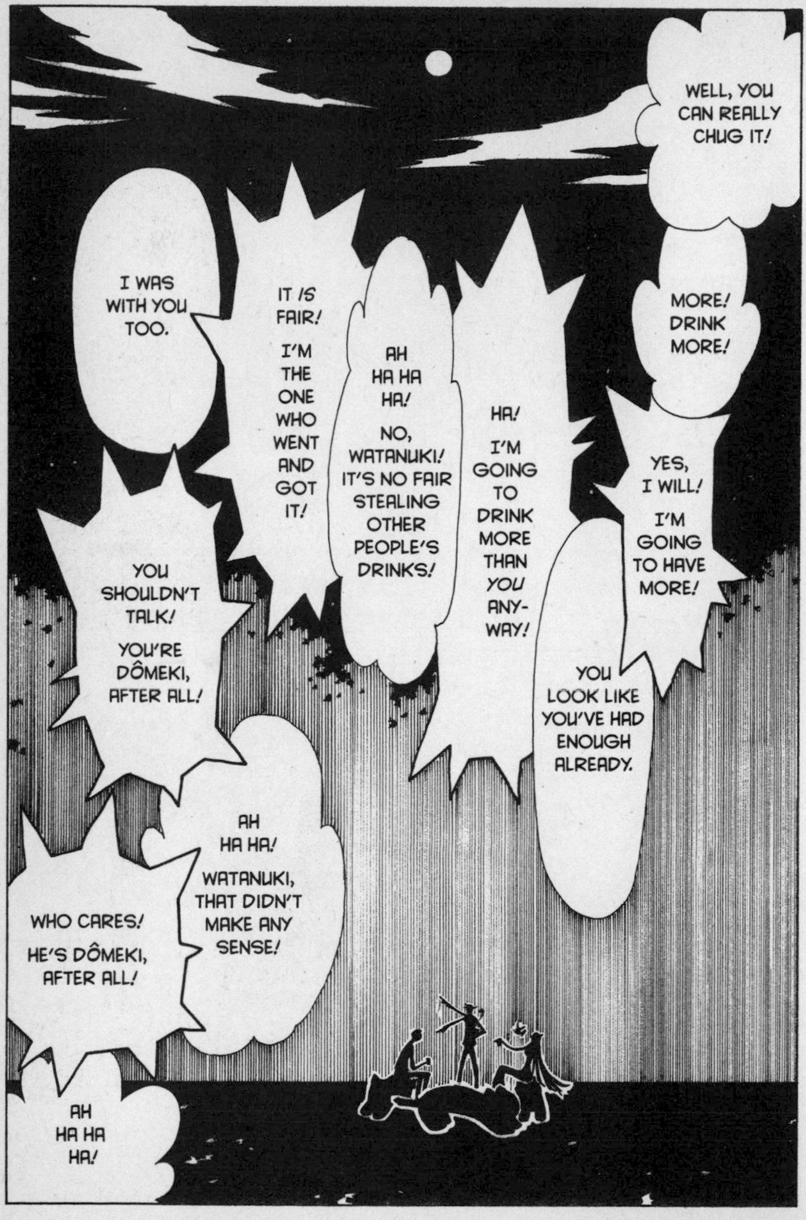
WELL, YOU CAN REALLY CHUG IT!
MORE! DRINK MORE!
YES, I WILL! I'M GOING TO HAVE MORE!
HA! I'M GOING TO DRINK MORE THAN YOU ANY-WAY!
YOU LOOK LIKE YOU'VE HAD ENOUGH ALREADY.
AH HA HA HA! NO, WATANUKI! IT'S NO FAIR STEALING OTHER PEOPLE'S DRINKS!
IT IS FAIR! I'M THE ONE WHO WENT AND GOT IT!
I WAS WITH YOU TOO.
YOU SHOULDN'T TALK! YOU'RE DÔMEKI, AFTER ALL!
AH HA HA! WATANUKI, THAT DIDN'T MAKE ANY SENSE!
WHO CARES! HE'S DÔMEKI, AFTER ALL!
AH HA HA HA!

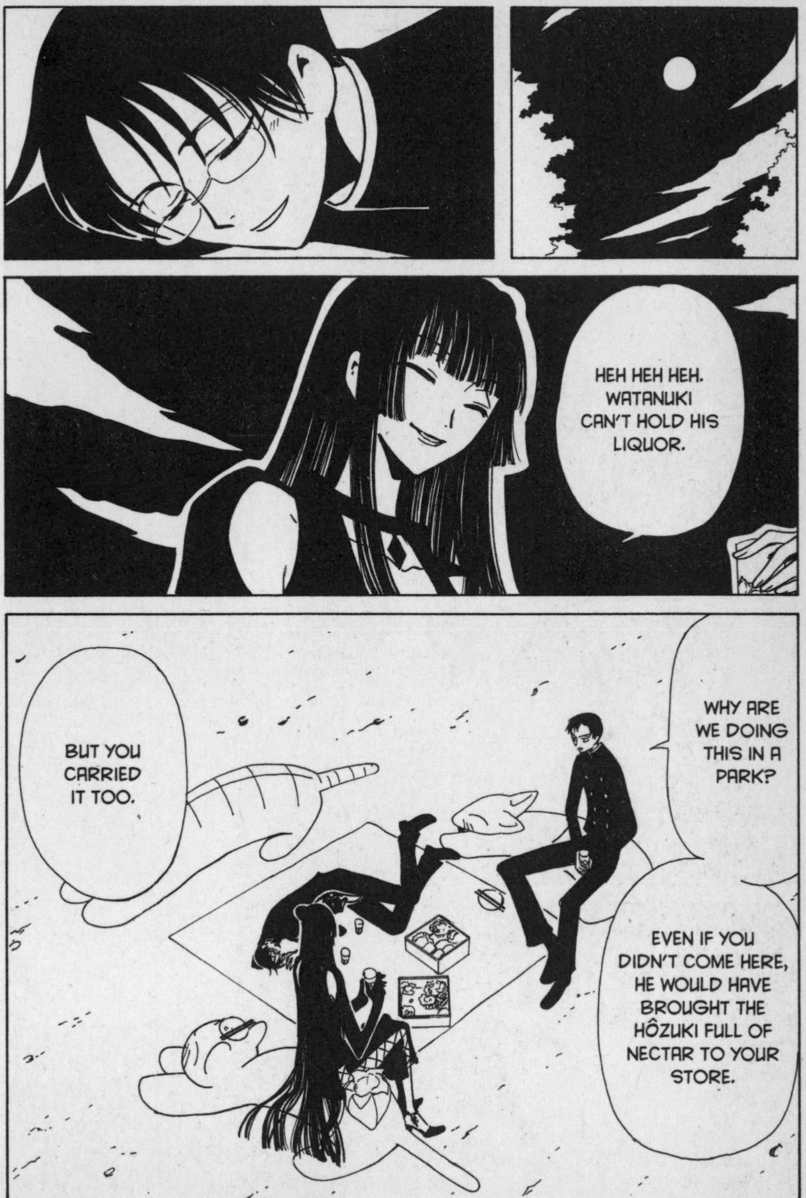
HEH HEH HEH. WATANUKI CAN'T HOLD HIS LIQUOR.
WHY ARE WE DOING THIS IN A PARK?
EVEN IF YOU DIDN'T COME HERE, HE WOULD HAVE BROUGHT THE HÔZUKI FULL OF NECTAR TO YOUR STORE.
BUT YOU CARRIED IT TOO.

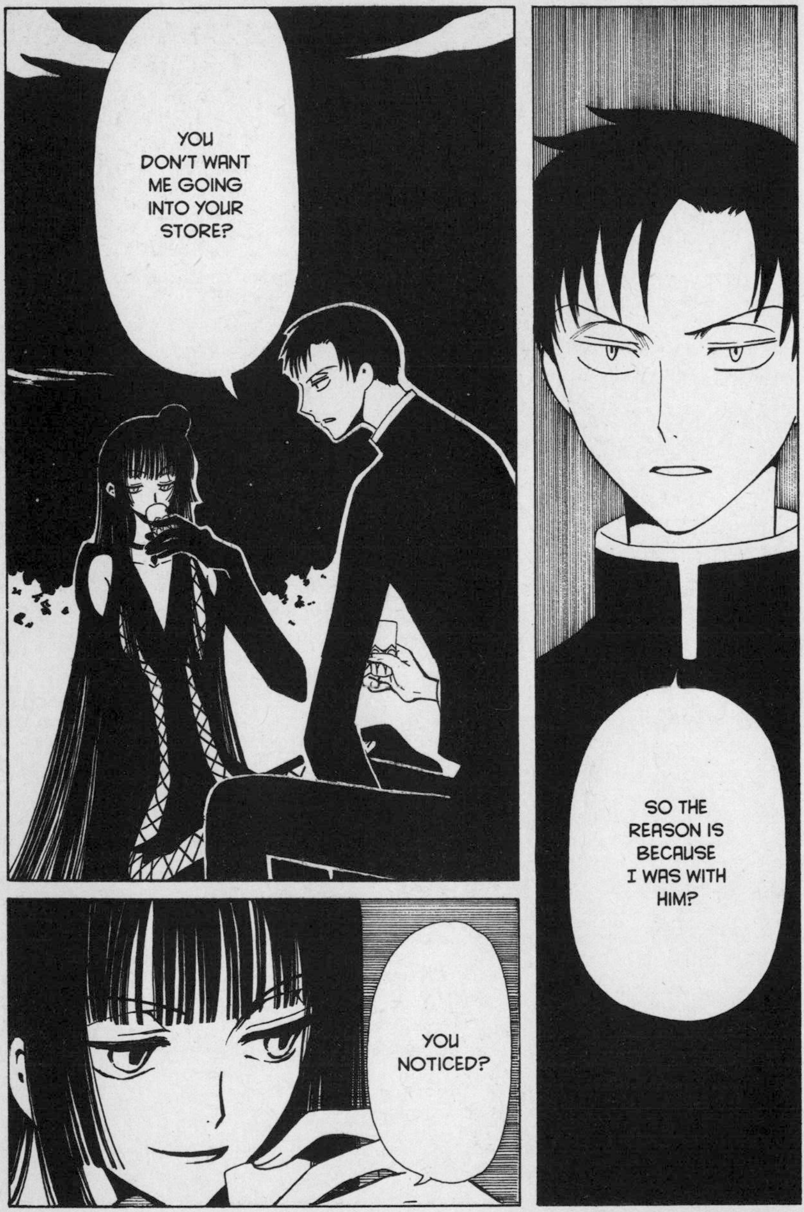
SO THE REASON IS BECAUSE I WAS WITH HIM?
YOU DON'T WANT ME GOING INTO YOUR STORE?
YOU NOTICED?

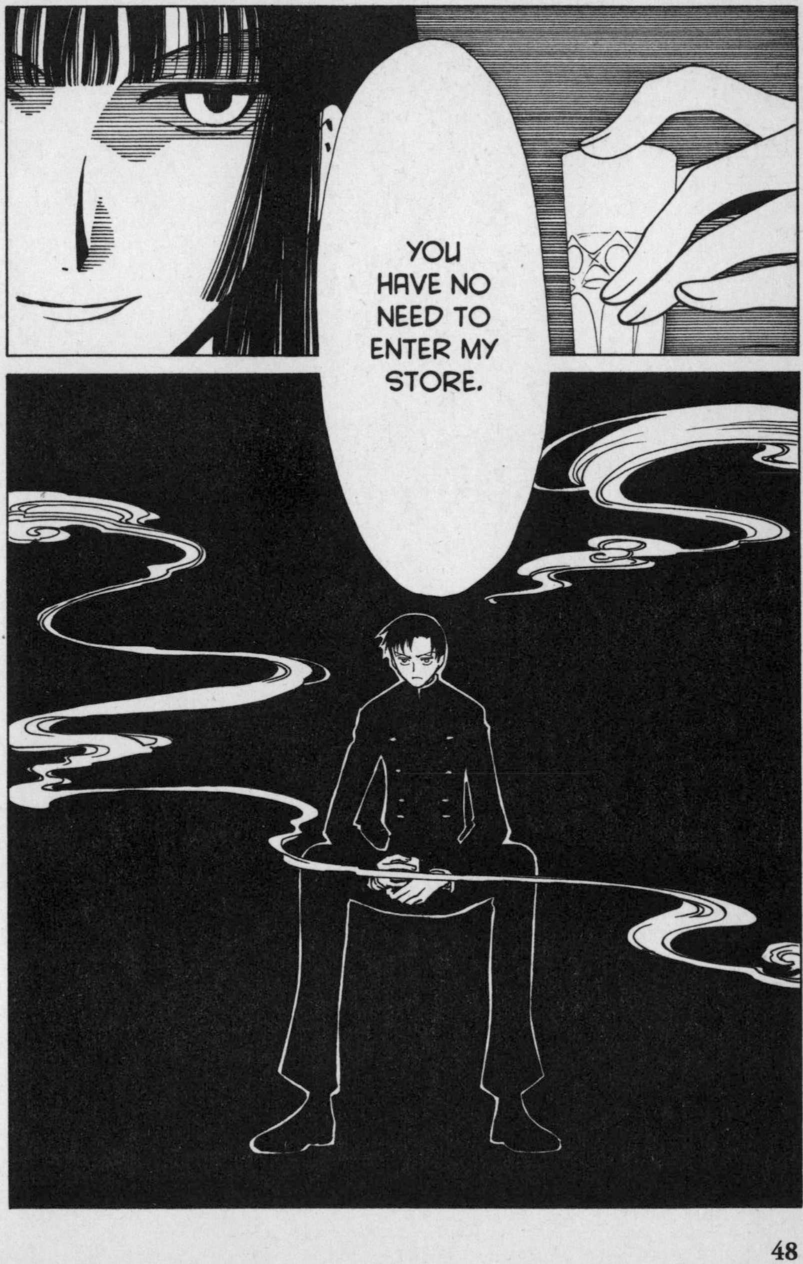
YOU HAVE NO NEED TO ENTER MY STORE.

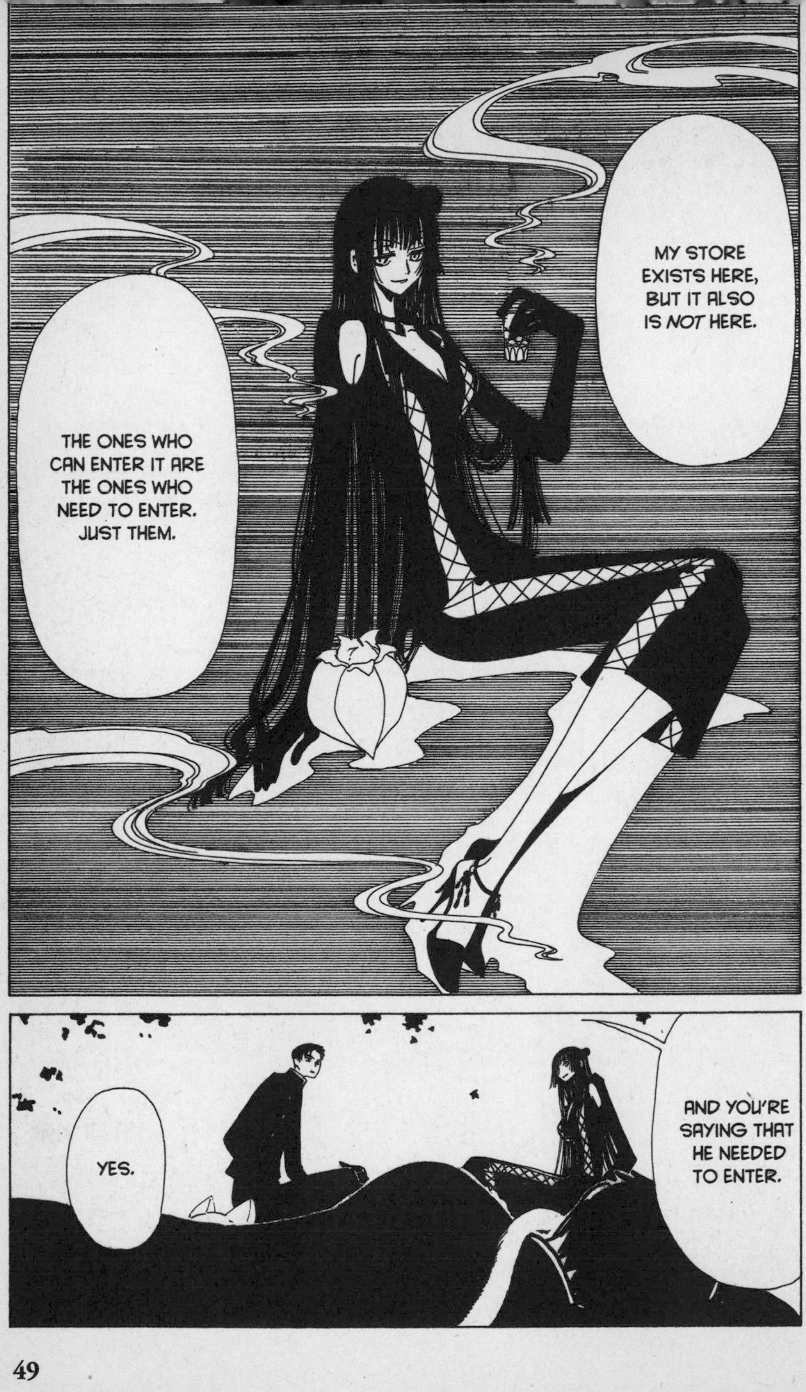
MY STORE EXISTS HERE, BUT IT ALSO IS *NOT* HERE.
THE ONES WHO CAN ENTER IT ARE THE ONES WHO NEED TO ENTER. JUST THEM.
AND YOU'RE SAYING THAT HE NEEDED TO ENTER.
YES.

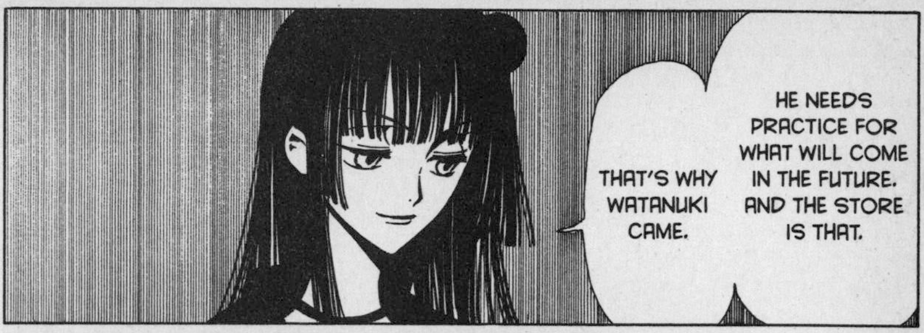
HE NEEDS PRACTICE FOR WHAT WILL COME IN THE FUTURE. AND THE STORE IS THAT.
THAT'S WHY WATANUKI CAME.
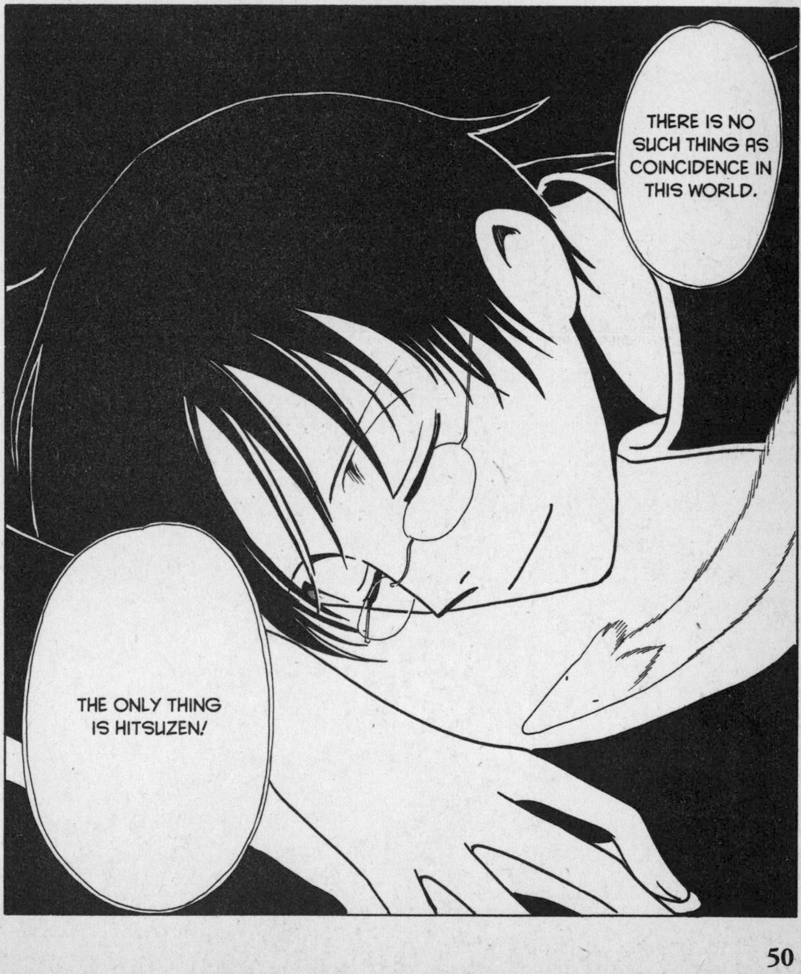
THERE IS NO SUCH THING AS COINCIDENCE IN THIS WORLD.
THE ONLY THING IS HITSUZEN!

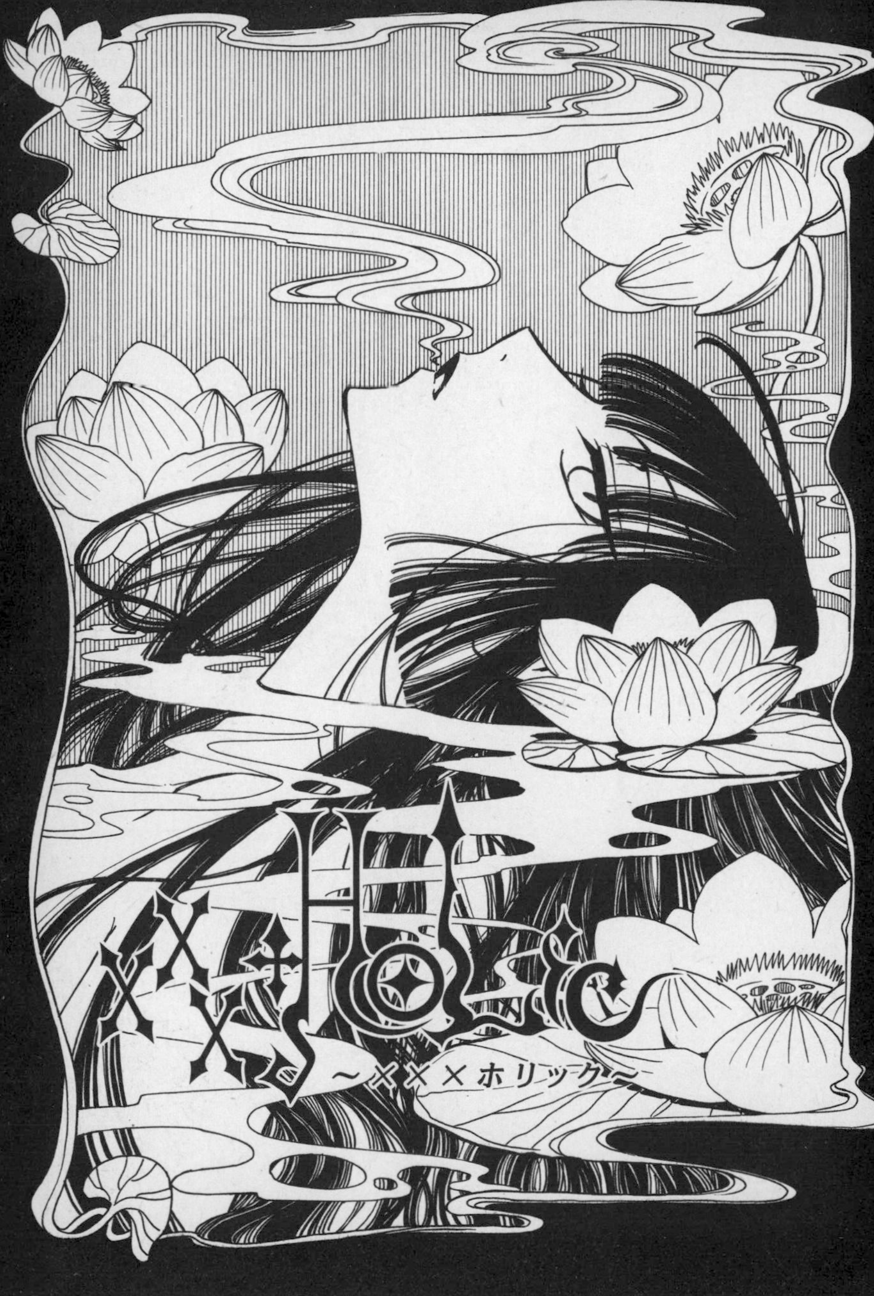
xxxHOLiC
〜×××ホリック〜

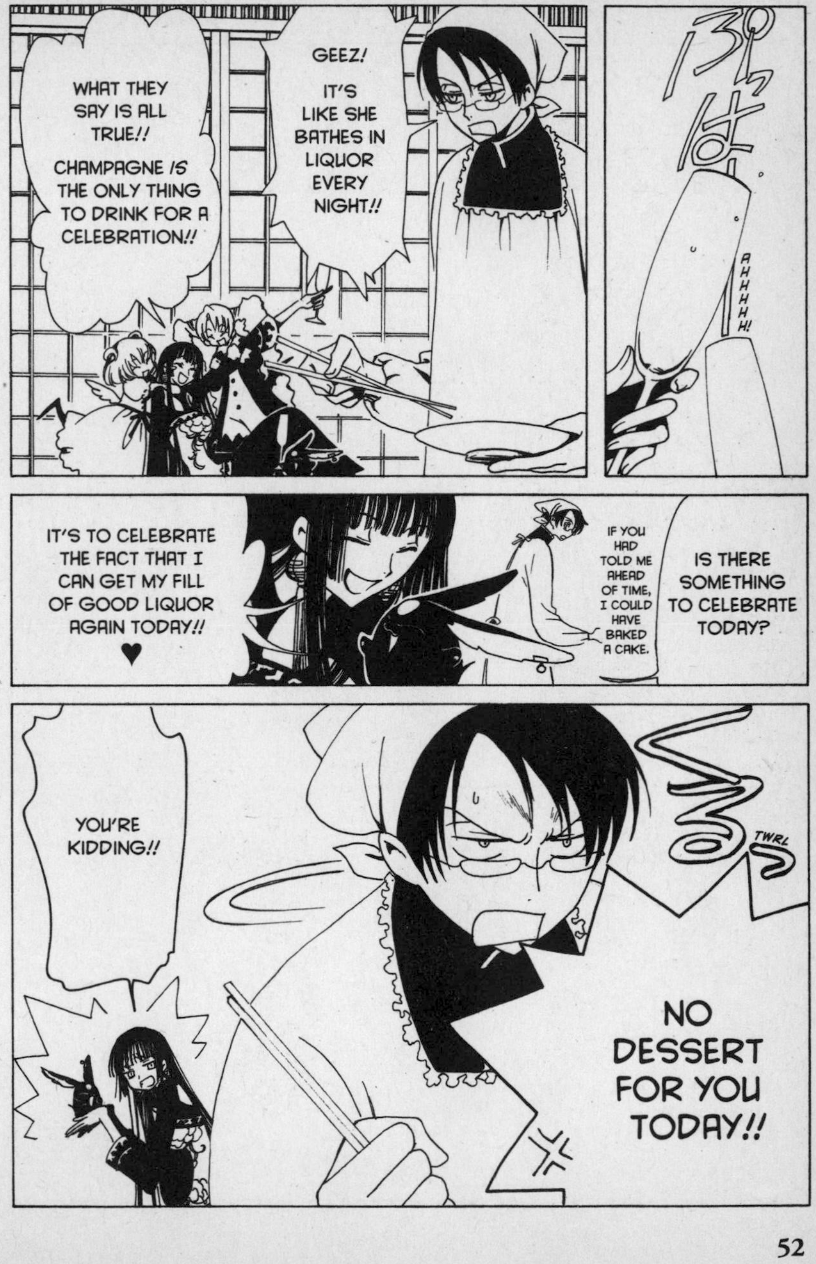
AHHHHHH!
GEEZ!
IT'S LIKE SHE BATHES IN LIQUOR EVERY NIGHT!!
WHAT THEY SAY IS ALL TRUE!!
CHAMPAGNE IS THE ONLY THING TO DRINK FOR A CELEBRATION!!
IS THERE SOMETHING TO CELEBRATE TODAY?
IF YOU HAD TOLD ME AHEAD OF TIME, I COULD HAVE BAKED A CAKE.
IT'S TO CELEBRATE THE FACT THAT I CAN GET MY FILL OF GOOD LIQUOR AGAIN TODAY!! ♥
くるっ
TWRL
NO DESSERT FOR YOU TODAY!!
YOU'RE KIDDING!!

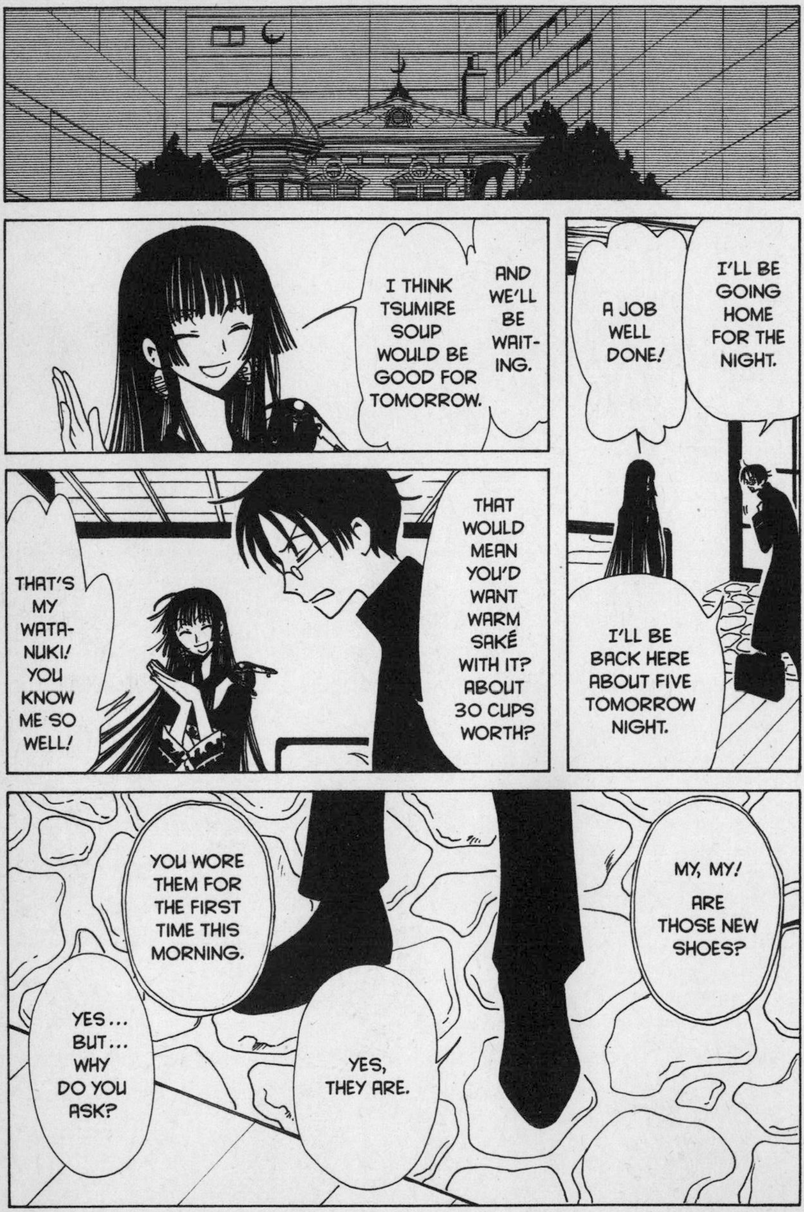
I'LL BE GOING HOME FOR THE NIGHT.
A JOB WELL DONE!
I'LL BE BACK HERE ABOUT FIVE TOMORROW NIGHT.
AND WE'LL BE WAIT-ING.
I THINK TSUMIRE SOUP WOULD BE GOOD FOR TOMORROW.
THAT WOULD MEAN YOU'D WANT WARM SAKÉ WITH IT? ABOUT 30 CUPS WORTH?
THAT'S MY WATA-NUKI! YOU KNOW ME SO WELL!
MY, MY!
ARE THOSE NEW SHOES?
YES, THEY ARE.
YOU WORE THEM FOR THE FIRST TIME THIS MORNING.
YES... BUT... WHY DO YOU ASK?

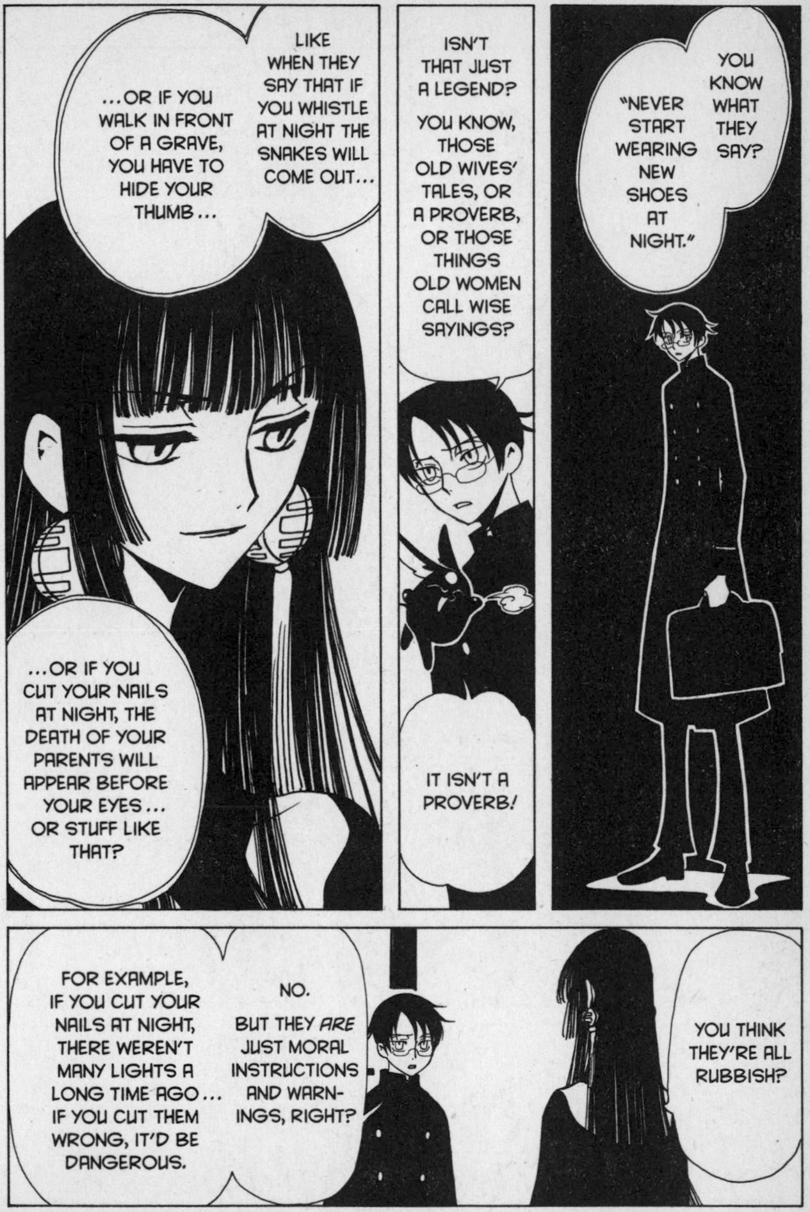
YOU KNOW WHAT THEY SAY?
"NEVER START WEARING NEW SHOES AT NIGHT."
ISN'T THAT JUST A LEGEND?
YOU KNOW, THOSE OLD WIVES' TALES, OR A PROVERB, OR THOSE THINGS OLD WOMEN CALL WISE SAYINGS?
IT ISN'T A PROVERB!
LIKE WHEN THEY SAY THAT IF YOU WHISTLE AT NIGHT THE SNAKES WILL COME OUT...
...OR IF YOU WALK IN FRONT OF A GRAVE, YOU HAVE TO HIDE YOUR THUMB...
...OR IF YOU CUT YOUR NAILS AT NIGHT, THE DEATH OF YOUR PARENTS WILL APPEAR BEFORE YOUR EYES... OR STUFF LIKE THAT?
YOU THINK THEY'RE ALL RUBBISH?
NO.
BUT THEY *ARE* JUST MORAL INSTRUCTIONS AND WARNINGS, RIGHT?
FOR EXAMPLE, IF YOU CUT YOUR NAILS AT NIGHT, THERE WEREN'T MANY LIGHTS A LONG TIME AGO... IF YOU CUT THEM WRONG, IT'D BE DANGEROUS.

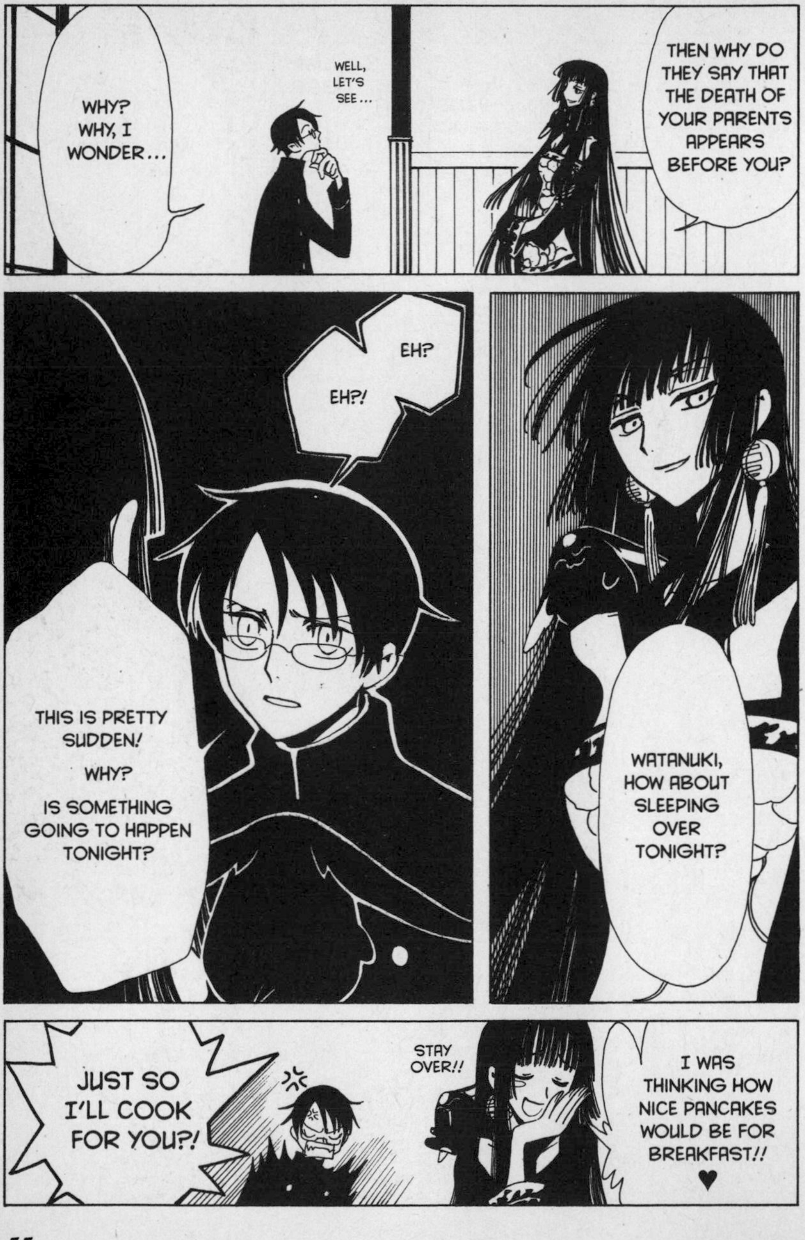
THEN WHY DO THEY SAY THAT THE DEATH OF YOUR PARENTS APPEARS BEFORE YOU?
WELL, LET'S SEE...
WHY? WHY, I WONDER...
WATANUKI, HOW ABOUT SLEEPING OVER TONIGHT?
EH?
EH?!
THIS IS PRETTY SUDDEN!
WHY?
IS SOMETHING GOING TO HAPPEN TONIGHT?
I WAS THINKING HOW NICE PANCAKES WOULD BE FOR BREAKFAST!! ♥
STAY OVER!!
JUST SO I'LL COOK FOR YOU?!

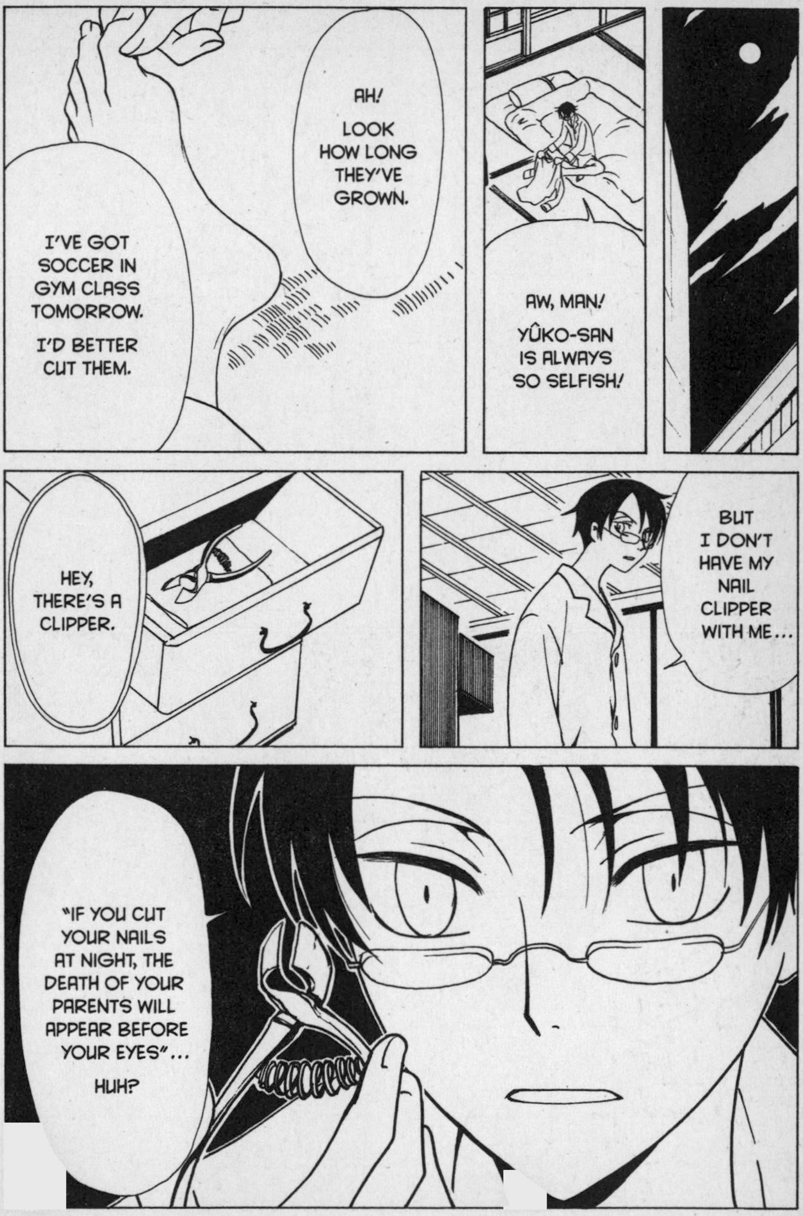
AW, MAN! YÛKO-SAN IS ALWAYS SO SELFISH!
AH! LOOK HOW LONG THEY'VE GROWN.
I'VE GOT SOCCER IN GYM CLASS TOMORROW. I'D BETTER CUT THEM.
BUT I DON'T HAVE MY NAIL CLIPPER WITH ME...
HEY, THERE'S A CLIPPER.
"IF YOU CUT YOUR NAILS AT NIGHT, THE DEATH OF YOUR PARENTS WILL APPEAR BEFORE YOUR EYES"... HUH?

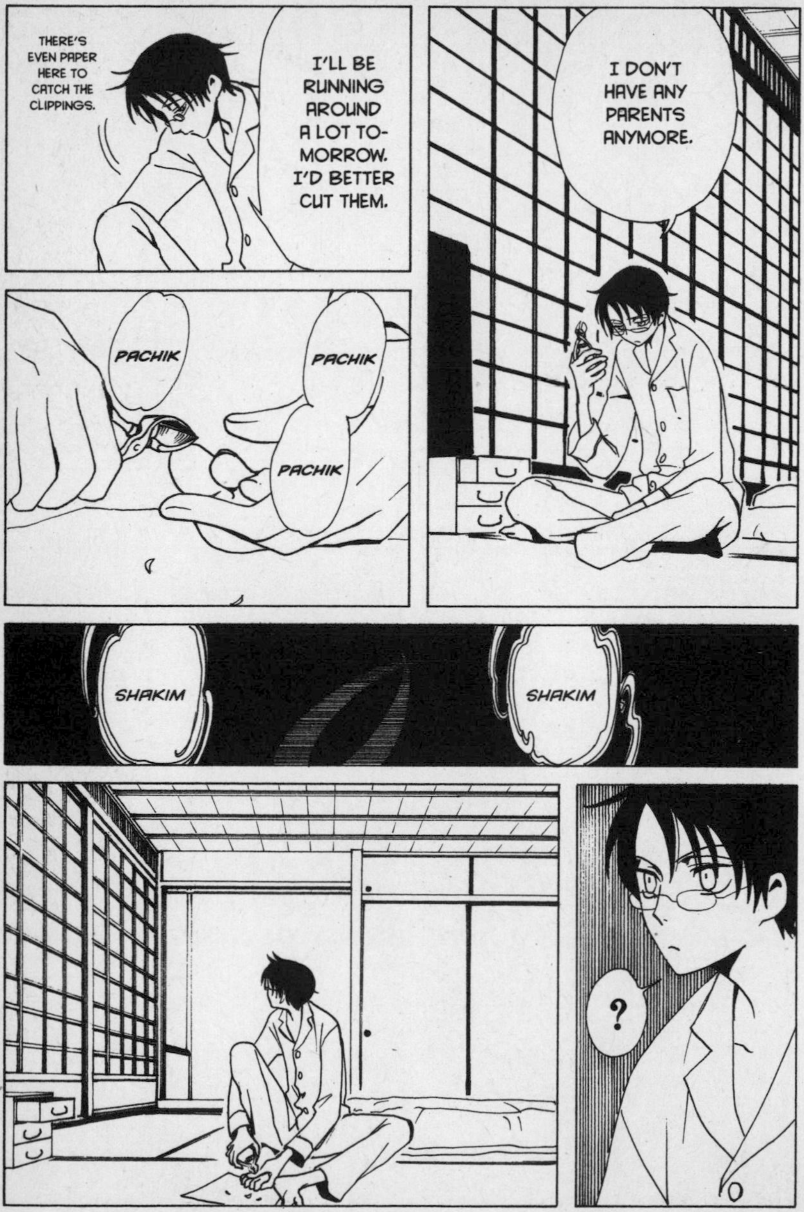
I DON'T HAVE ANY PARENTS ANYMORE.
I'LL BE RUNNING AROUND A LOT TO-MORROW. I'D BETTER CUT THEM.
THERE'S EVEN PAPER HERE TO CATCH THE CLIPPINGS.
PACHIK
PACHIK
PACHIK
SHAKIM
SHAKIM
?

PACHIK
PACHIK
SHAKIM
?
SHAKIM
PACHIK
SHAKIM

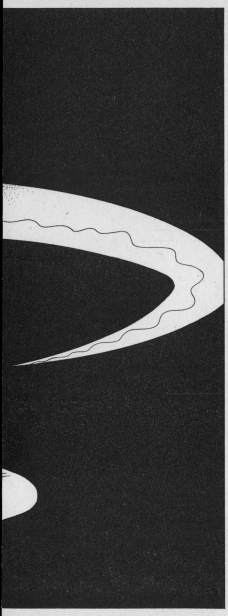

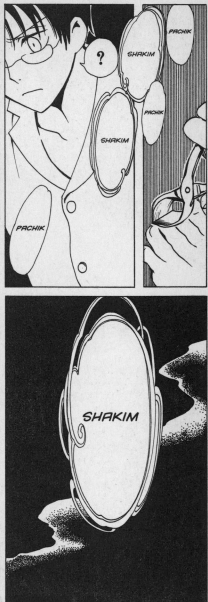

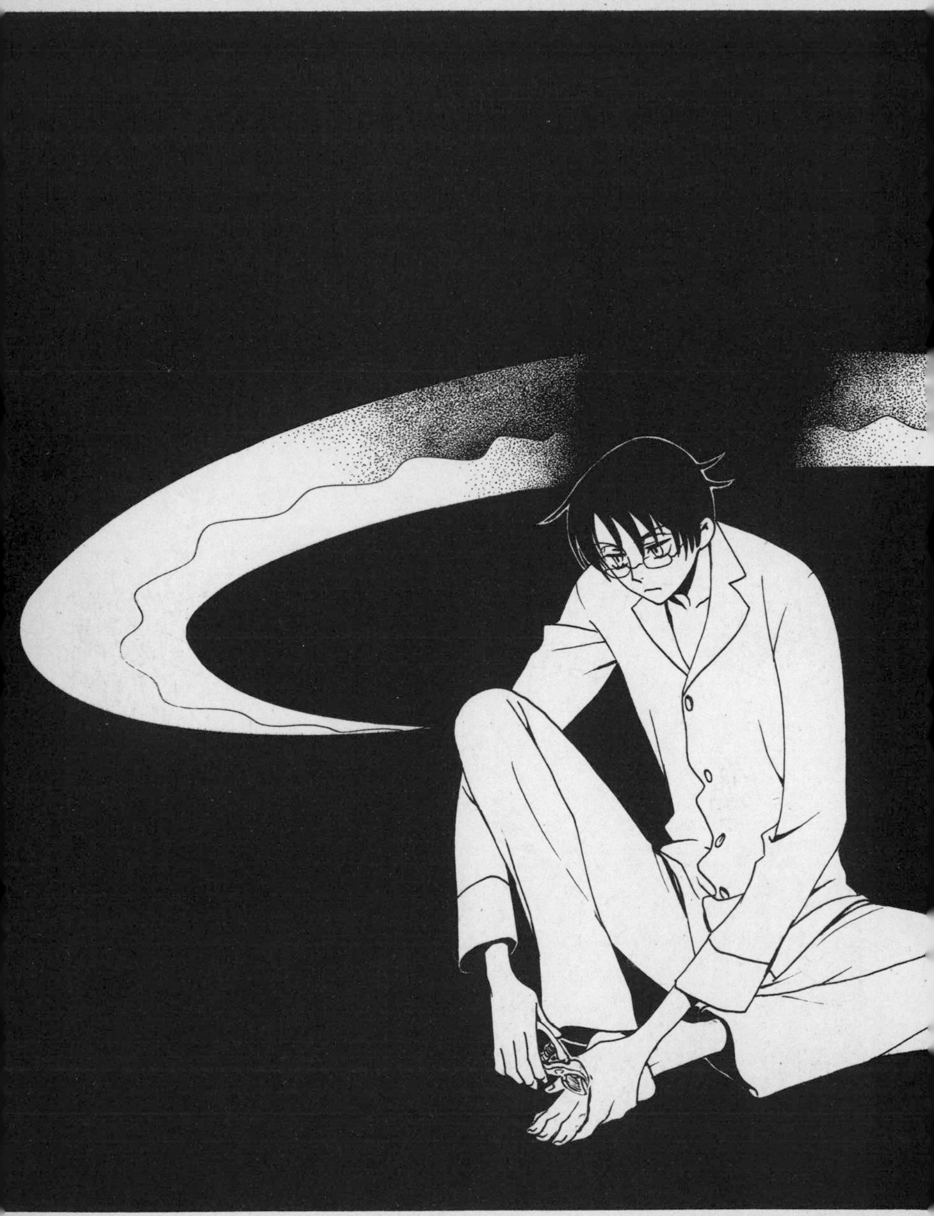

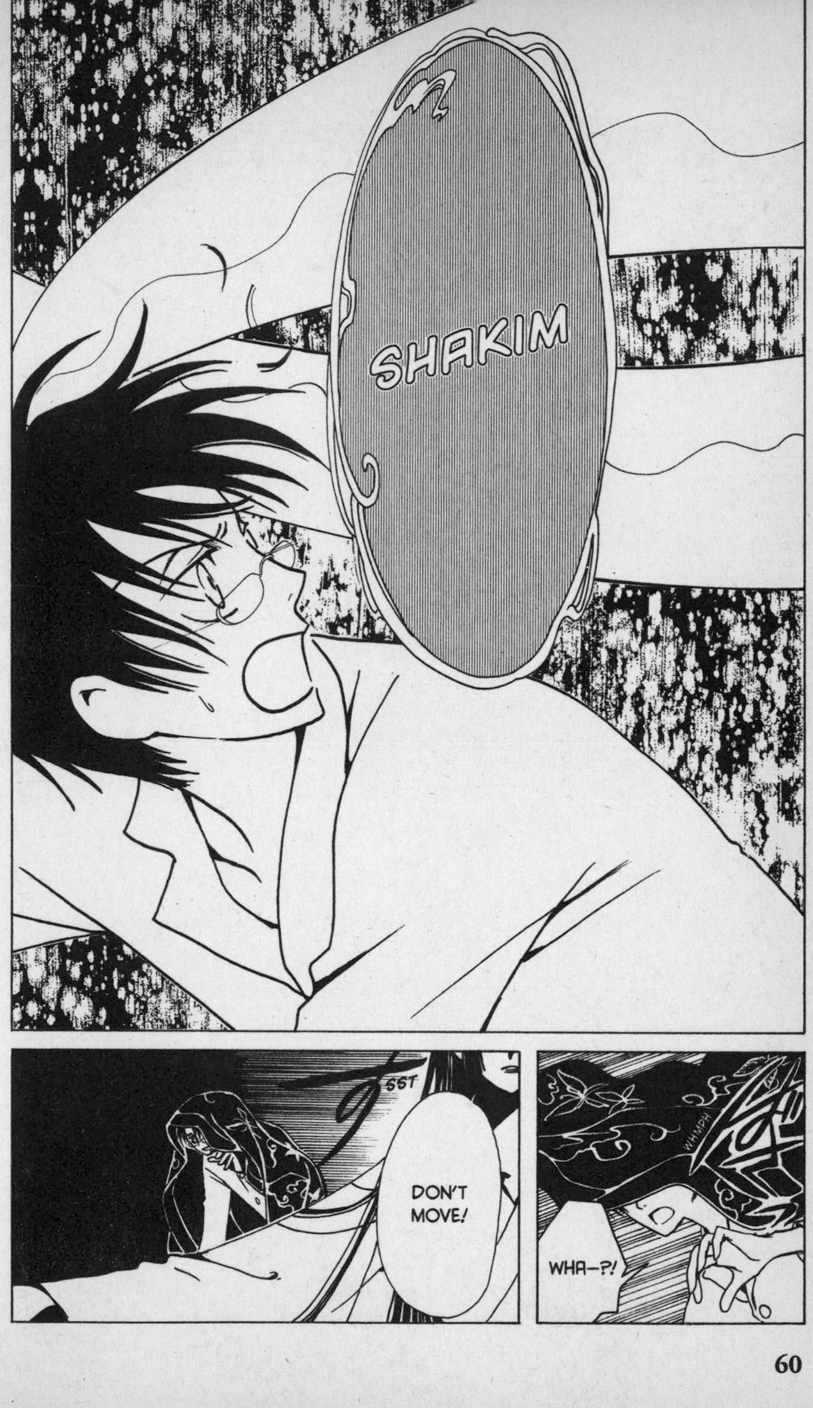
SHAKIM
WHMPH
WHA-?!
SST
DON'T
MOVE!

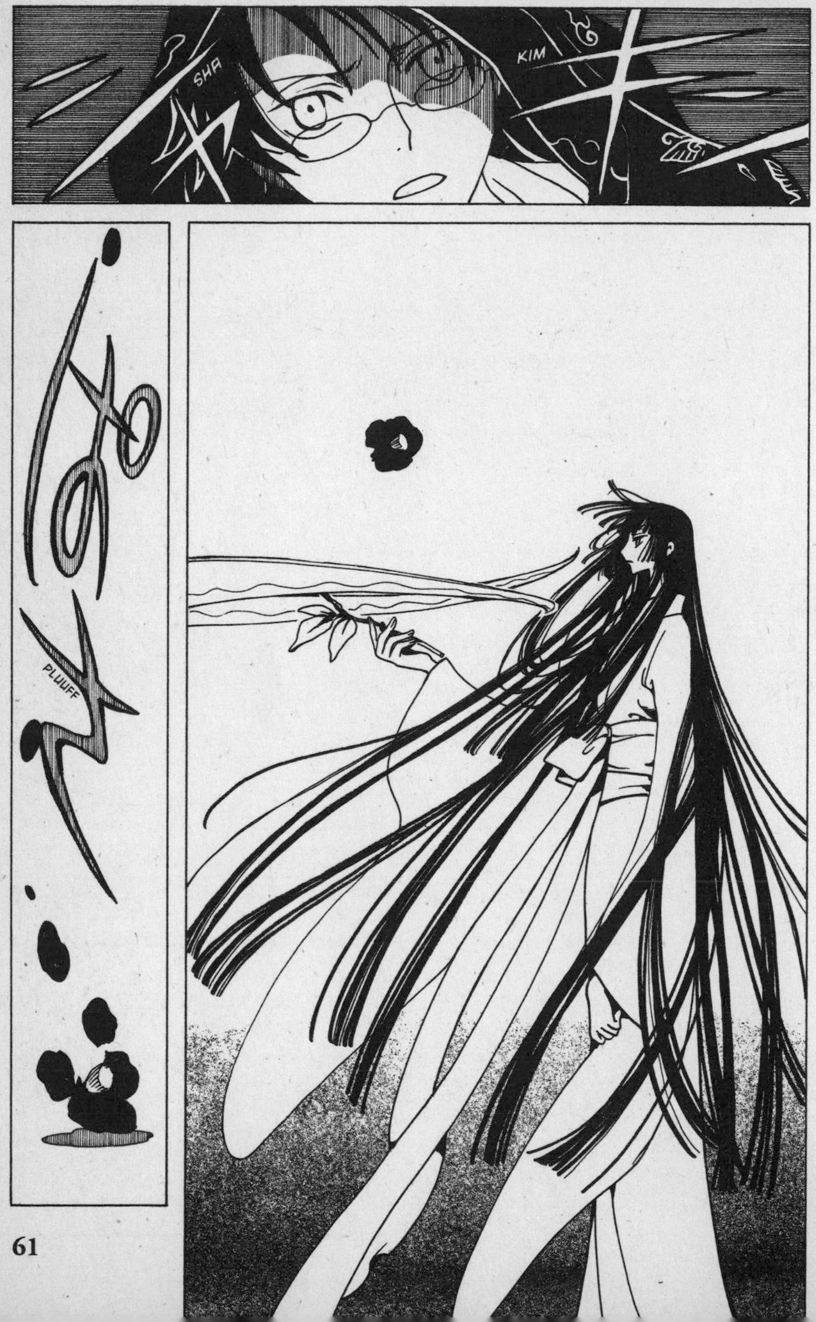
KIM
SHA
PLUUFF

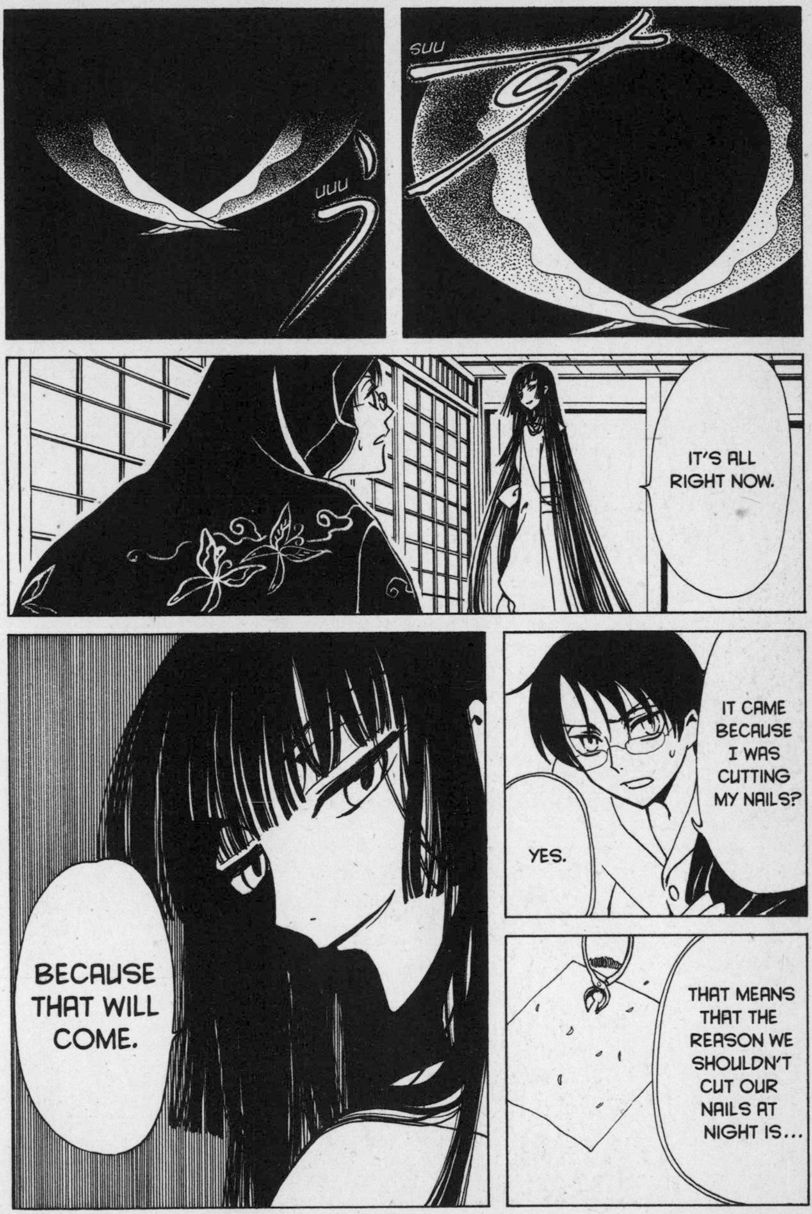
SUU
UUU
IT'S ALL RIGHT NOW.
IT CAME BECAUSE I WAS CUTTING MY NAILS?
YES.
THAT MEANS THAT THE REASON WE SHOULDN'T CUT OUR NAILS AT NIGHT IS...
BECAUSE THAT WILL COME.

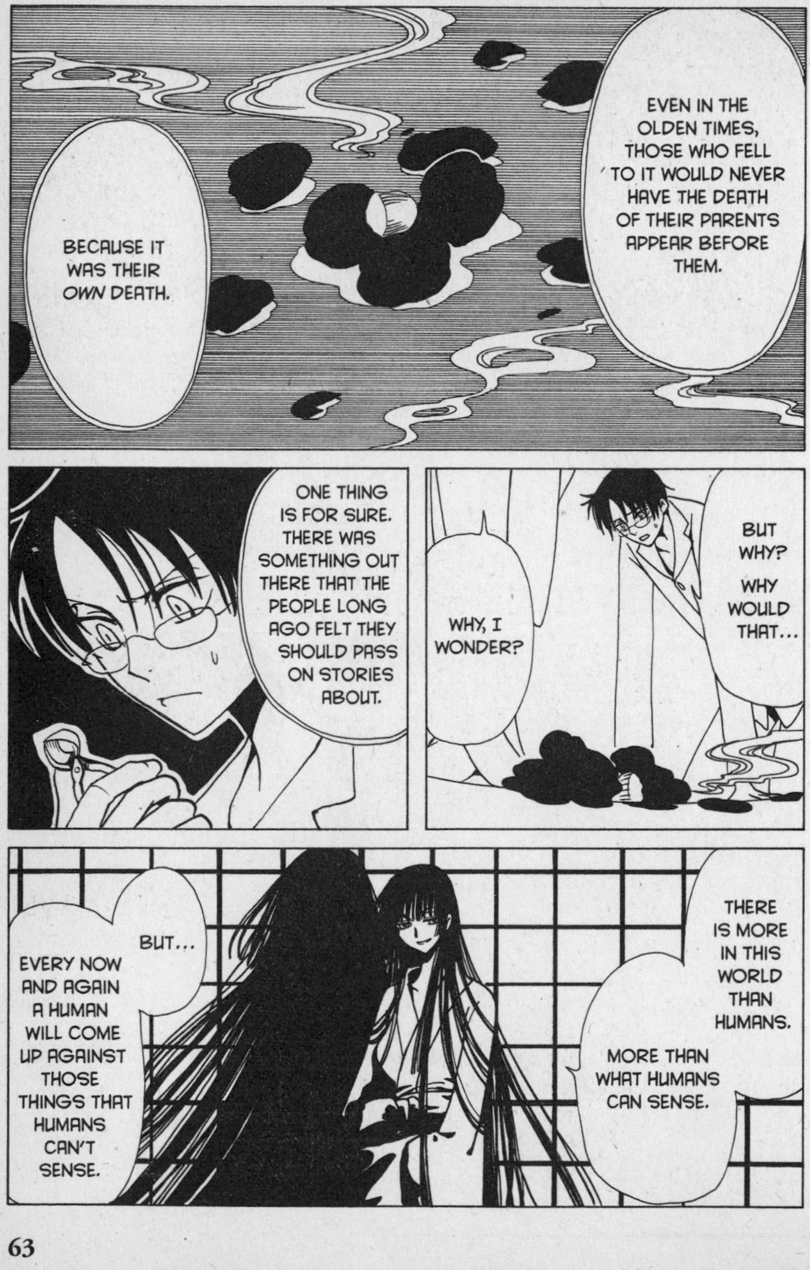
EVEN IN THE OLDEN TIMES, THOSE WHO FELL TO IT WOULD NEVER HAVE THE DEATH OF THEIR PARENTS APPEAR BEFORE THEM.
BECAUSE IT WAS THEIR *OWN* DEATH.
BUT WHY?
WHY WOULD THAT...
WHY, I WONDER?
ONE THING IS FOR SURE. THERE WAS SOMETHING OUT THERE THAT THE PEOPLE LONG AGO FELT THEY SHOULD PASS ON STORIES ABOUT.
THERE IS MORE IN THIS WORLD THAN HUMANS.
MORE THAN WHAT HUMANS CAN SENSE.
BUT...
EVERY NOW AND AGAIN A HUMAN WILL COME UP AGAINST THOSE THINGS THAT HUMANS CAN'T SENSE.

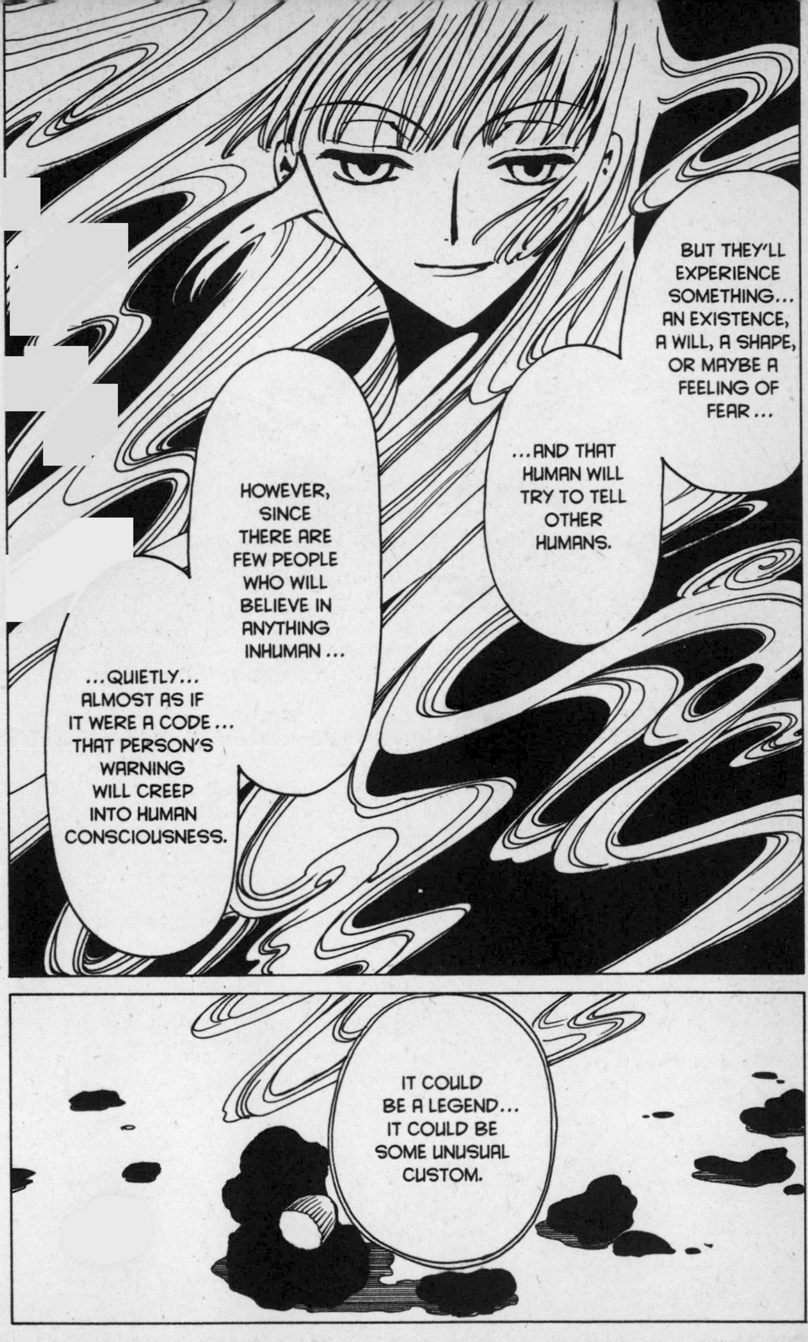
BUT THEY'LL EXPERIENCE SOMETHING... AN EXISTENCE, A WILL, A SHAPE, OR MAYBE A FEELING OF FEAR...
...AND THAT HUMAN WILL TRY TO TELL OTHER HUMANS.
HOWEVER, SINCE THERE ARE FEW PEOPLE WHO WILL BELIEVE IN ANYTHING INHUMAN...
...QUIETLY... ALMOST AS IF IT WERE A CODE... THAT PERSON'S WARNING WILL CREEP INTO HUMAN CONSCIOUSNESS.
IT COULD BE A LEGEND... IT COULD BE SOME UNUSUAL CUSTOM.

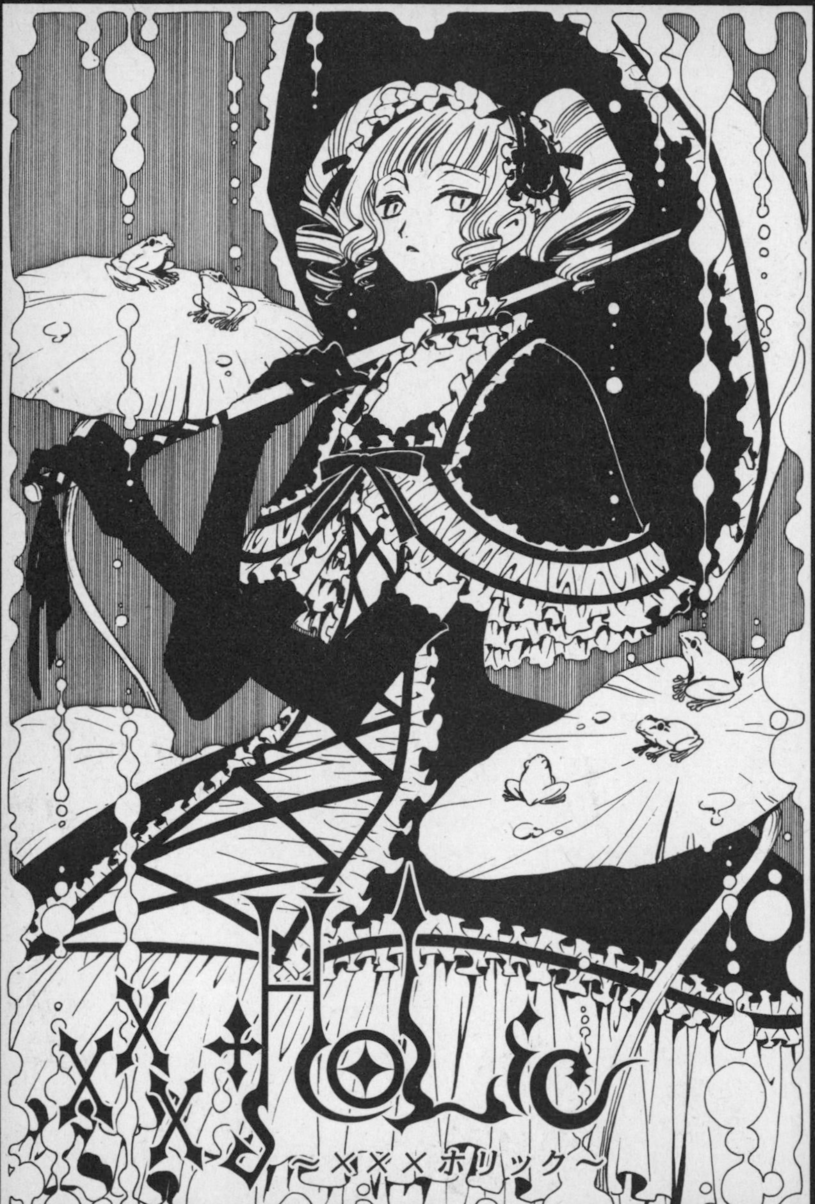
xxxHOLiC
〜×××ホリック〜

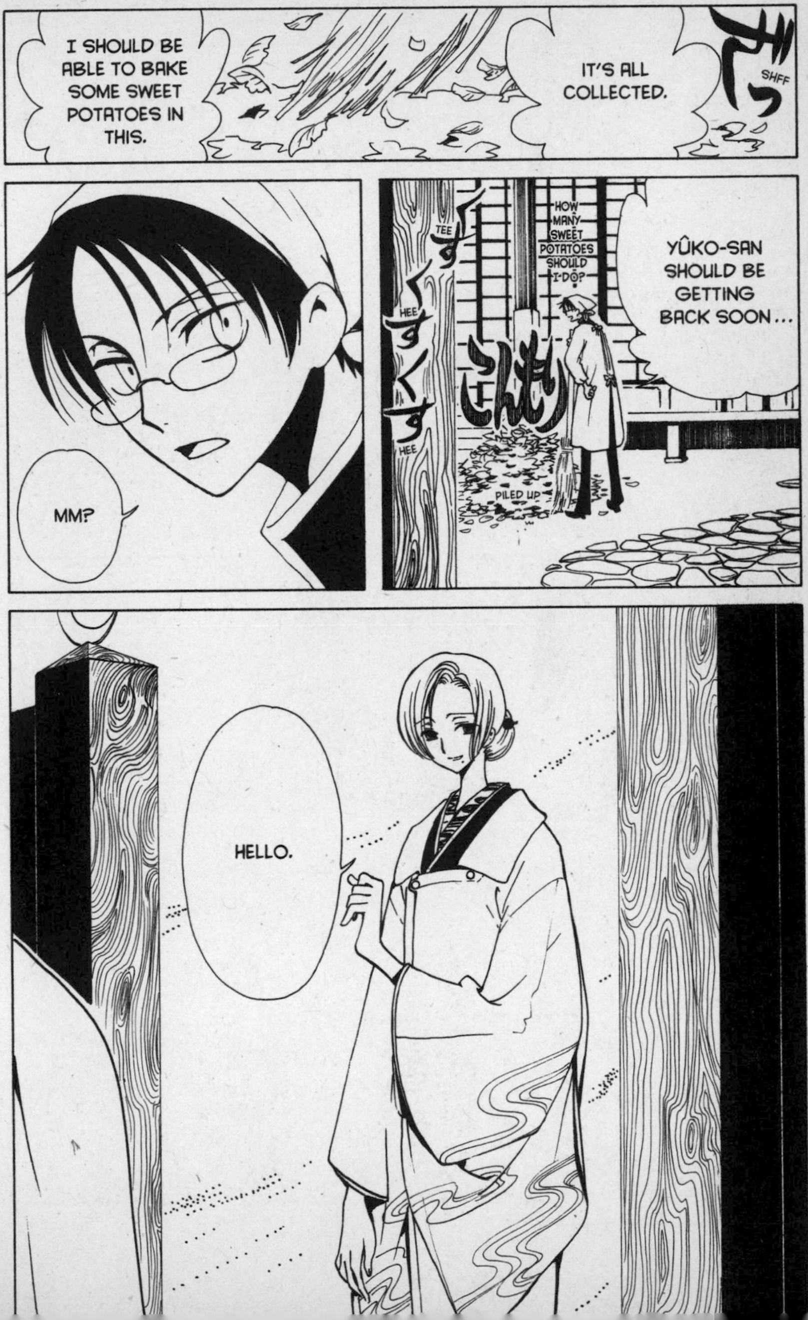
SHFF
IT'S ALL COLLECTED.
I SHOULD BE ABLE TO BAKE SOME SWEET POTATOES IN THIS.
YÛKO-SAN SHOULD BE GETTING BACK SOON...
HOW MANY SWEET POTATOES SHOULD I DO?
TEE
HEE
HEE
PILED UP
MM?
HELLO.

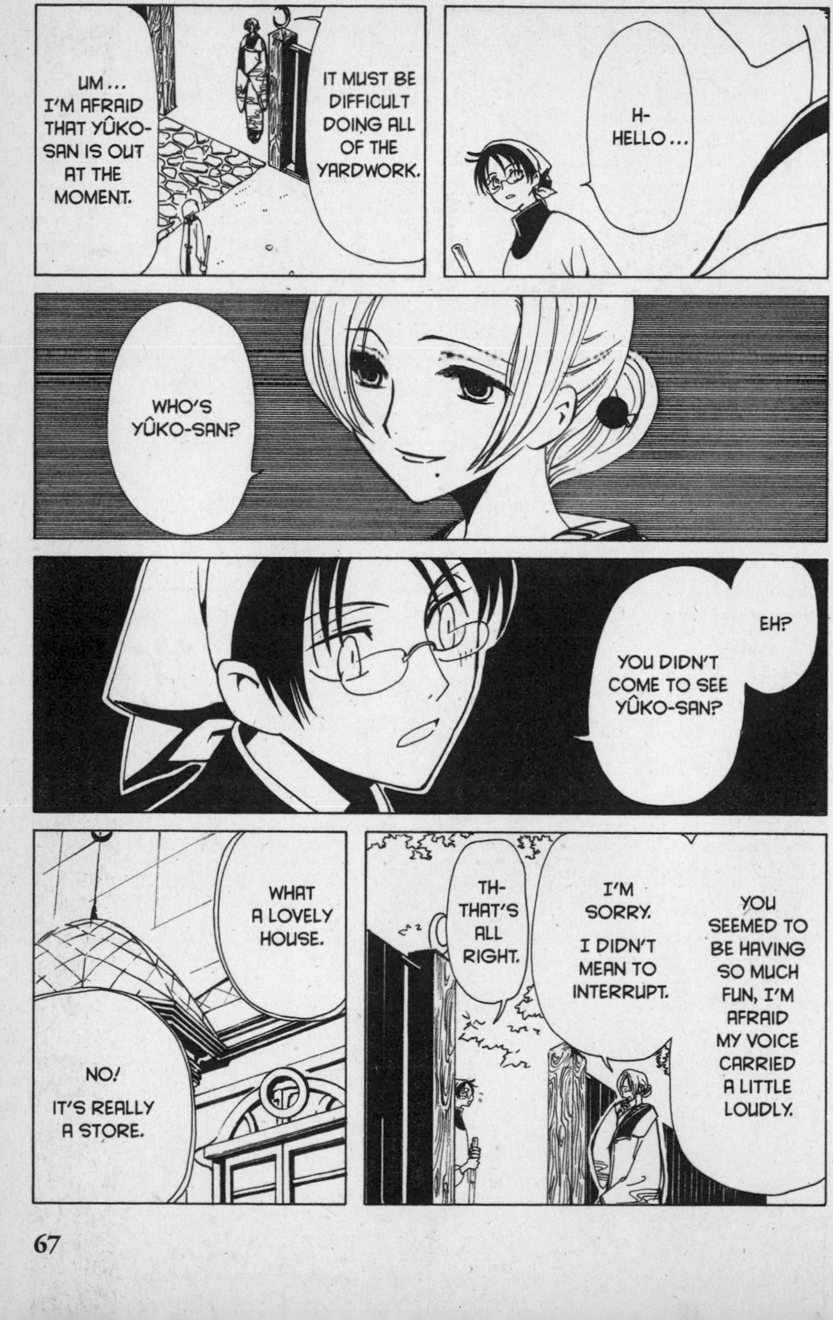
H- HELLO...
IT MUST BE DIFFICULT DOING ALL OF THE YARDWORK.
UM... I'M AFRAID THAT YÛKO-SAN IS OUT AT THE MOMENT.
WHO'S YÛKO-SAN?
EH?
YOU DIDN'T COME TO SEE YÛKO-SAN?
YOU SEEMED TO BE HAVING SO MUCH FUN, I'M AFRAID MY VOICE CARRIED A LITTLE LOUDLY.
I'M SORRY.
I DIDN'T MEAN TO INTERRUPT.
TH- THAT'S ALL RIGHT.
WHAT A LOVELY HOUSE.
NO!
IT'S REALLY A STORE.

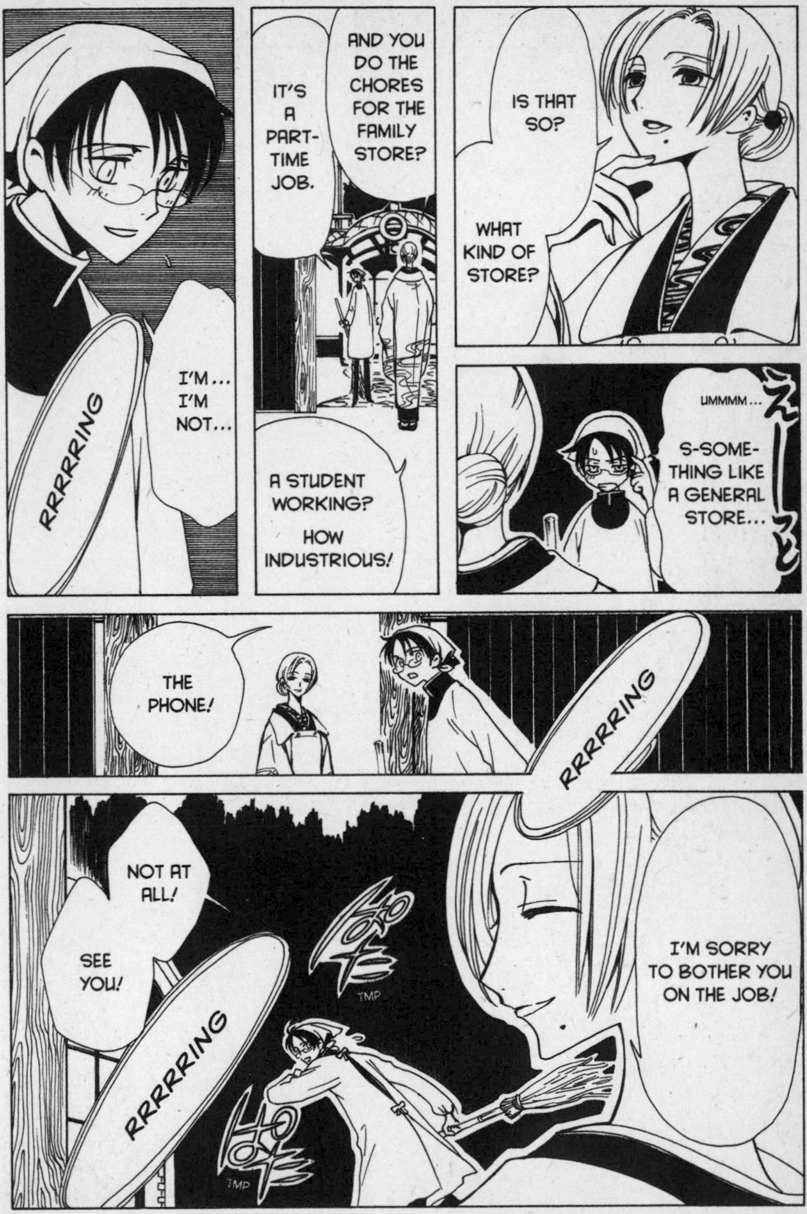
IS THAT SO?
WHAT KIND OF STORE?
UMMMM...
S-SOMETHING LIKE A GENERAL STORE...
えーっと
AND YOU DO THE CHORES FOR THE FAMILY STORE?
IT'S A PART-TIME JOB.
A STUDENT WORKING?
HOW INDUSTRIOUS!
I'M... I'M NOT...
RRRRRING
RRRRRING
THE PHONE!
I'M SORRY TO BOTHER YOU ON THE JOB!
RRRRRING
NOT AT ALL!
SEE YOU!
TMP
TMP

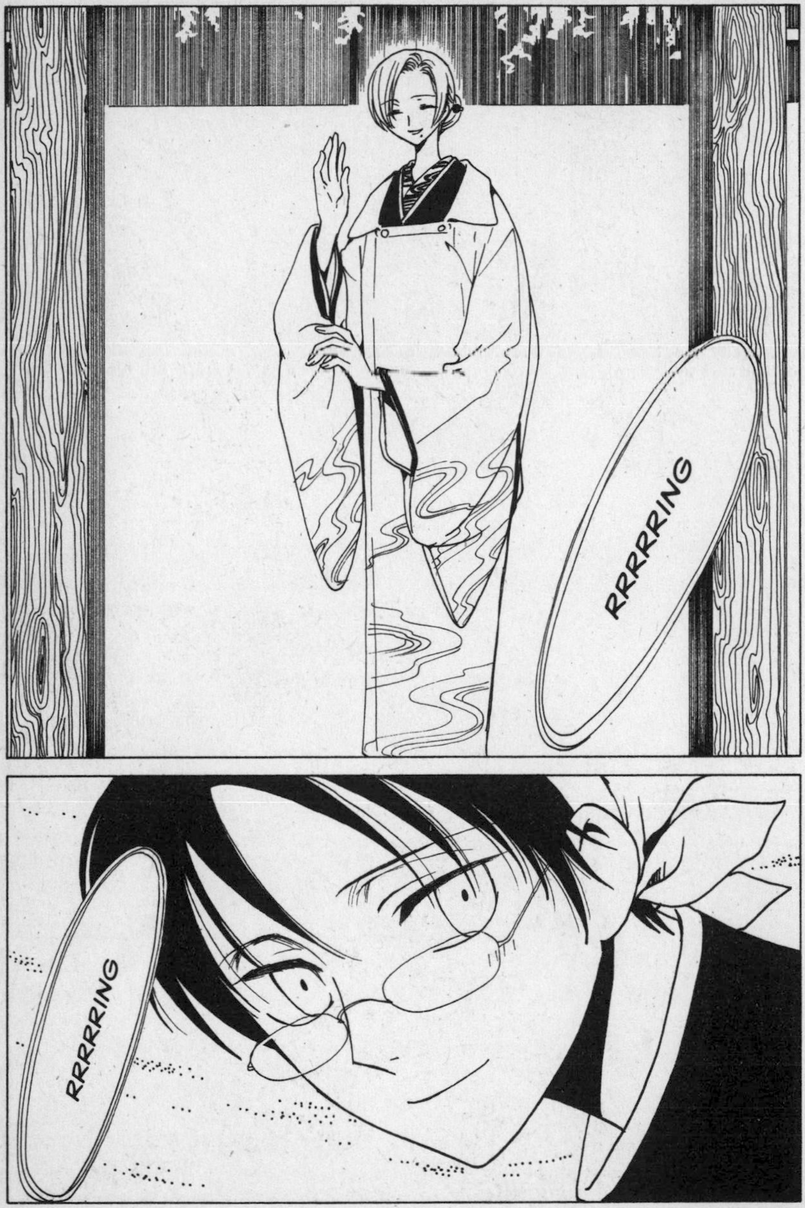
RRRRRING
RRRRRING

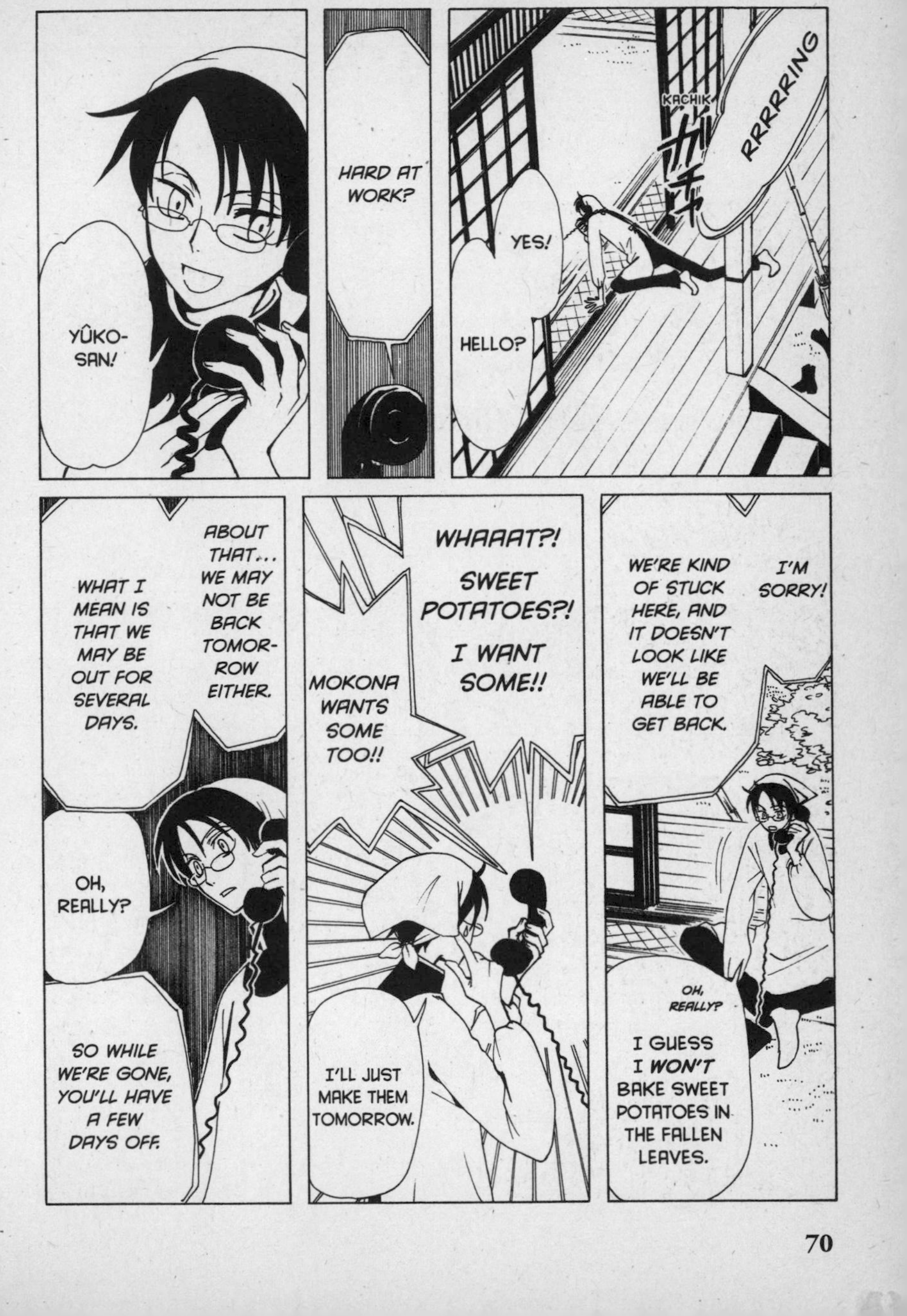
RRRRRING
KACHIK
ガチャ
YES!
HELLO?
HARD AT WORK?
YÛKO-SAN!
I'M SORRY!
WE'RE KIND OF STUCK HERE, AND IT DOESN'T LOOK LIKE WE'LL BE ABLE TO GET BACK.
OH, REALLY?
I GUESS I *WON'T* BAKE SWEET POTATOES IN THE FALLEN LEAVES.
WHAAAT?!
SWEET POTATOES?!
I WANT SOME!!
MOKONA WANTS SOME TOO!!
I'LL JUST MAKE THEM TOMORROW.
ABOUT THAT... WE MAY NOT BE BACK TOMORROW EITHER.
WHAT I MEAN IS THAT WE MAY BE OUT FOR SEVERAL DAYS.
OH, REALLY?
SO WHILE WE'RE GONE, YOU'LL HAVE A FEW DAYS OFF.

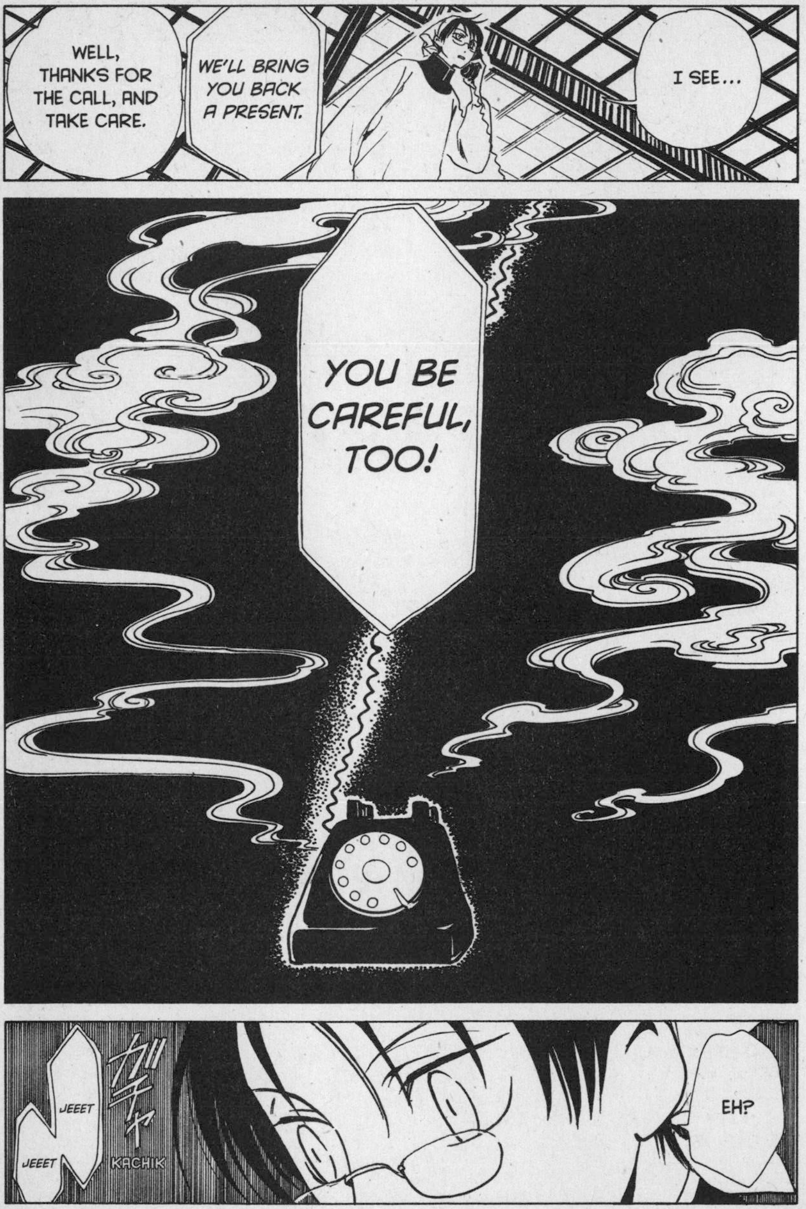
I SEE...
WE'LL BRING YOU BACK A PRESENT.
WELL, THANKS FOR THE CALL, AND TAKE CARE.
YOU BE CAREFUL, TOO!
EH?
KACHIK
JEEET
JEEET

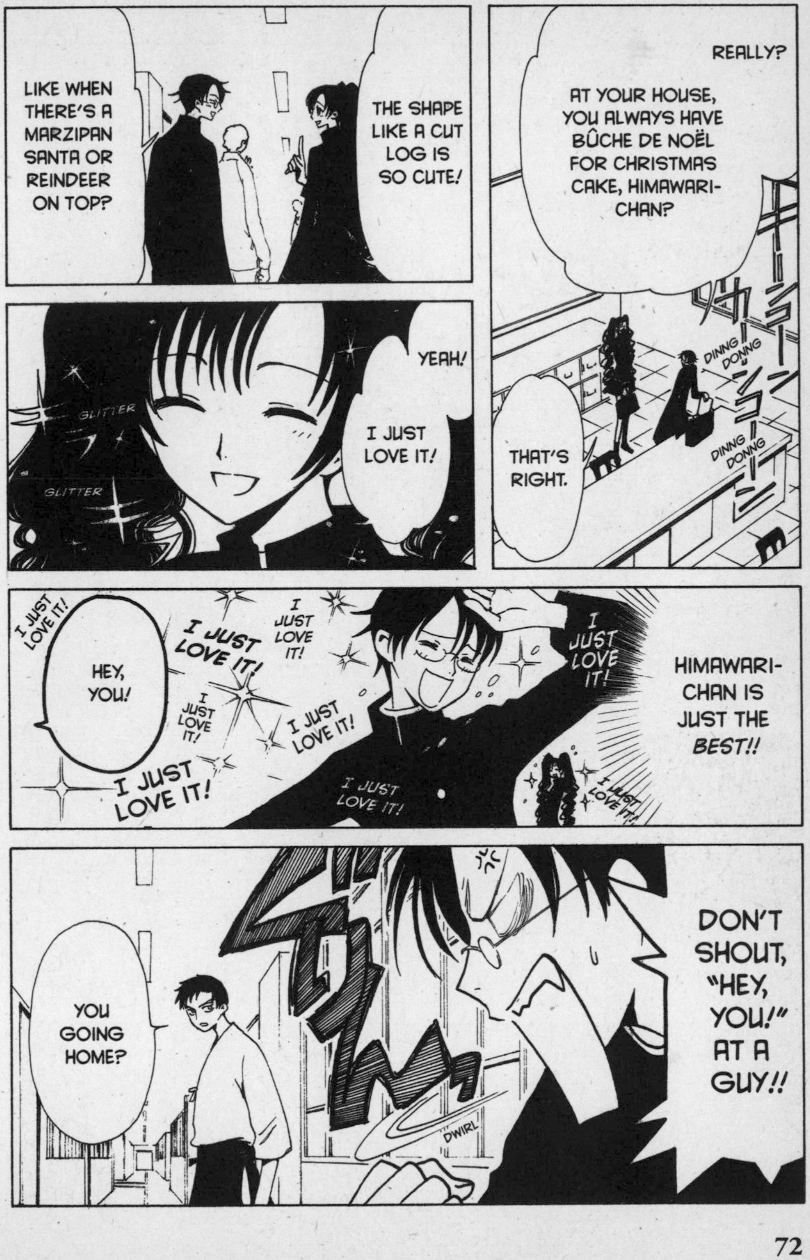
REALLY?
AT YOUR HOUSE, YOU ALWAYS HAVE BÛCHE DE NOËL FOR CHRISTMAS CAKE, HIMAWARI-CHAN?
DINNG DONNG
DINNG DONNG
THAT'S RIGHT.
THE SHAPE LIKE A CUT LOG IS SO CUTE!
LIKE WHEN THERE'S A MARZIPAN SANTA OR REINDEER ON TOP?
YEAH!
I JUST LOVE IT!
GLITTER
GLITTER
HIMAWARI-CHAN IS JUST THE BEST!!
I JUST LOVE IT!
I JUST LOVE IT!
I JUST LOVE IT!
I JUST LOVE IT!
I JUST LOVE IT!
I JUST LOVE IT!
I JUST LOVE IT!
I JUST LOVE IT!
I JUST LOVE IT!
HEY, YOU!
DON'T SHOUT, "HEY, YOU!" AT A GUY!!
DWIRL
YOU GOING HOME?

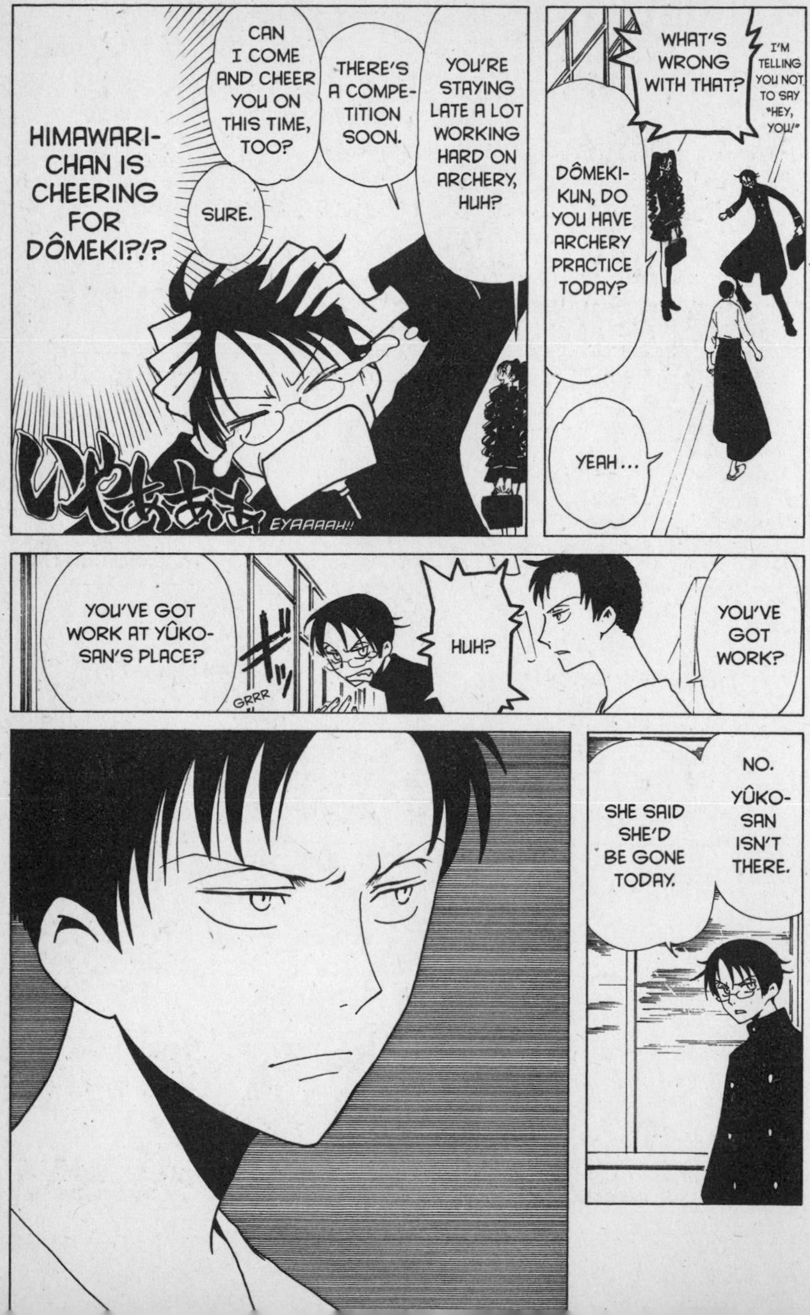
I'M TELLING YOU NOT TO SAY "HEY, YOU!"
WHAT'S WRONG WITH THAT?
DÔMEKI-KUN, DO YOU HAVE ARCHERY PRACTICE TODAY?
YEAH...
YOU'RE STAYING LATE A LOT WORKING HARD ON ARCHERY, HUH?
THERE'S A COMPETITION SOON.
CAN I COME AND CHEER YOU ON THIS TIME, TOO?
SURE.
HIMAWARI-CHAN IS CHEERING FOR DÔMEKI?!?
いやあああ
EYAAAAAH!!
YOU'VE GOT WORK?
HUH?
ギッ
GRRR
YOU'VE GOT WORK AT YÛKO-SAN'S PLACE?
NO. YÛKO-SAN ISN'T THERE.
SHE SAID SHE'D BE GONE TODAY.

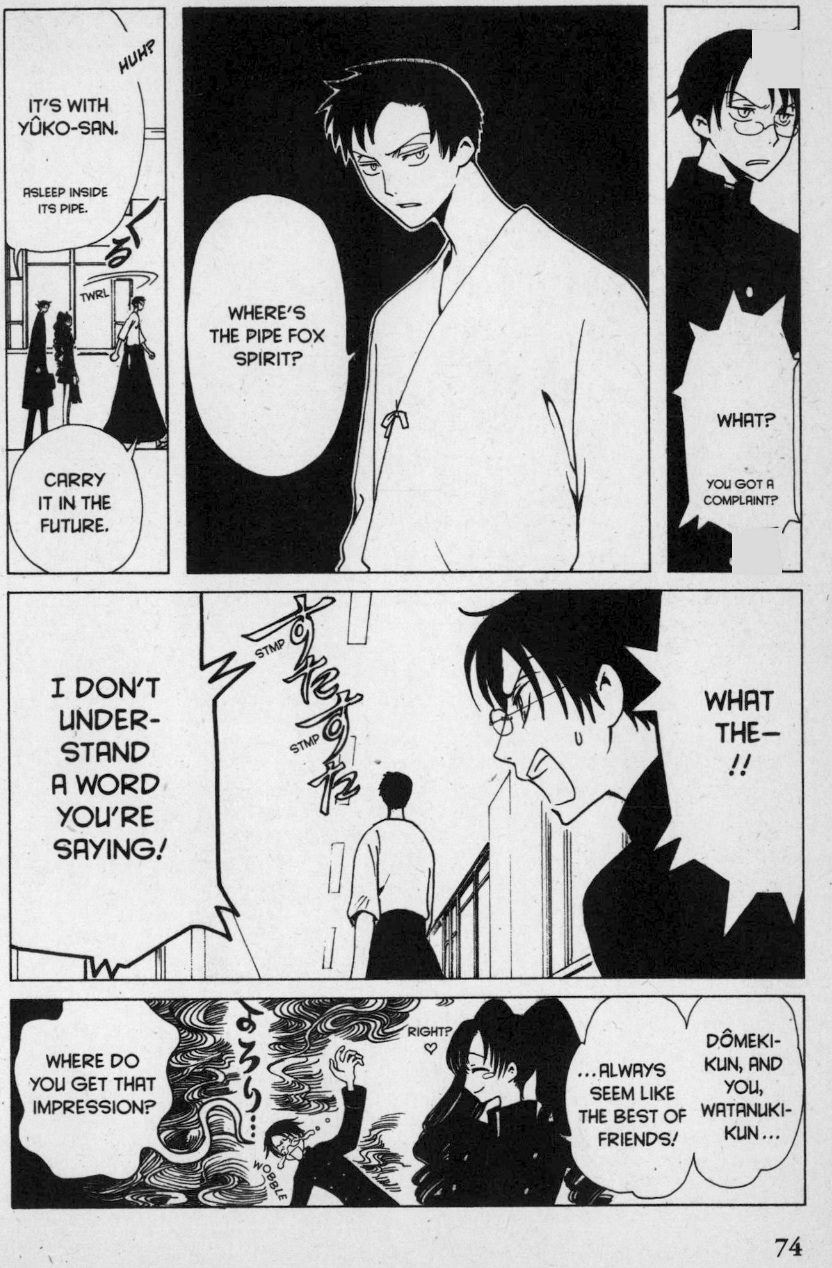
WHAT?
YOU GOT A COMPLAINT?
WHERE'S THE PIPE FOX SPIRIT?
HUH?
IT'S WITH YÛKO-SAN.
ASLEEP INSIDE ITS PIPE.
TWRL
CARRY IT IN THE FUTURE.
WHAT THE—!!
STMP
STMP
I DON'T UNDER-STAND A WORD YOU'RE SAYING!
DÔMEKI-KUN, AND YOU, WATANUKI-KUN...
...ALWAYS SEEM LIKE THE BEST OF FRIENDS!
RIGHT? ♡
WOBBLE
WHERE DO YOU GET THAT IMPRESSION?

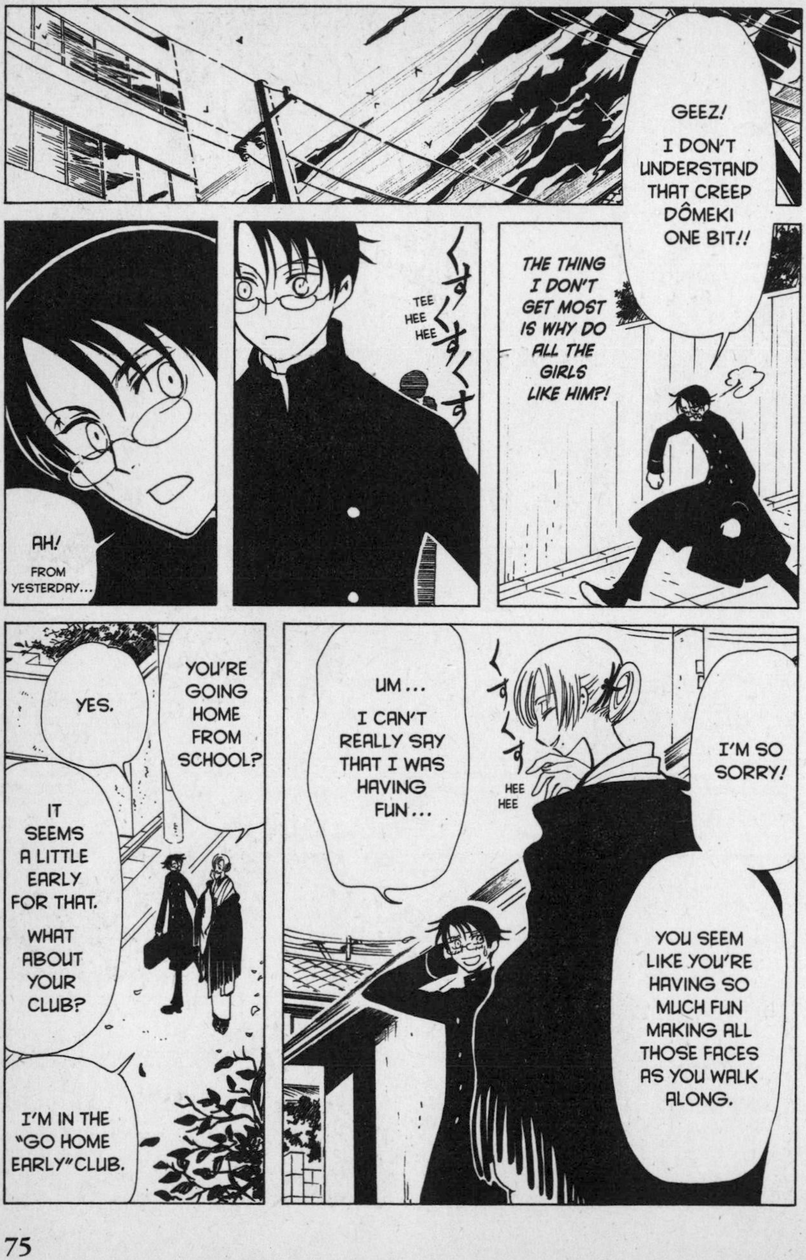
GEEZ! I DON'T UNDERSTAND THAT CREEP DÔMEKI ONE BIT!!
THE THING I DON'T GET MOST IS WHY DO ALL THE GIRLS LIKE HIM?!
くすくすくす
TEE HEE HEE
AH! FROM YESTERDAY...
I'M SO SORRY!
YOU SEEM LIKE YOU'RE HAVING SO MUCH FUN MAKING ALL THOSE FACES AS YOU WALK ALONG.
くすくす
HEE HEE
UM... I CAN'T REALLY SAY THAT I WAS HAVING FUN...
YOU'RE GOING HOME FROM SCHOOL?
YES.
IT SEEMS A LITTLE EARLY FOR THAT. WHAT ABOUT YOUR CLUB?
I'M IN THE "GO HOME EARLY" CLUB.

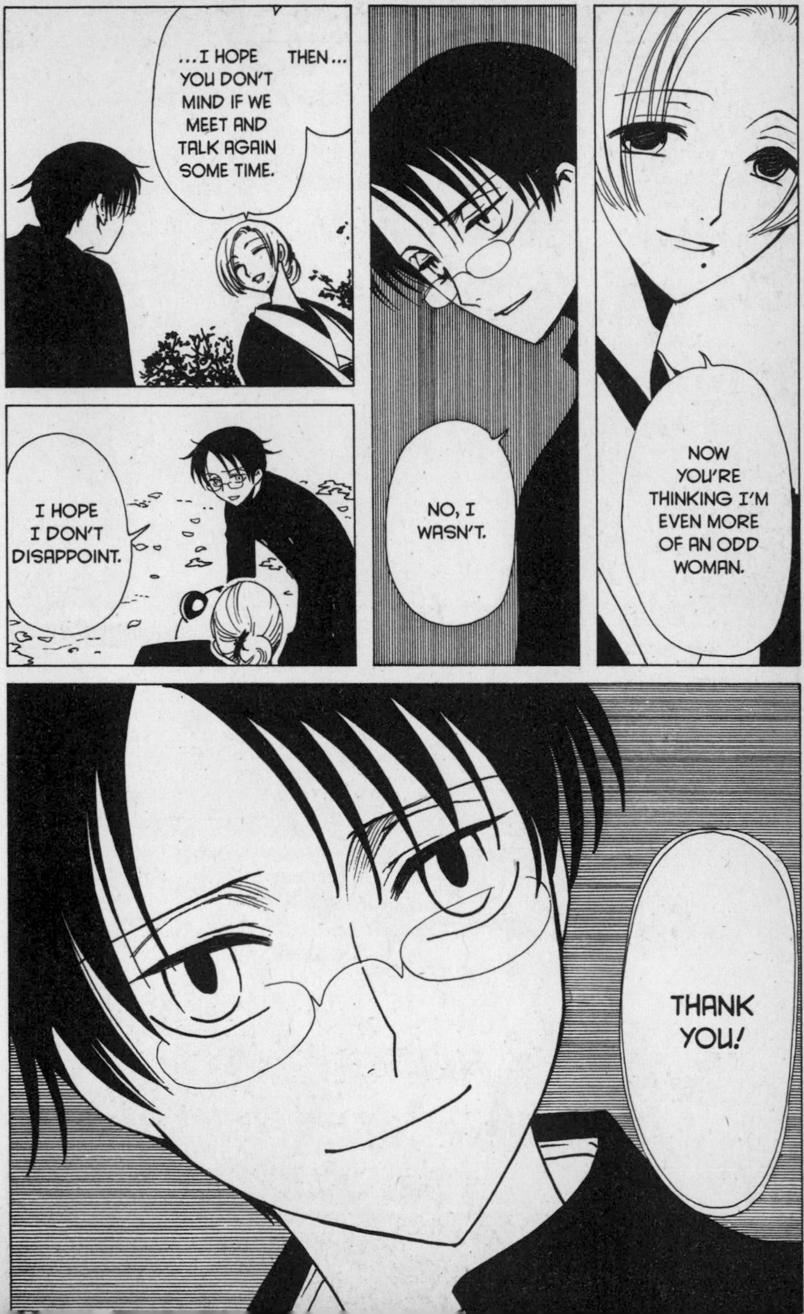
NOW YOU'RE THINKING I'M EVEN MORE OF AN ODD WOMAN.
NO, I WASN'T.
THEN... ...I HOPE YOU DON'T MIND IF WE MEET AND TALK AGAIN SOME TIME.
I HOPE I DON'T DISAPPOINT.
THANK YOU!

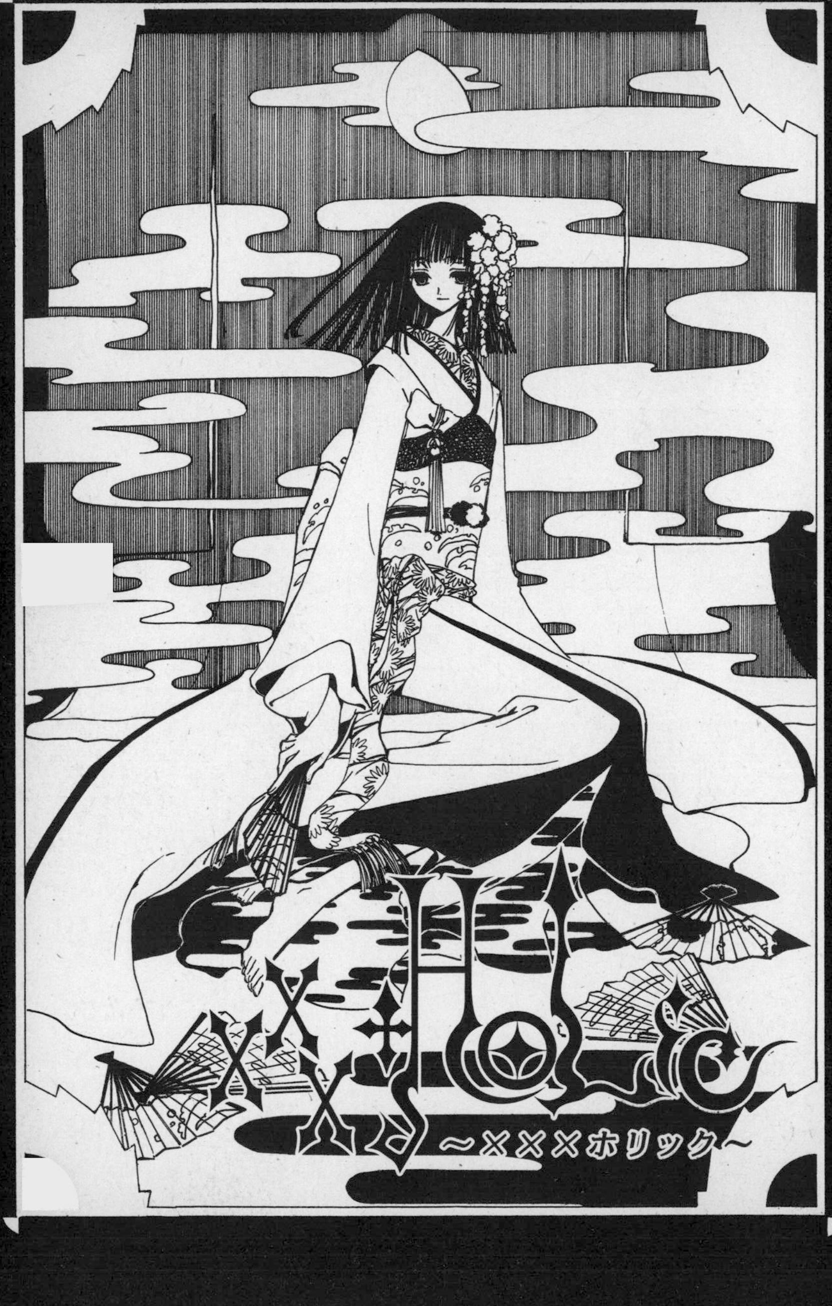
xxxHOLiC
～×××ホリック～

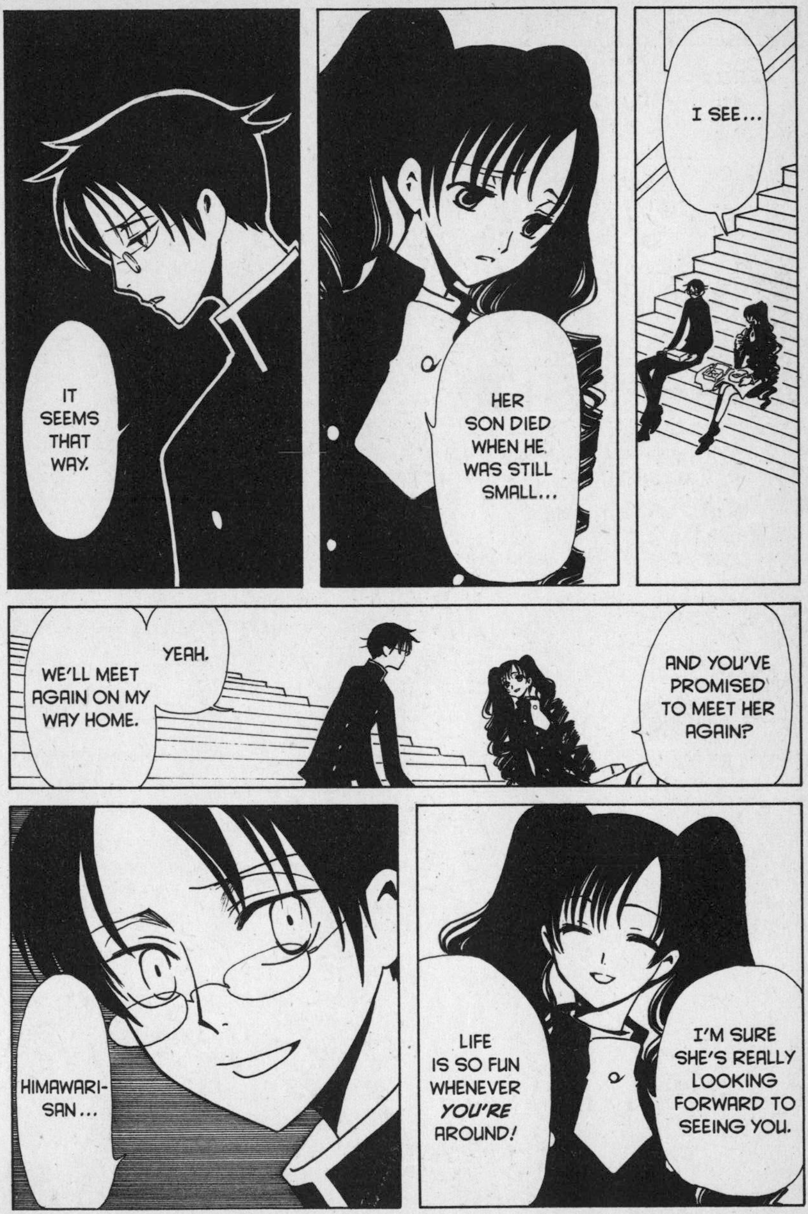
I SEE...
HER SON DIED WHEN HE WAS STILL SMALL...
IT SEEMS THAT WAY.
AND YOU'VE PROMISED TO MEET HER AGAIN?
YEAH. WE'LL MEET AGAIN ON MY WAY HOME.
I'M SURE SHE'S REALLY LOOKING FORWARD TO SEEING YOU.
LIFE IS SO FUN WHENEVER *YOU'RE* AROUND!
HIMAWARI-SAN...

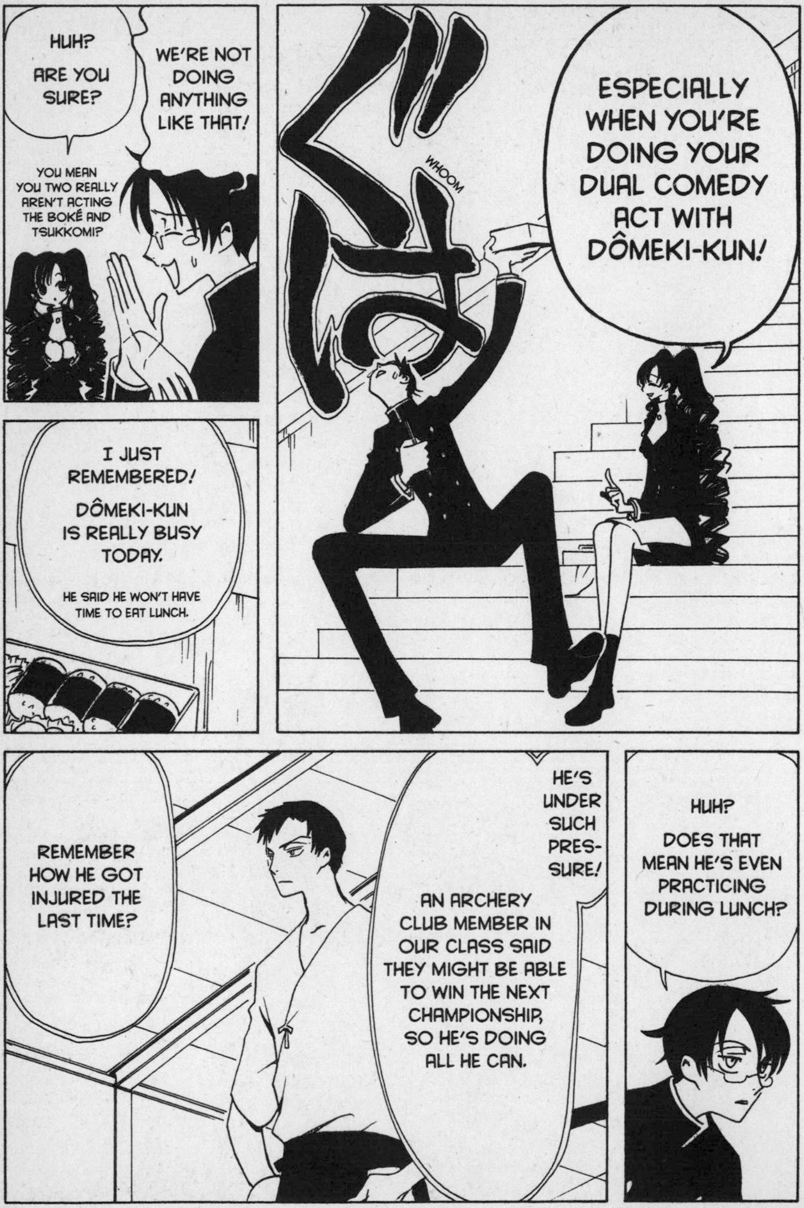
ESPECIALLY WHEN YOU'RE DOING YOUR DUAL COMEDY ACT WITH DÔMEKI-KUN!
WHOOM
WE'RE NOT DOING ANYTHING LIKE THAT!
HUH? ARE YOU SURE?
YOU MEAN YOU TWO REALLY AREN'T ACTING THE BOKÉ AND TSUKKOMI?
I JUST REMEMBERED! DÔMEKI-KUN IS REALLY BUSY TODAY.
HE SAID HE WON'T HAVE TIME TO EAT LUNCH.
HUH? DOES THAT MEAN HE'S EVEN PRACTICING DURING LUNCH?
HE'S UNDER SUCH PRES-SURE!
AN ARCHERY CLUB MEMBER IN OUR CLASS SAID THEY MIGHT BE ABLE TO WIN THE NEXT CHAMPIONSHIP, SO HE'S DOING ALL HE CAN.
REMEMBER HOW HE GOT INJURED THE LAST TIME?

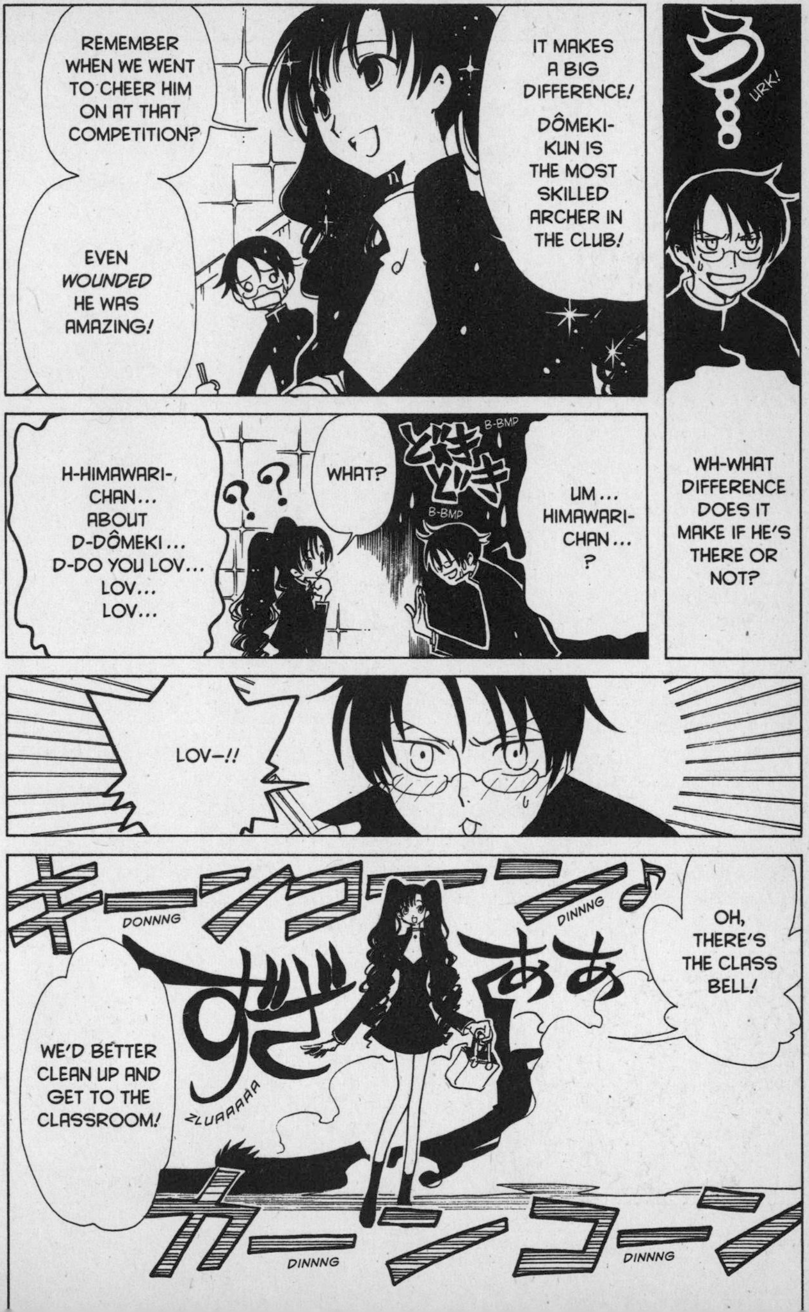
URK!
IT MAKES A BIG DIFFERENCE!
DÔMEKI-KUN IS THE MOST SKILLED ARCHER IN THE CLUB!
REMEMBER WHEN WE WENT TO CHEER HIM ON AT THAT COMPETITION?
EVEN *WOUNDED* HE WAS AMAZING!
WH-WHAT DIFFERENCE DOES IT MAKE IF HE'S THERE OR NOT?
B-BMP
B-BMP
UM ... HIMAWARI-CHAN ... ?
WHAT?
H-HIMAWARI-CHAN... ABOUT D-DÔMEKI... D-DO YOU LOV... LOV... LOV...
LOV—!!
OH, THERE'S THE CLASS BELL!
DINNNG
DONNNG
ZLUAAAAA
WE'D BETTER CLEAN UP AND GET TO THE CLASSROOM!
DINNNG
DINNNG

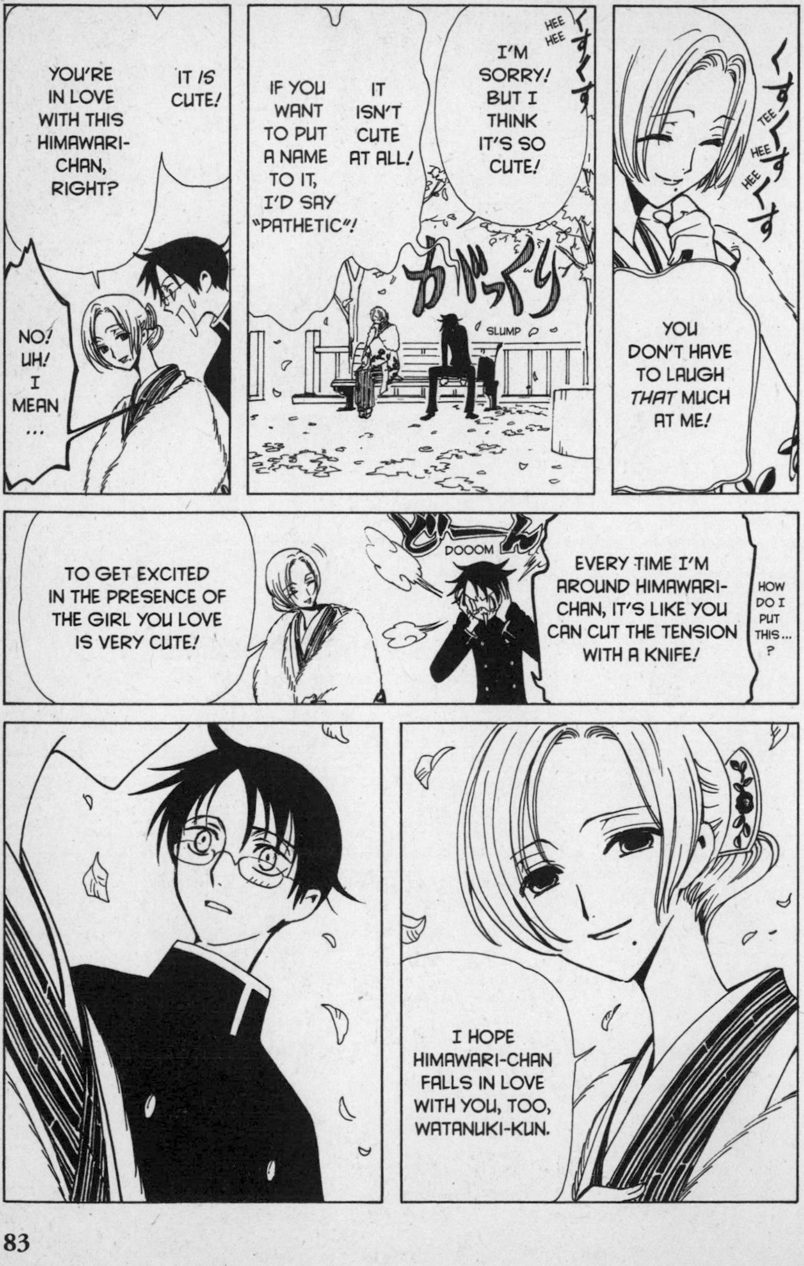
くすくす
TEE HEE HEE
YOU DON'T HAVE TO LAUGH *THAT* MUCH AT ME!
HEE HEE
くすくす
I'M SORRY! BUT I THINK IT'S SO CUTE!
IT ISN'T CUTE AT ALL!
IF YOU WANT TO PUT A NAME TO IT, I'D SAY "PATHETIC"!
がっくり
SLUMP
IT *IS* CUTE!
YOU'RE IN LOVE WITH THIS HIMAWARI-CHAN, RIGHT?
NO! UH! I MEAN ...
HOW DO I PUT THIS...?
EVERY TIME I'M AROUND HIMAWARI-CHAN, IT'S LIKE YOU CAN CUT THE TENSION WITH A KNIFE!
DOOOM
TO GET EXCITED IN THE PRESENCE OF THE GIRL YOU LOVE IS VERY CUTE!
I HOPE HIMAWARI-CHAN FALLS IN LOVE WITH YOU, TOO, WATANUKI-KUN.

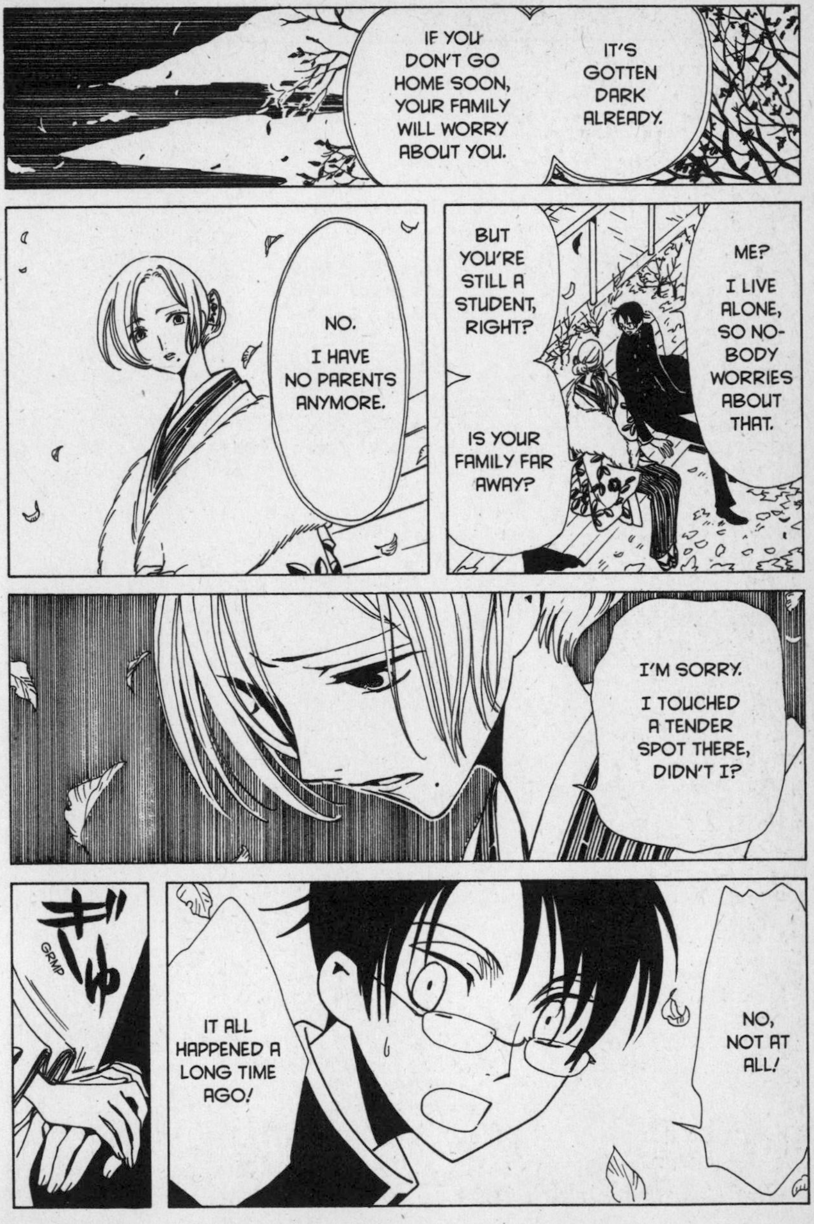
IT'S GOTTEN DARK ALREADY.
IF YOU DON'T GO HOME SOON, YOUR FAMILY WILL WORRY ABOUT YOU.
ME? I LIVE ALONE, SO NO-BODY WORRIES ABOUT THAT.
BUT YOU'RE STILL A STUDENT, RIGHT?
IS YOUR FAMILY FAR AWAY?
NO. I HAVE NO PARENTS ANYMORE.
I'M SORRY. I TOUCHED A TENDER SPOT THERE, DIDN'T I?
NO, NOT AT ALL!
IT ALL HAPPENED A LONG TIME AGO!
ぎゅ
GRMP

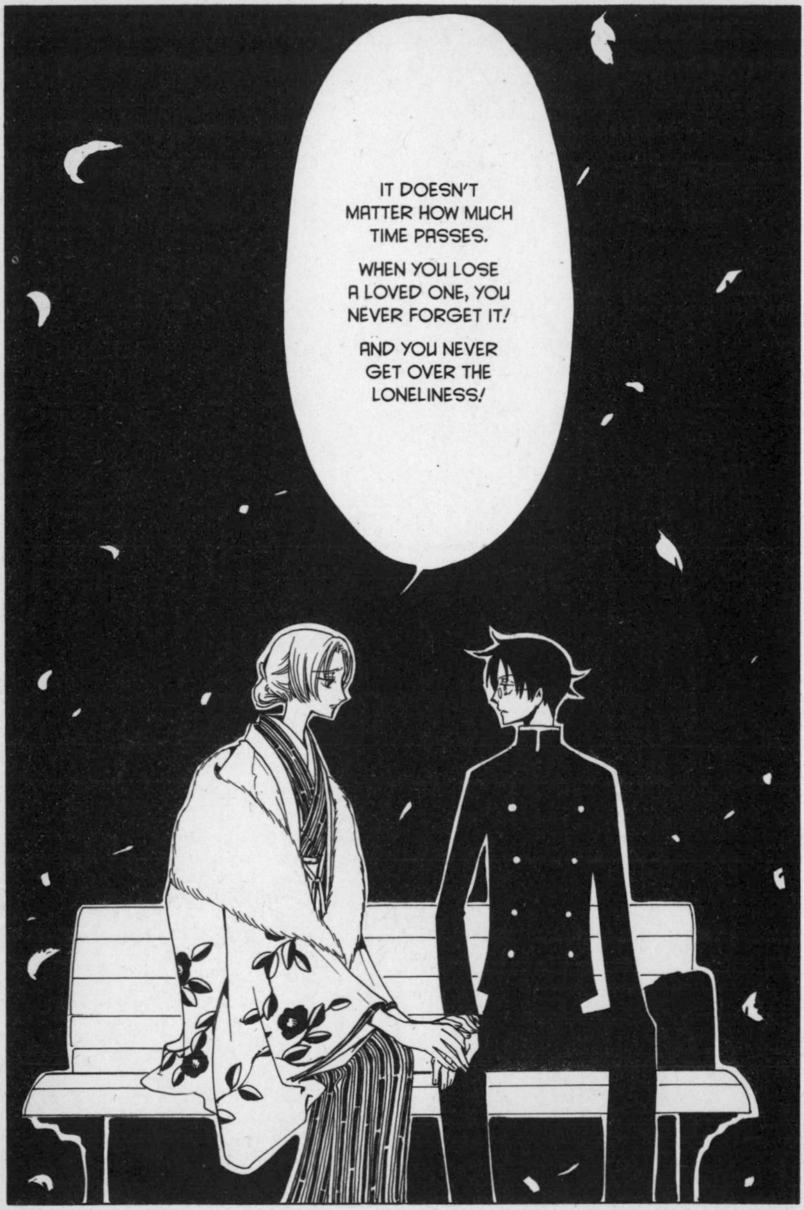
IT DOESN'T MATTER HOW MUCH TIME PASSES.
WHEN YOU LOSE A LOVED ONE, YOU NEVER FORGET IT!
AND YOU NEVER GET OVER THE LONELINESS!

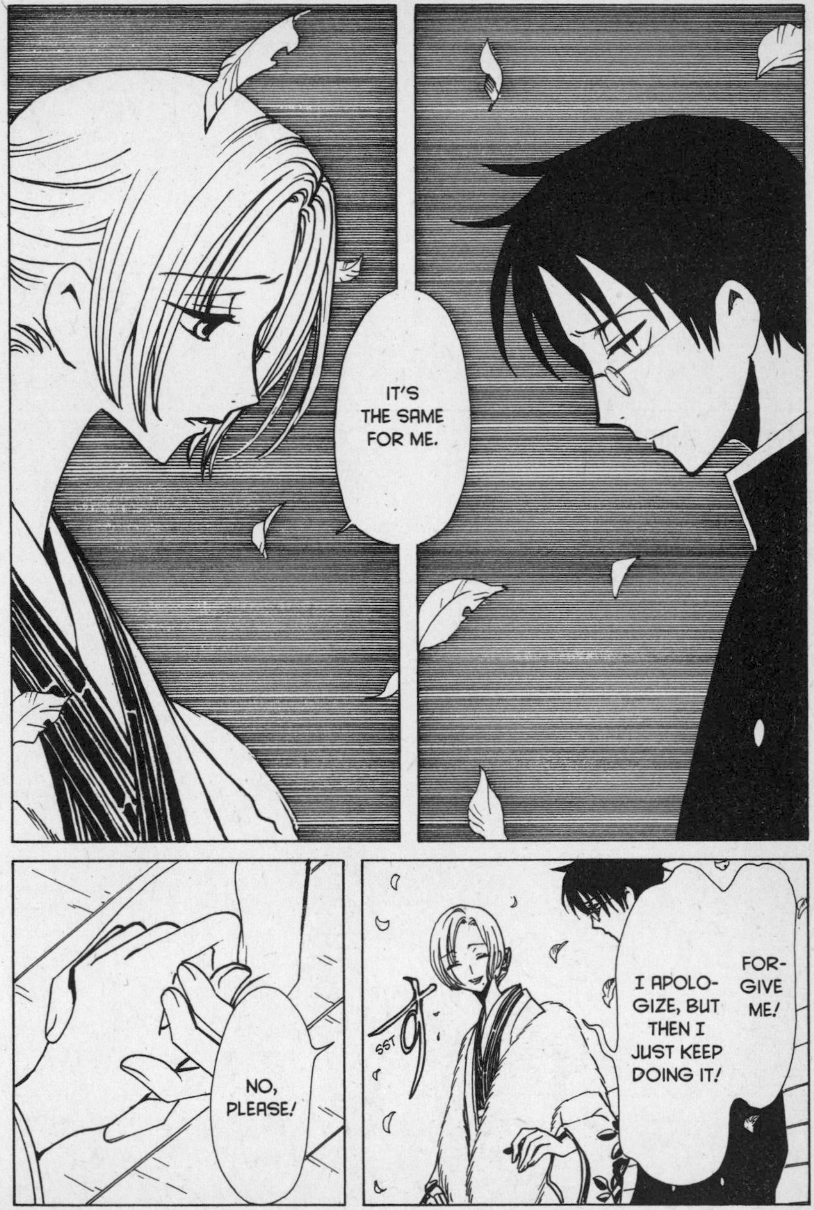
IT'S THE SAME FOR ME.
FOR-GIVE ME!
I APOLO-GIZE, BUT THEN I JUST KEEP DOING IT!
SST
NO, PLEASE!

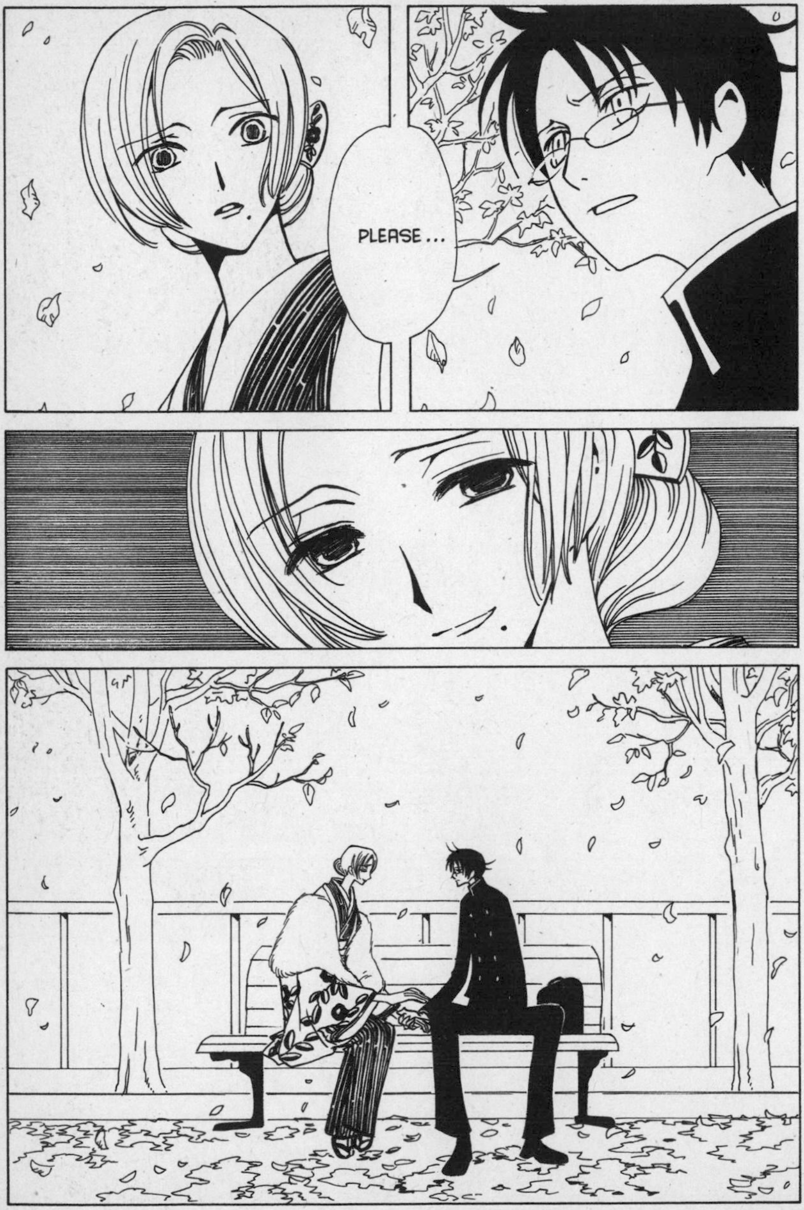
PLEASE...

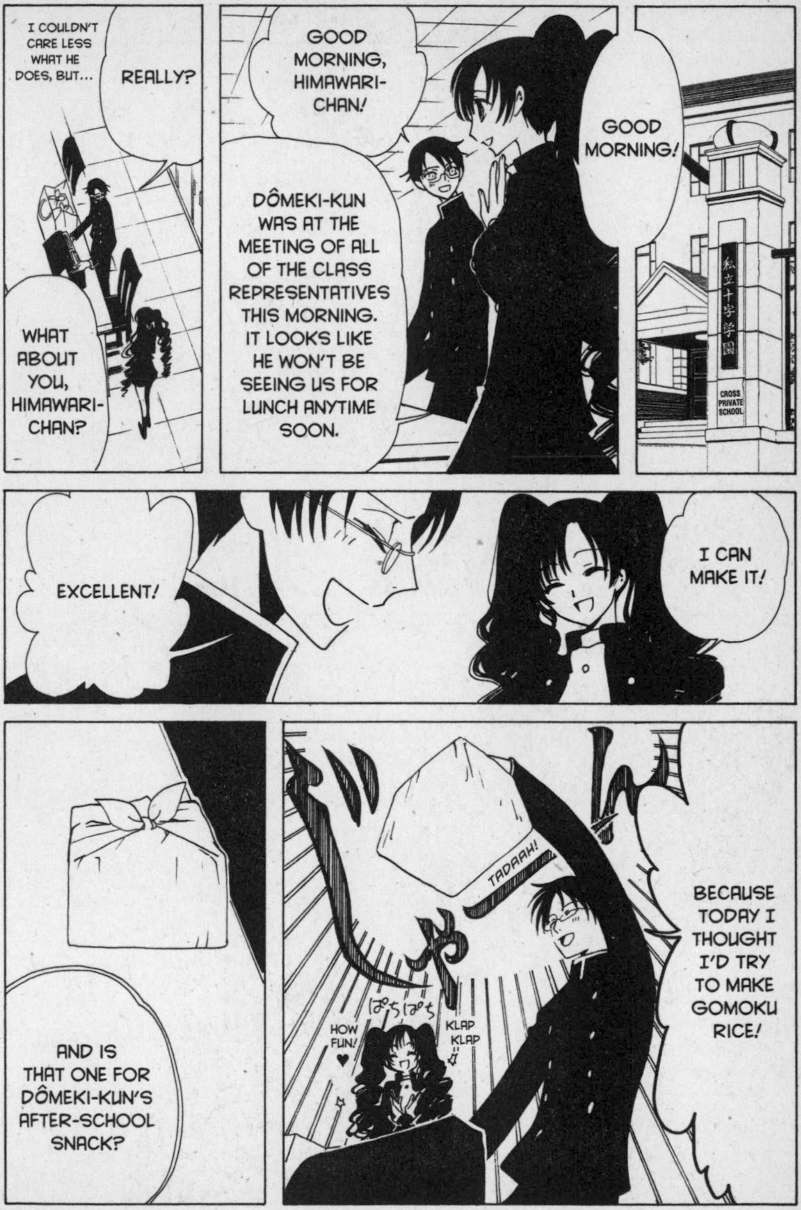
GOOD MORNING!
私立十字学園
CROSS PRIVATE SCHOOL
GOOD MORNING, HIMAWARI-CHAN!
DÔMEKI-KUN WAS AT THE MEETING OF ALL OF THE CLASS REPRESENTATIVES THIS MORNING. IT LOOKS LIKE HE WON'T BE SEEING US FOR LUNCH ANYTIME SOON.
REALLY?
I COULDN'T CARE LESS WHAT HE DOES, BUT...
WHAT ABOUT YOU, HIMAWARI-CHAN?
I CAN MAKE IT!
EXCELLENT!
BECAUSE TODAY I THOUGHT I'D TRY TO MAKE GOMOKU RICE!
TADAAH!
ぱちぱち
KLAP KLAP
HOW FUN!
AND IS THAT ONE FOR DÔMEKI-KUN'S AFTER-SCHOOL SNACK?

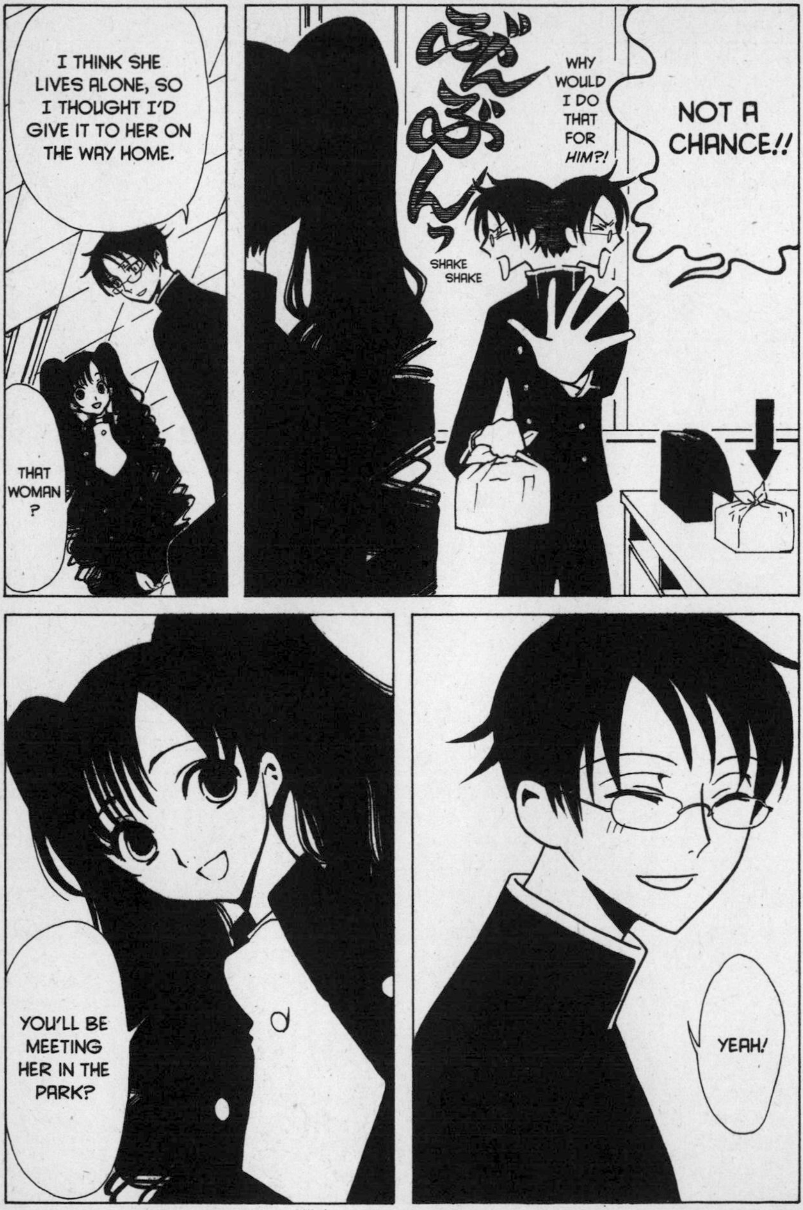
NOT A CHANCE!!
WHY WOULD I DO THAT FOR *HIM*?!
ぶんぶんっ
SHAKE SHAKE
I THINK SHE LIVES ALONE, SO I THOUGHT I'D GIVE IT TO HER ON THE WAY HOME.
THAT WOMAN?
YEAH!
YOU'LL BE MEETING HER IN THE PARK?

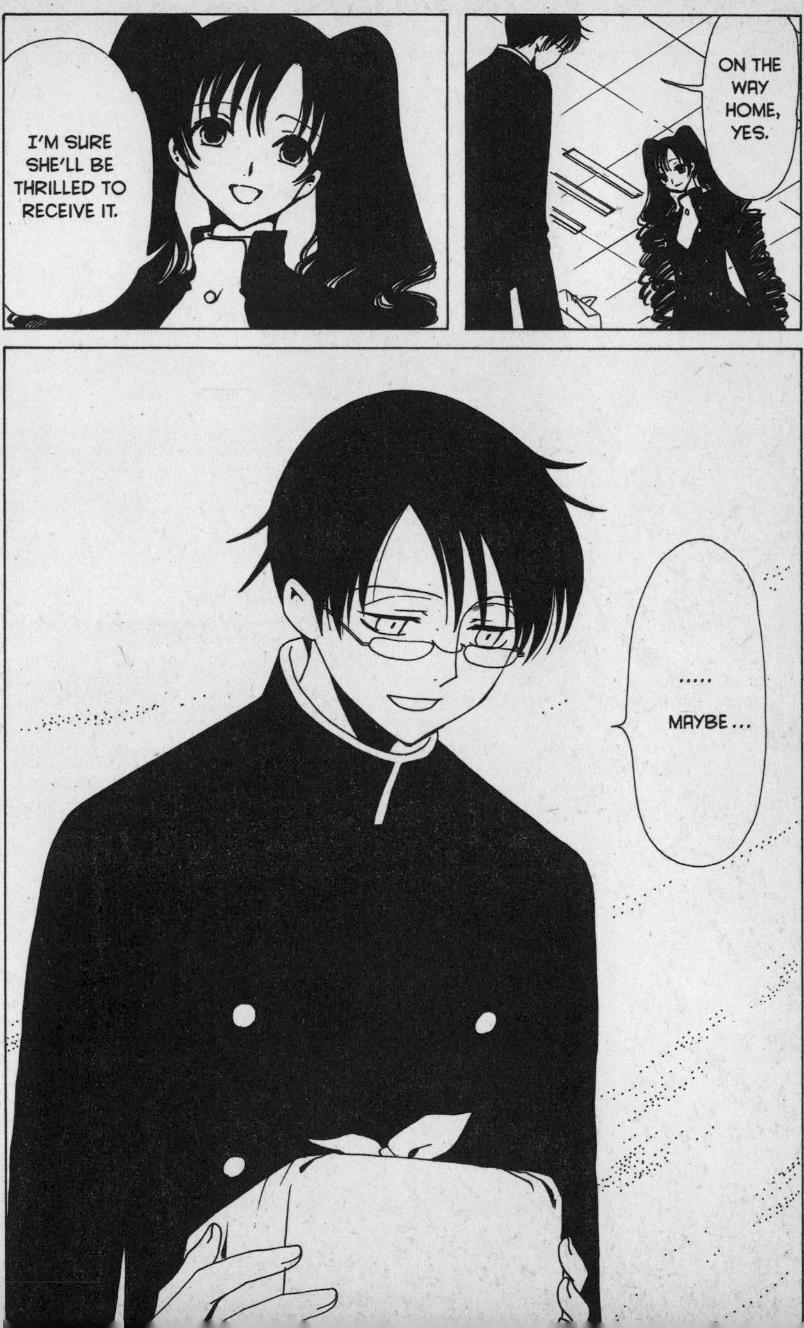
ON THE WAY HOME, YES.
I'M SURE SHE'LL BE THRILLED TO RECEIVE IT.
..... MAYBE...

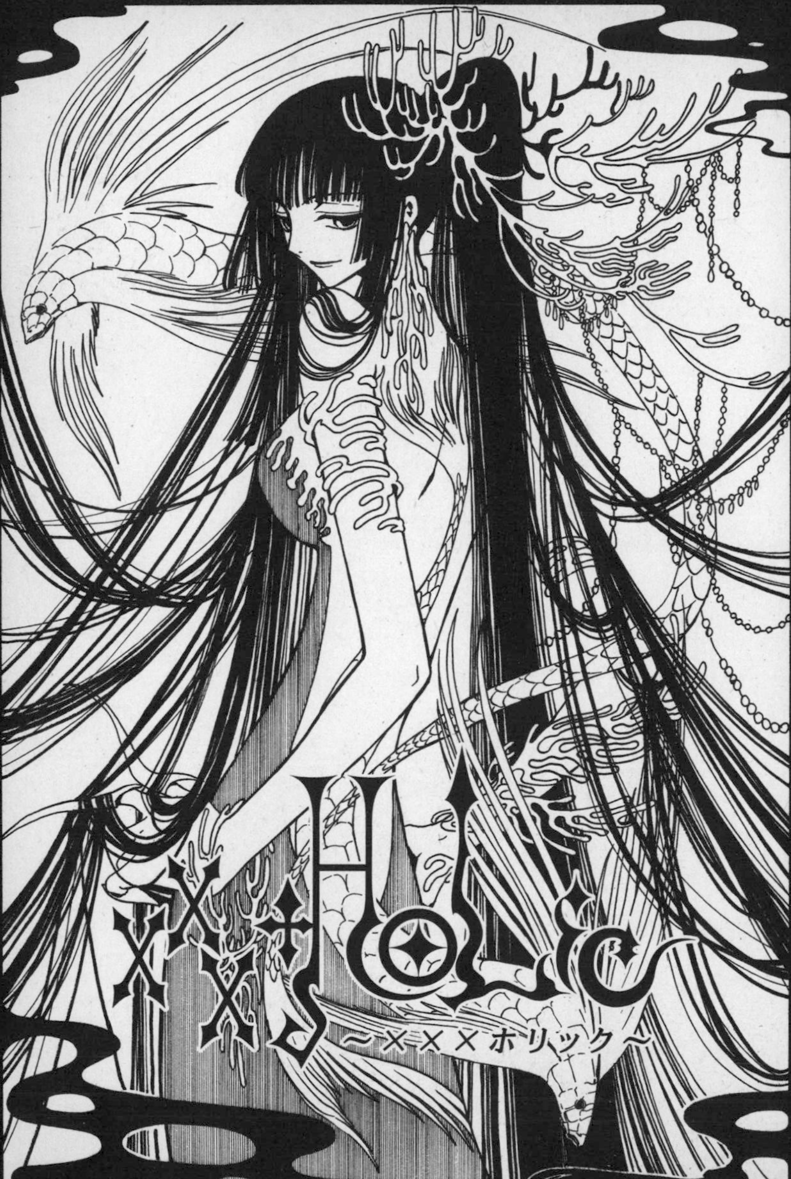
xxxHOLiC
〜×××ホリック〜

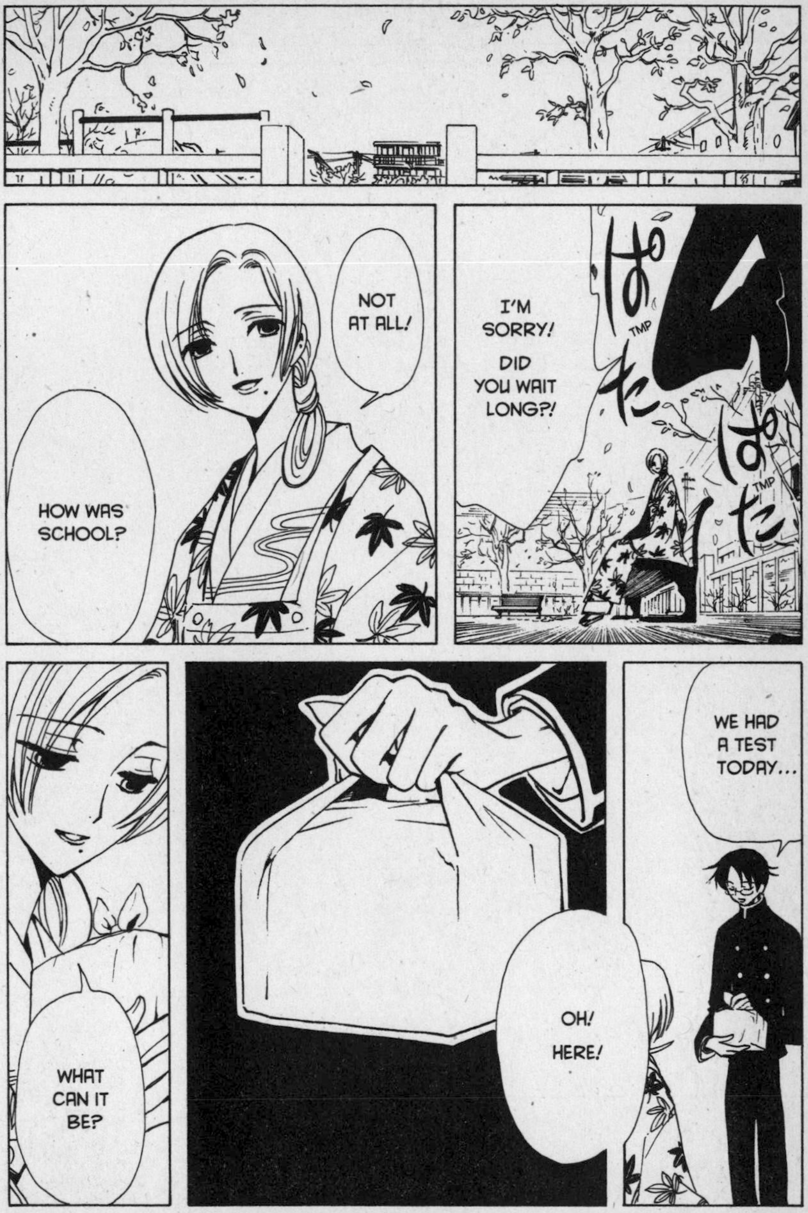
ぱた TMP
ぱた TMP
I'M SORRY!
DID YOU WAIT LONG?!
NOT AT ALL!
HOW WAS SCHOOL?
WE HAD A TEST TODAY...
OH! HERE!
WHAT CAN IT BE?

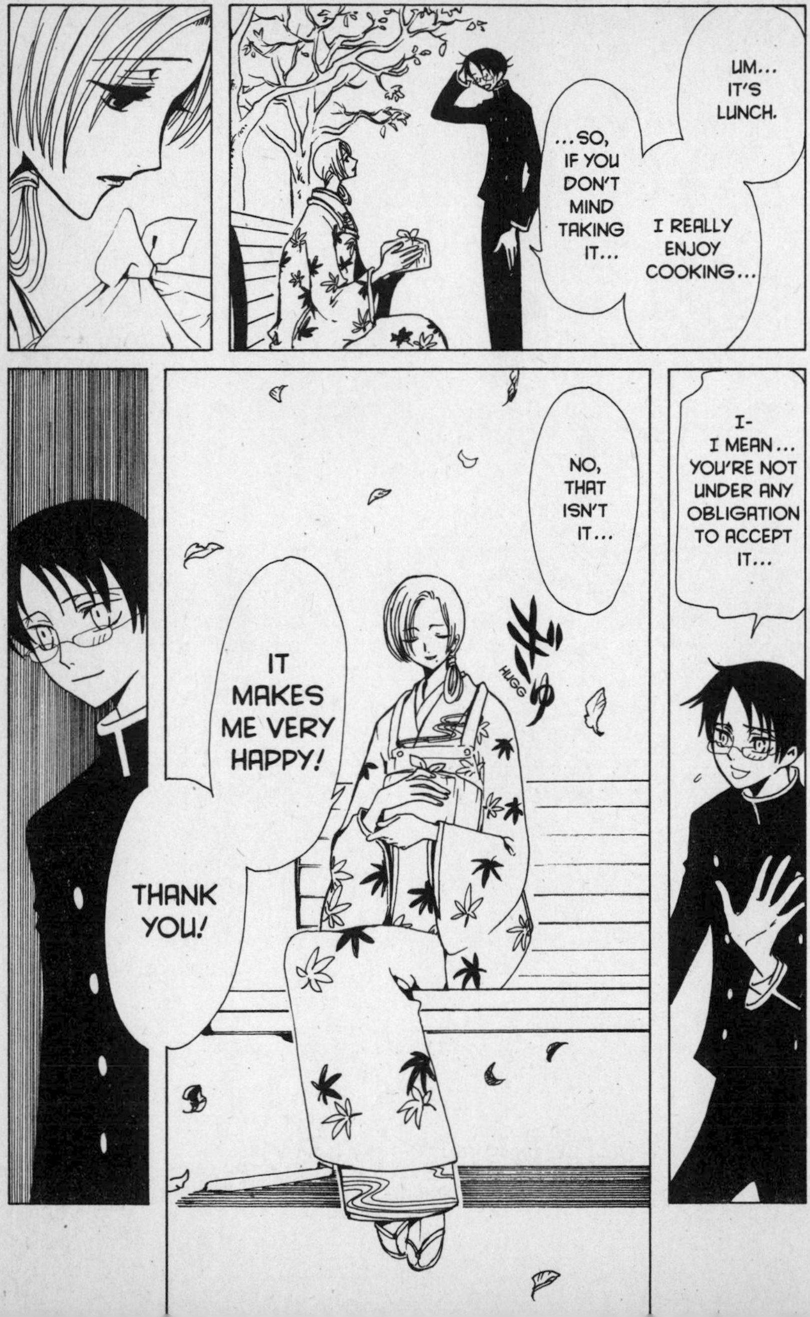
UM... IT'S LUNCH.
I REALLY ENJOY COOKING...
...SO, IF YOU DON'T MIND TAKING IT...
I- I MEAN... YOU'RE NOT UNDER ANY OBLIGATION TO ACCEPT IT...
NO, THAT ISN'T IT...
HUGG
IT MAKES ME VERY HAPPY!
THANK YOU!

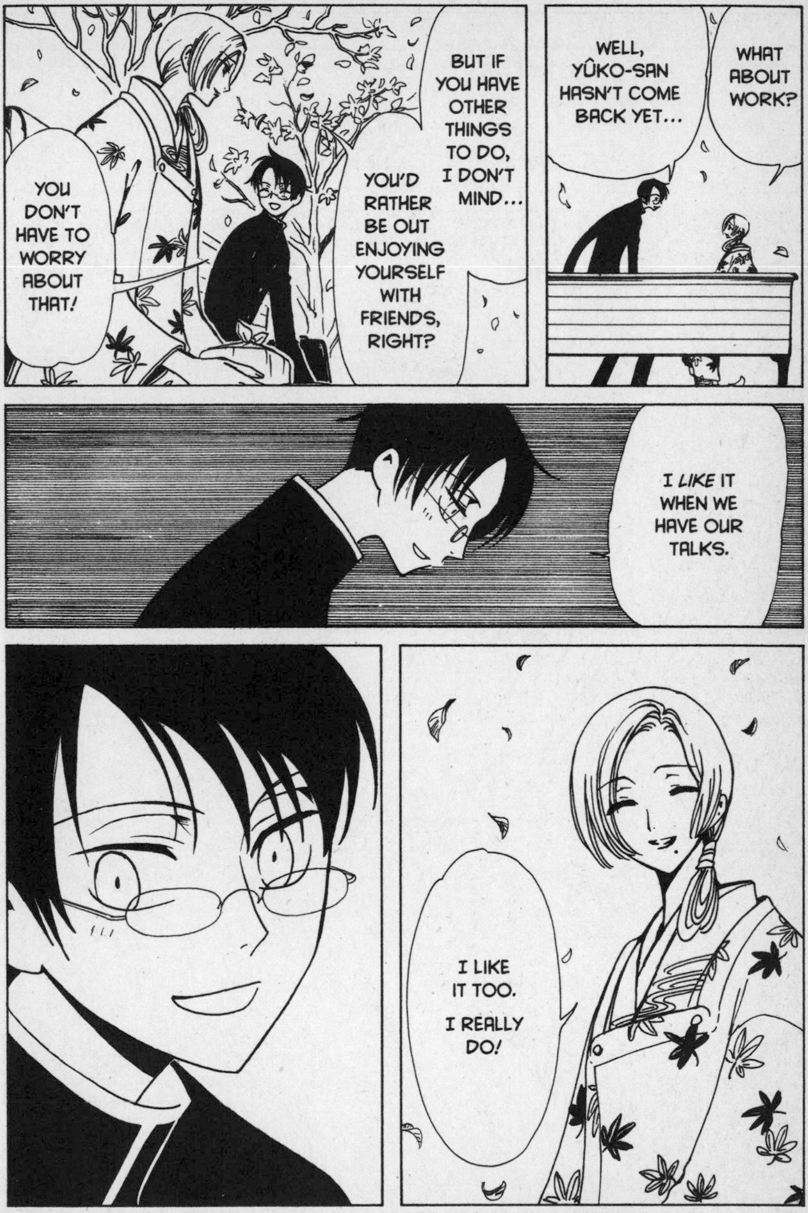
WHAT ABOUT WORK?
WELL, YÛKO-SAN HASN'T COME BACK YET...
BUT IF YOU HAVE OTHER THINGS TO DO, I DON'T MIND...
YOU'D RATHER BE OUT ENJOYING YOURSELF WITH FRIENDS, RIGHT?
YOU DON'T HAVE TO WORRY ABOUT THAT!
I *LIKE* IT WHEN WE HAVE OUR TALKS.
I LIKE IT TOO. I REALLY DO!

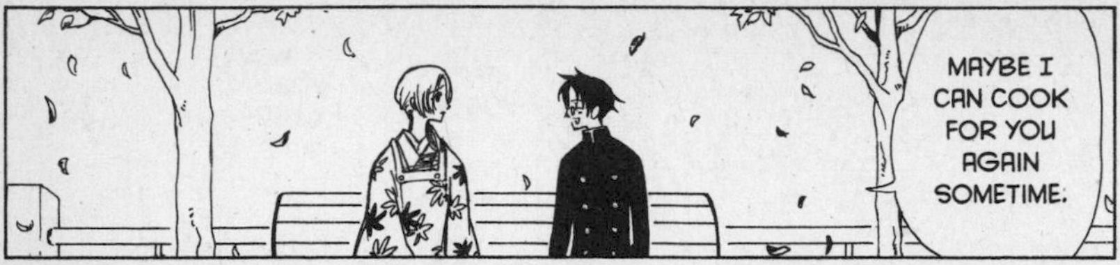
MAYBE I CAN COOK FOR YOU AGAIN SOMETIME.

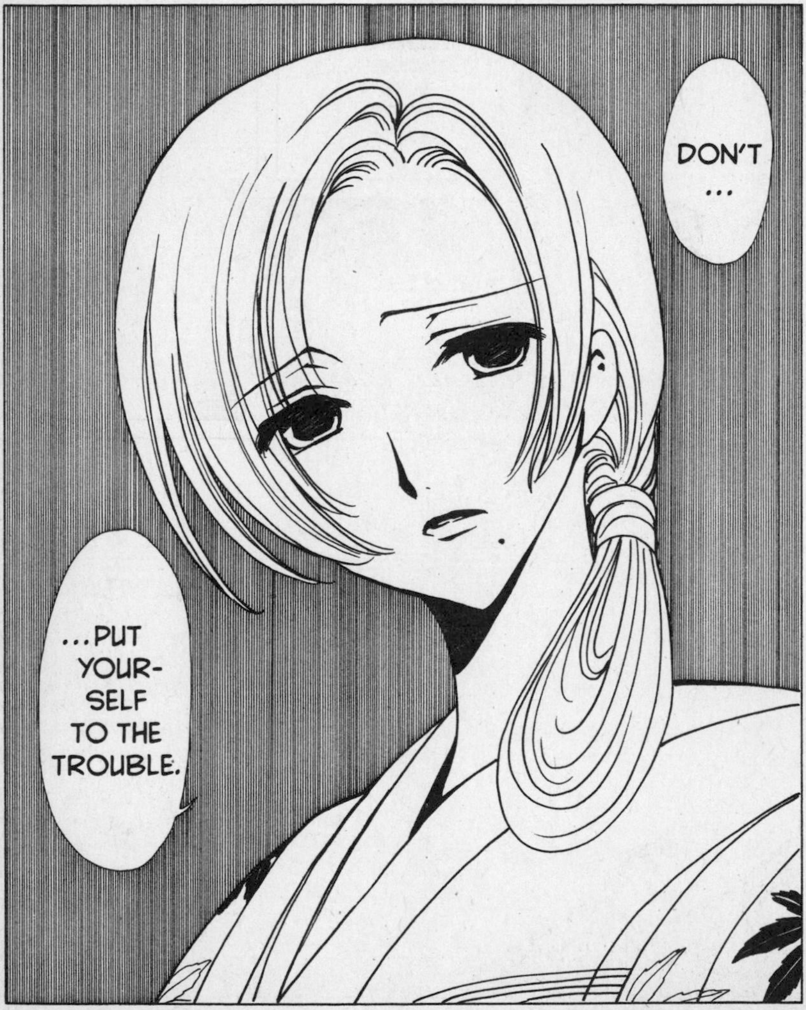
DON'T ...
...PUT YOURSELF TO THE TROUBLE.

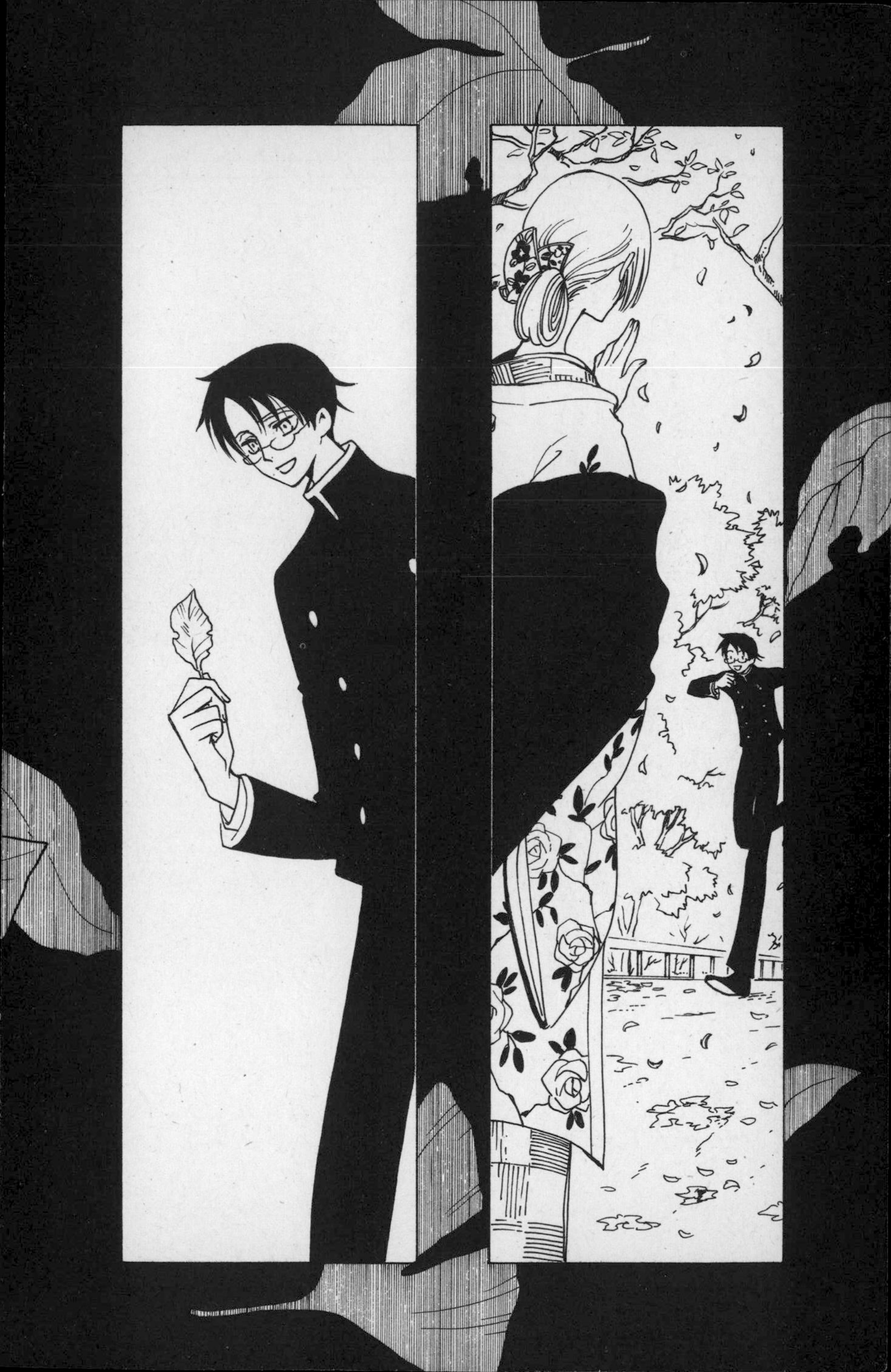

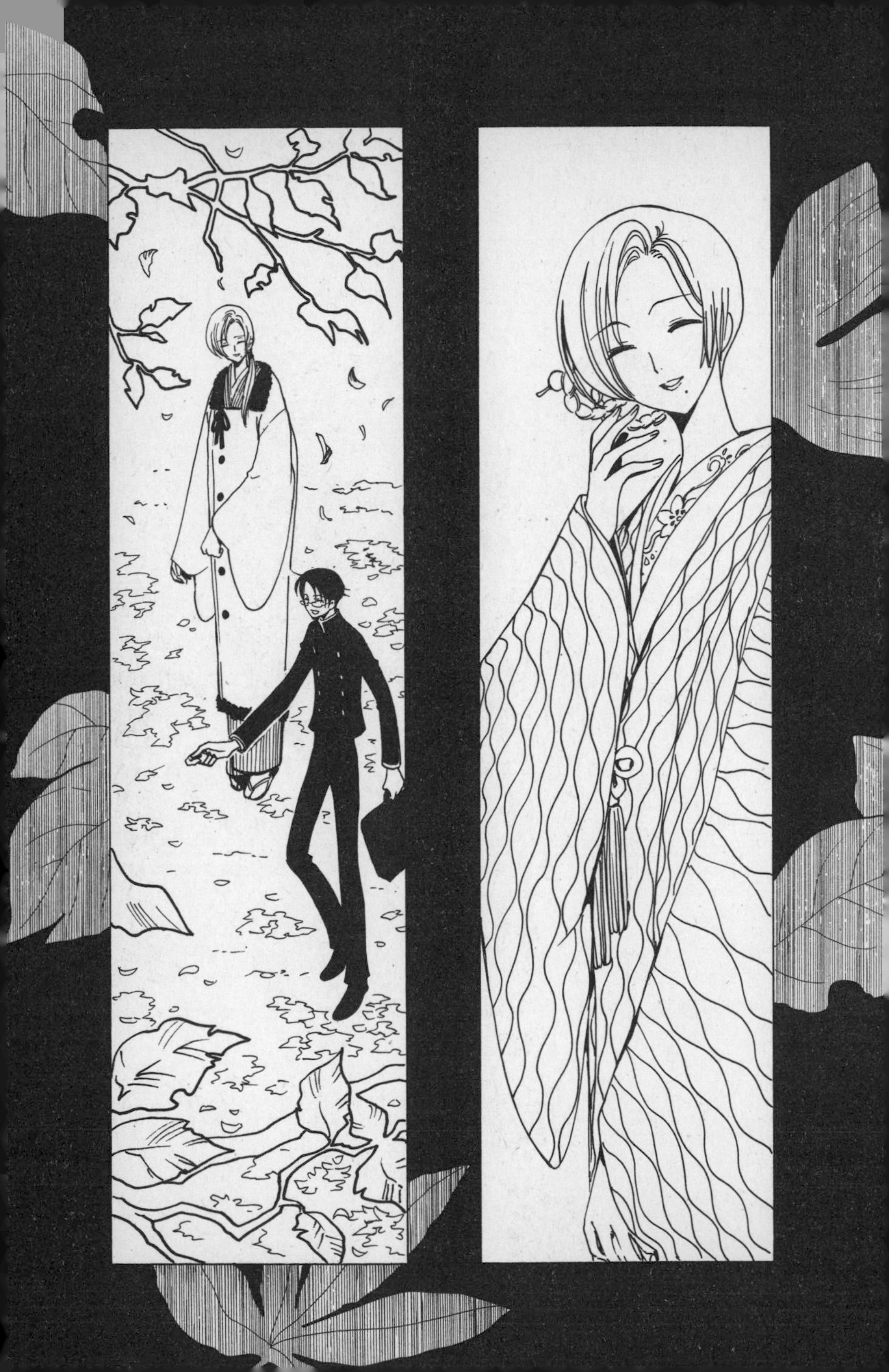

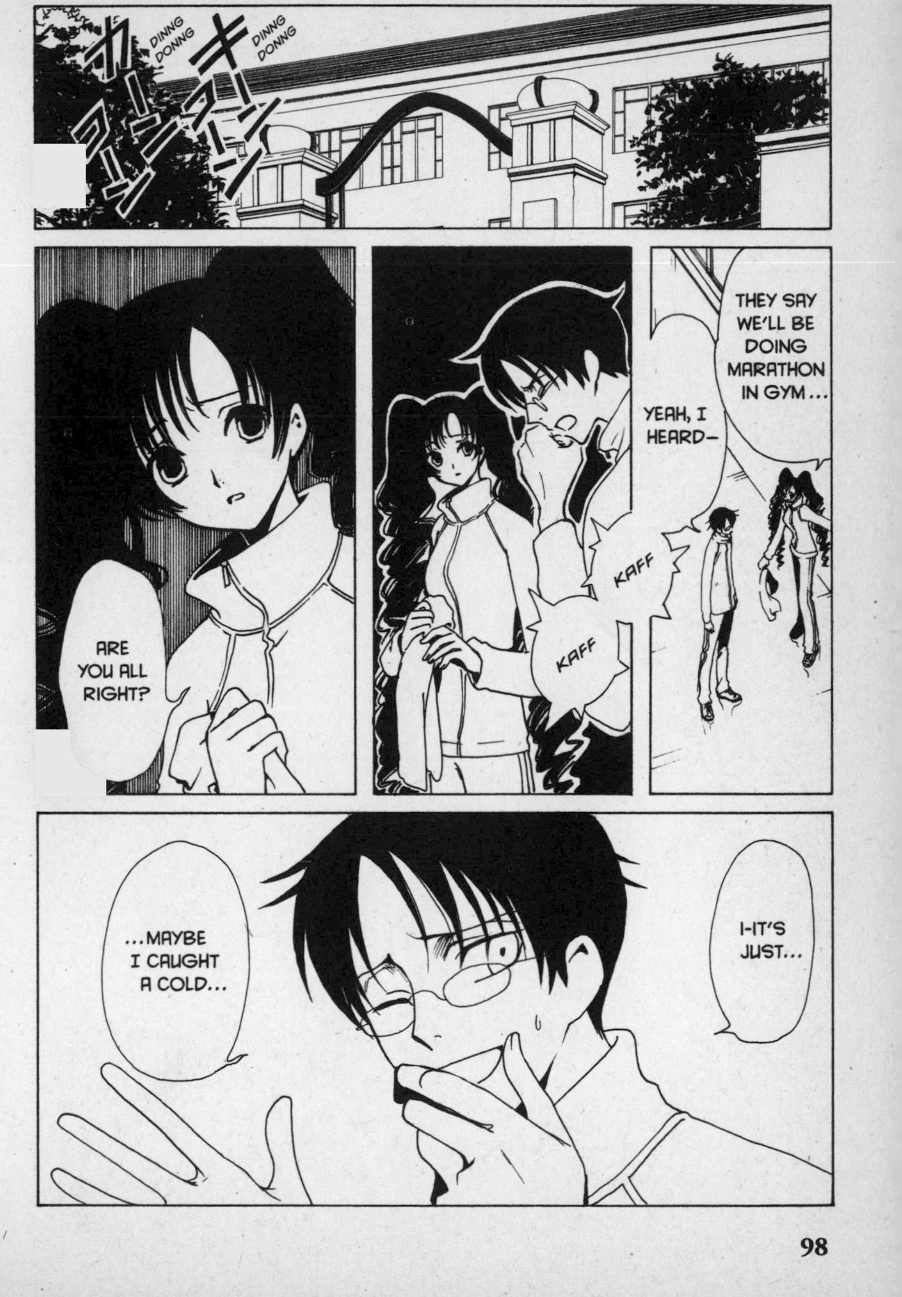
キーンコーン
DINNG DONNG
カーンコーン
DINNG DONNG
THEY SAY WE'LL BE DOING MARATHON IN GYM...
YEAH, I HEARD–
KAFF
KAFF
ARE YOU ALL RIGHT?
I-IT'S JUST...
...MAYBE I CAUGHT A COLD...

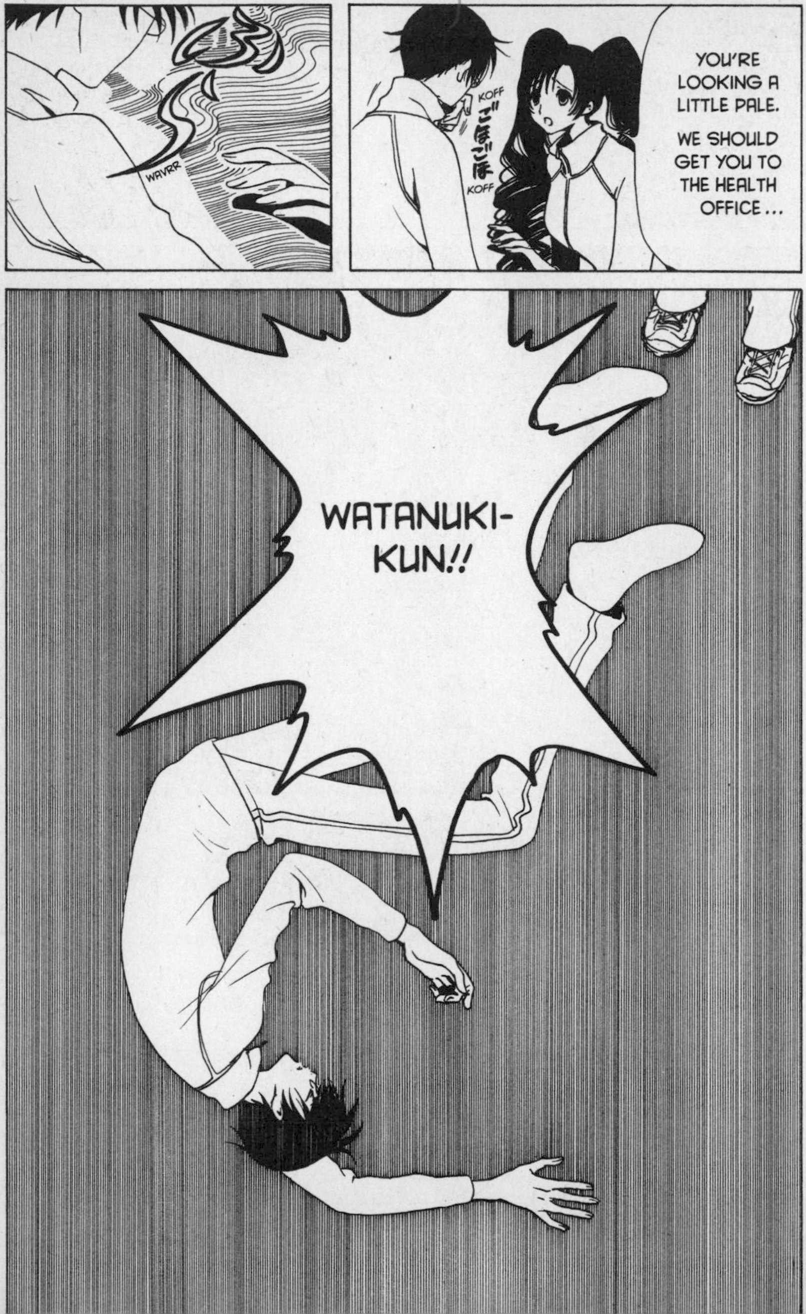
YOU'RE LOOKING A LITTLE PALE.
WE SHOULD GET YOU TO THE HEALTH OFFICE...
KOFF ごほごほ KOFF
WAVRR
WATANUKI-KUN!!

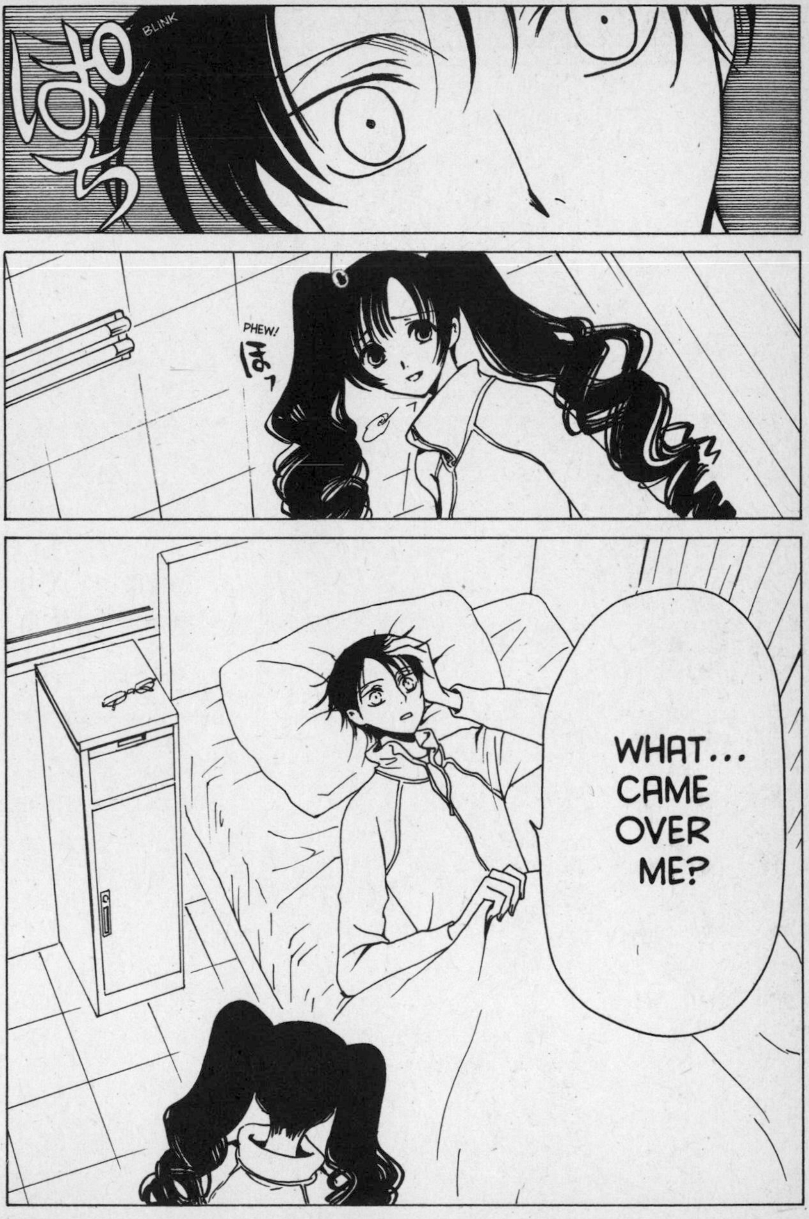
ぱち
BLINK
PHEW!
ほっ
WHAT... CAME OVER ME?

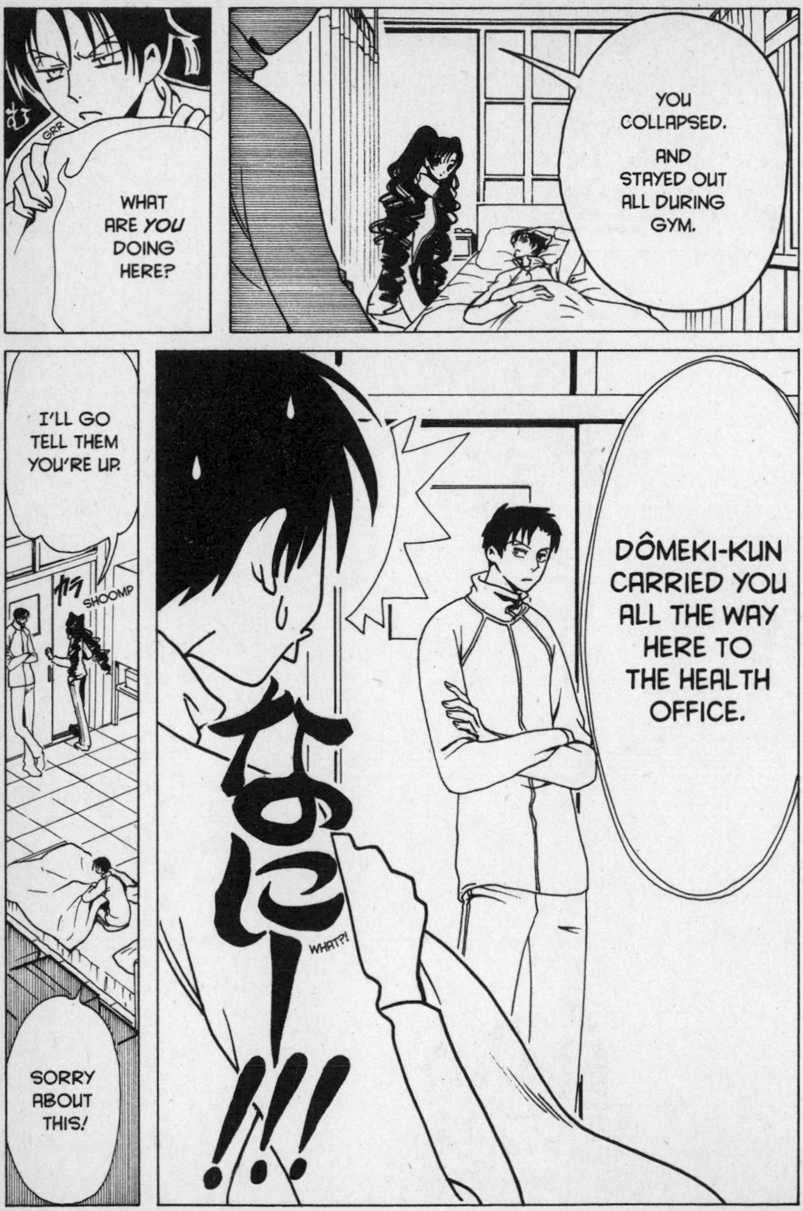
YOU COLLAPSED.
AND STAYED OUT ALL DURING GYM.
GRR
WHAT ARE *YOU* DOING HERE?
DÔMEKI-KUN CARRIED YOU ALL THE WAY HERE TO THE HEALTH OFFICE.
なにー!!!!
WHAT?!
I'LL GO TELL THEM YOU'RE UP.
SHOOMP
SORRY ABOUT THIS!

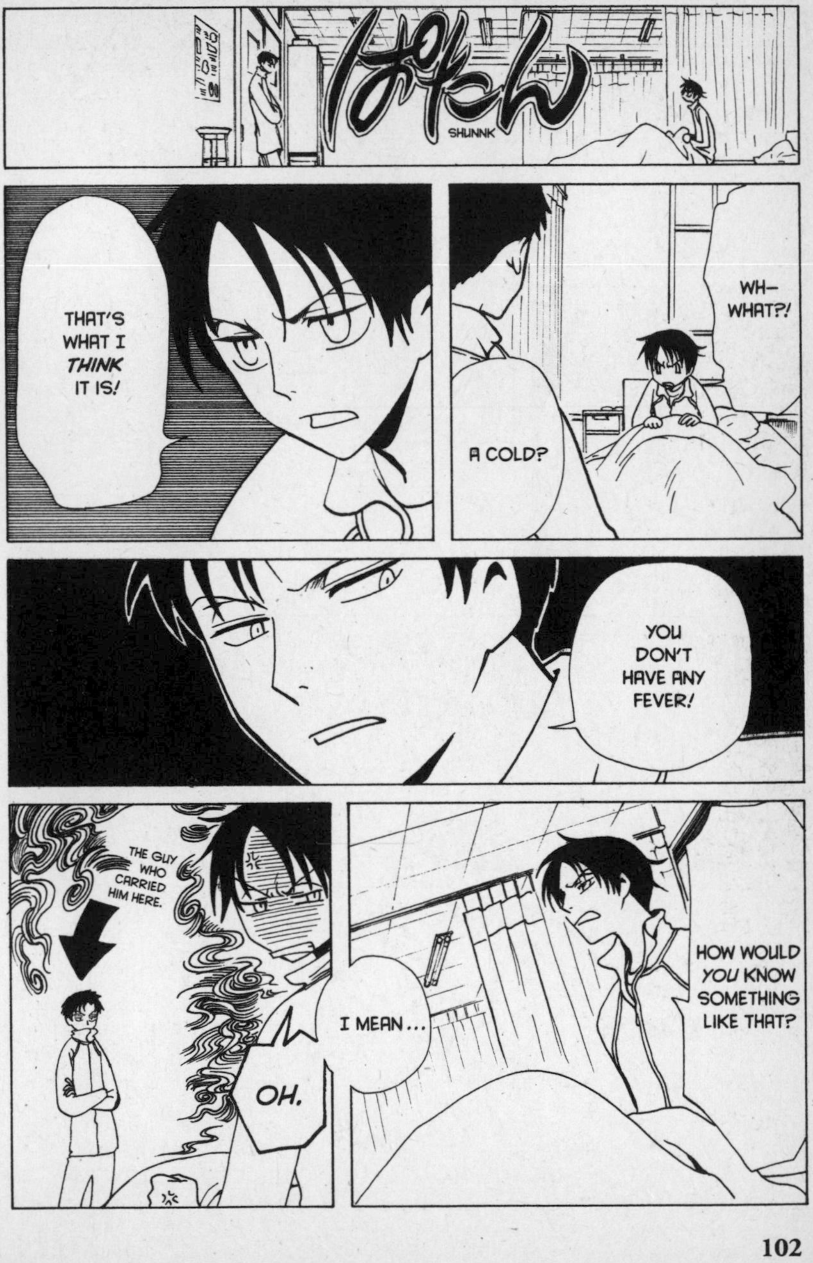
SHUNNK
WH— WHAT?!
A COLD?
THAT'S WHAT I *THINK* IT IS!
YOU DON'T HAVE ANY FEVER!
HOW WOULD *YOU* KNOW SOMETHING LIKE THAT?
I MEAN...
OH.
THE GUY WHO CARRIED HIM HERE.

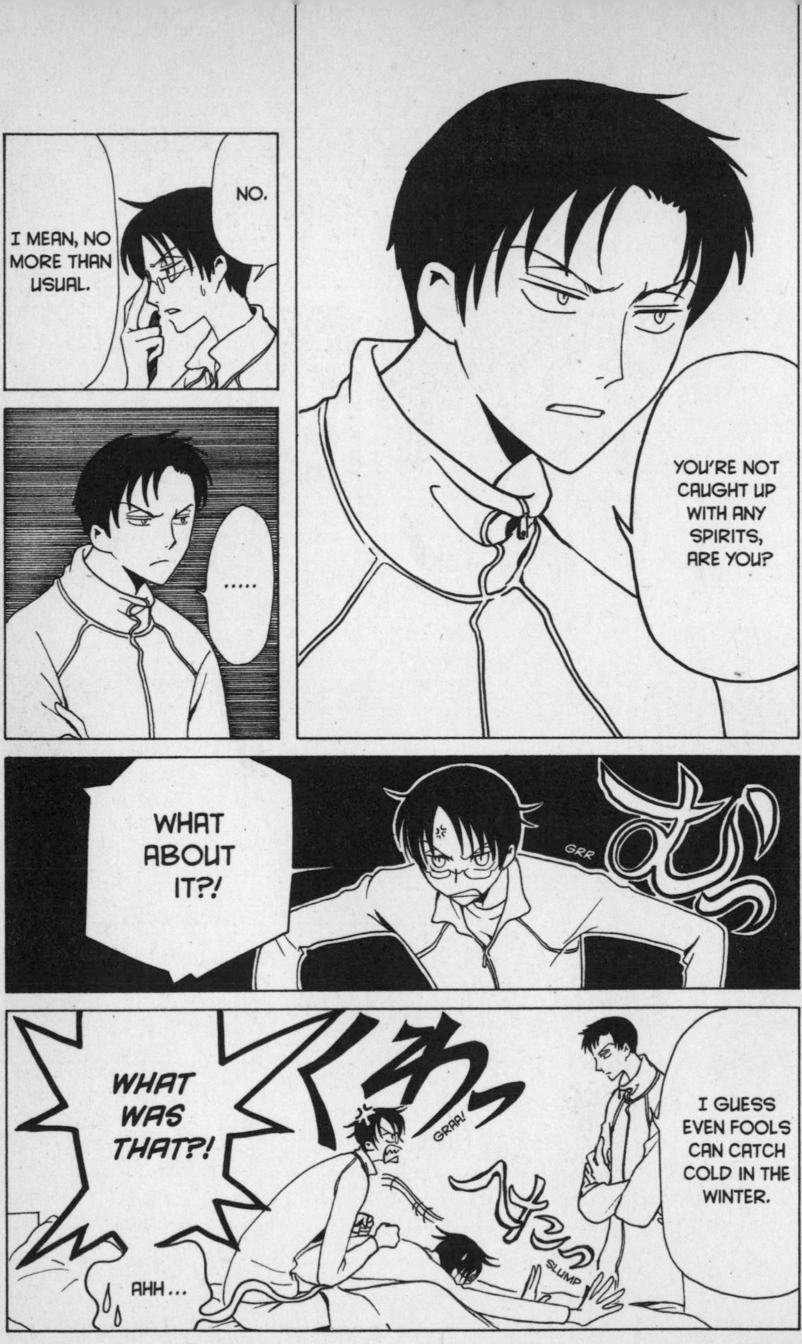
YOU'RE NOT CAUGHT UP WITH ANY SPIRITS, ARE YOU?
NO.
I MEAN, NO MORE THAN USUAL.
.....
WHAT ABOUT IT?!
GRR
I GUESS EVEN FOOLS CAN CATCH COLD IN THE WINTER.
WHAT WAS THAT?!
GRAR!
SLUMP
AHH...

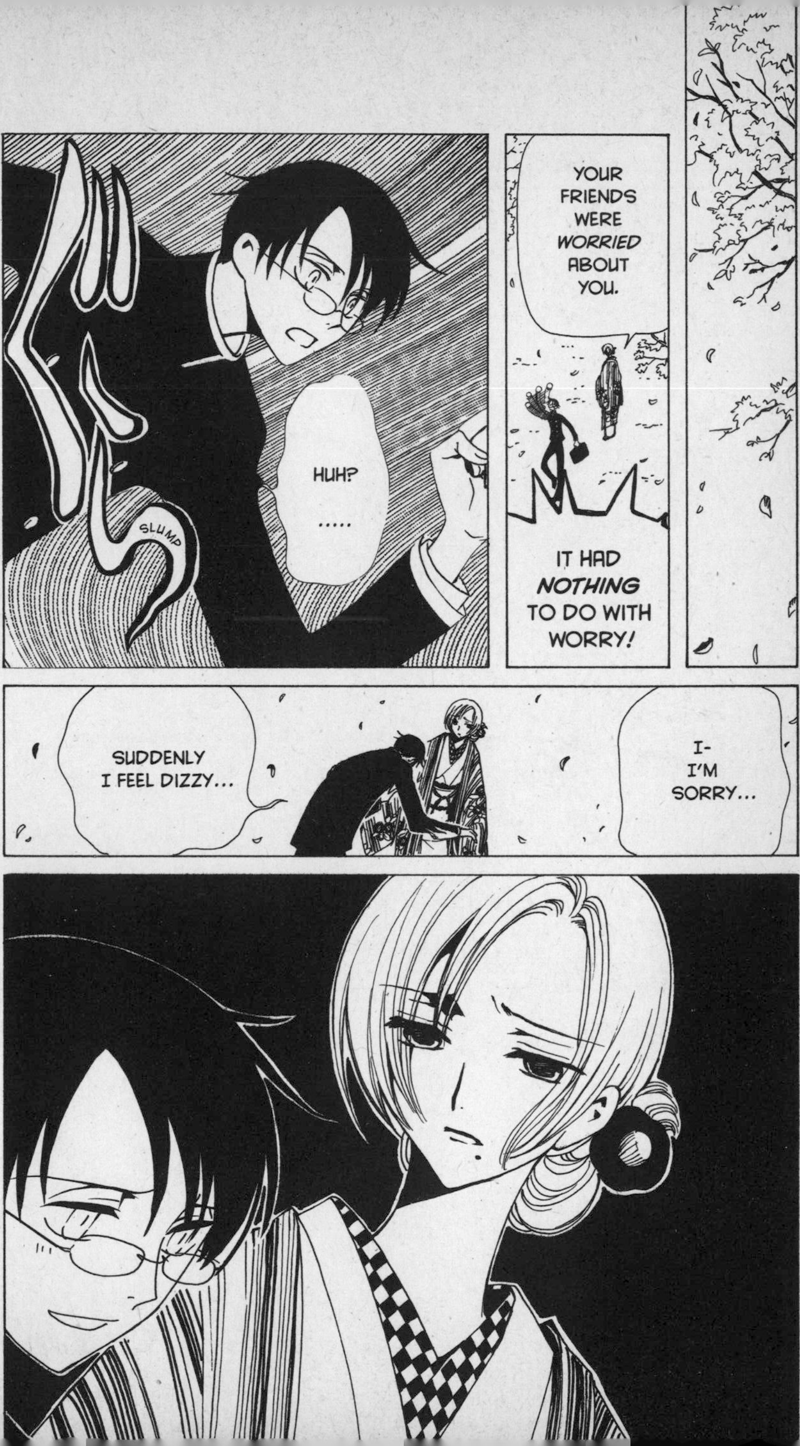
YOUR FRIENDS WERE WORRIED ABOUT YOU.
IT HAD NOTHING TO DO WITH WORRY!
HUH?
.....
SLUMP
I- I'M SORRY...
SUDDENLY I FEEL DIZZY...

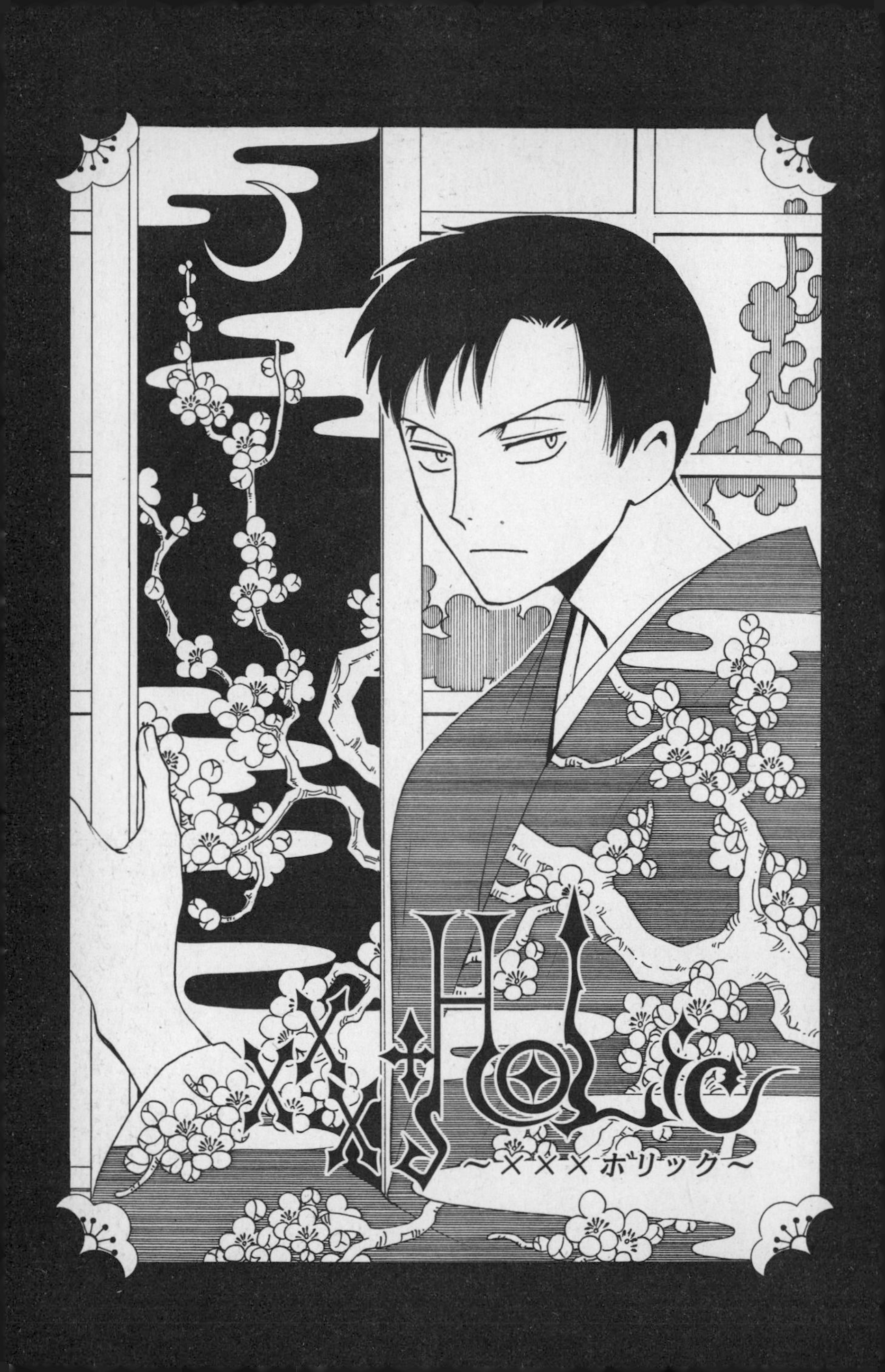
xxxHOLiC
～×××ホリック～

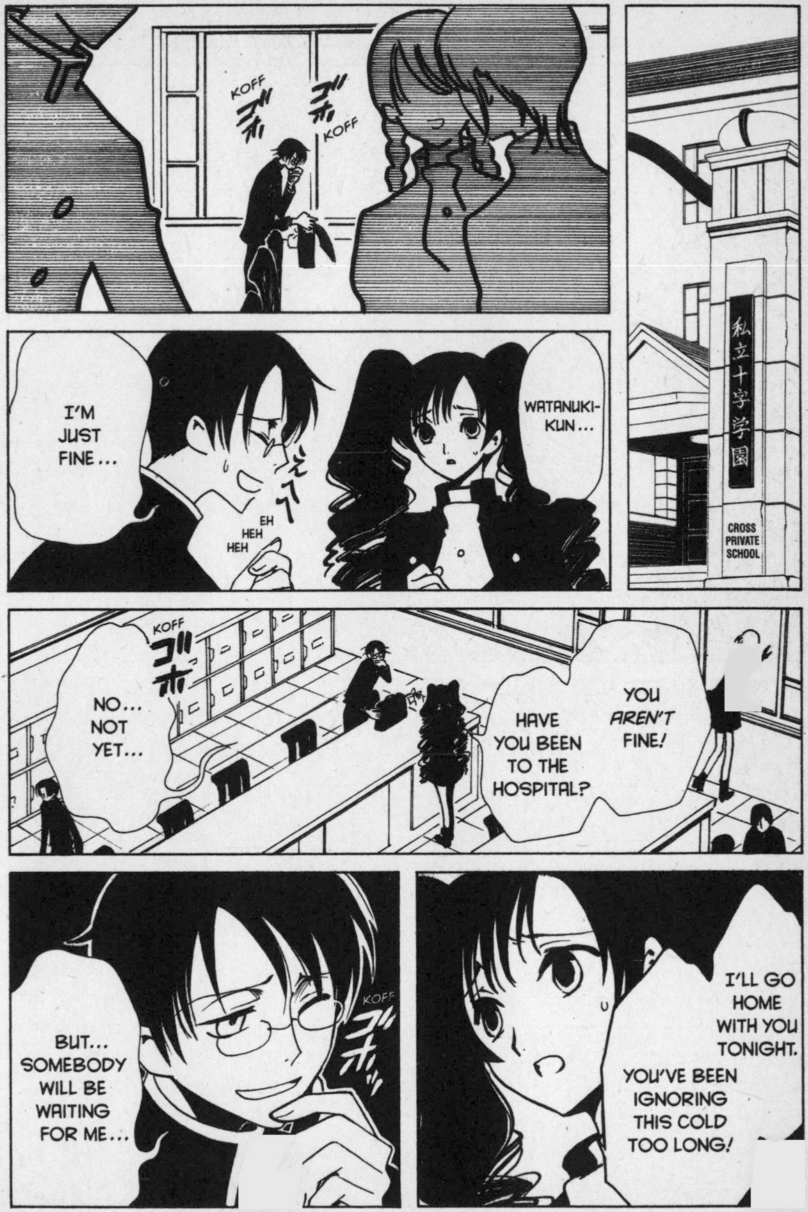
私立十字学園
CROSS PRIVATE SCHOOL
KOFF
ゴホ
ゴホ
KOFF
WATANUKI-KUN...
I'M JUST FINE...
EH HEH HEH
YOU AREN'T FINE!
HAVE YOU BEEN TO THE HOSPITAL?
NO... NOT YET...
KOFF
ゴホ
I'LL GO HOME WITH YOU TONIGHT.
YOU'VE BEEN IGNORING THIS COLD TOO LONG!
BUT... SOMEBODY WILL BE WAITING FOR ME...
KOFF
ゴホッ

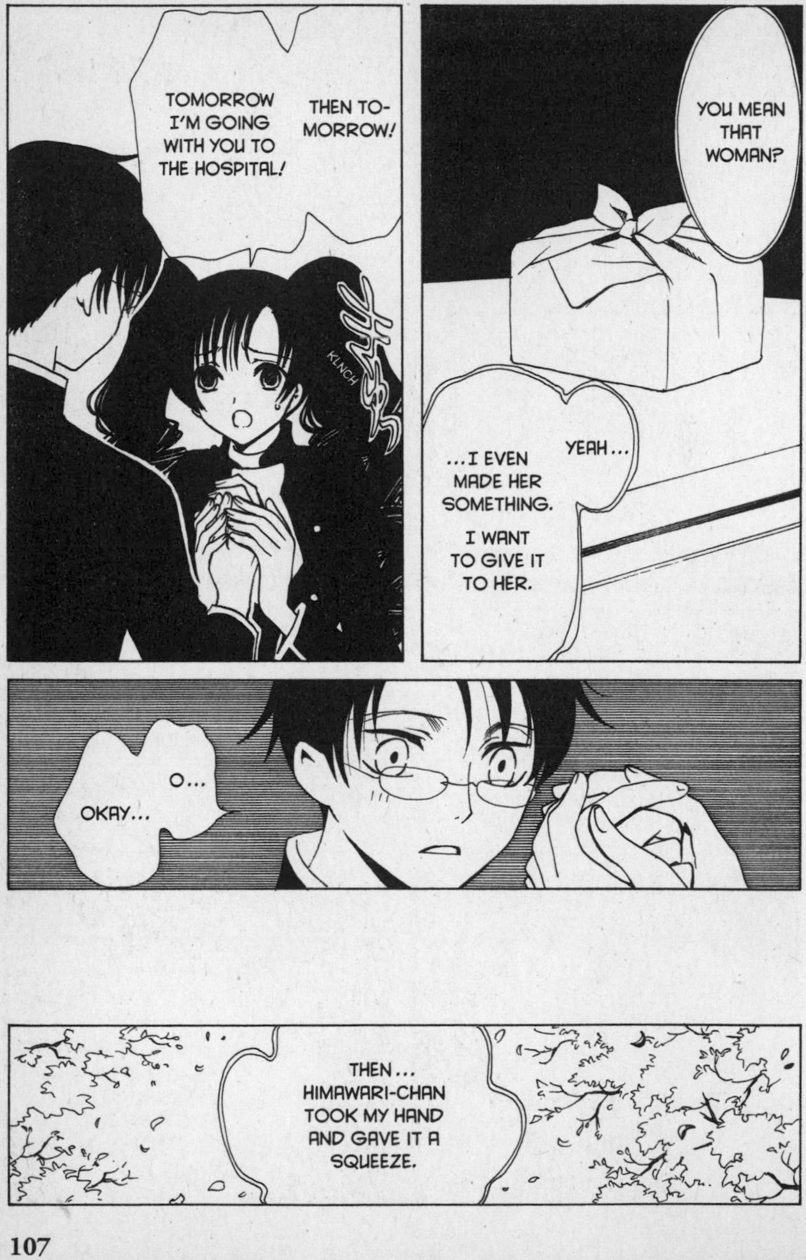
YOU MEAN THAT WOMAN?
YEAH...
...I EVEN MADE HER SOMETHING.
I WANT TO GIVE IT TO HER.
THEN TO-MORROW!
TOMORROW I'M GOING WITH YOU TO THE HOSPITAL!
KLNCH
O...
OKAY...
THEN... HIMAWARI-CHAN TOOK MY HAND AND GAVE IT A SQUEEZE.

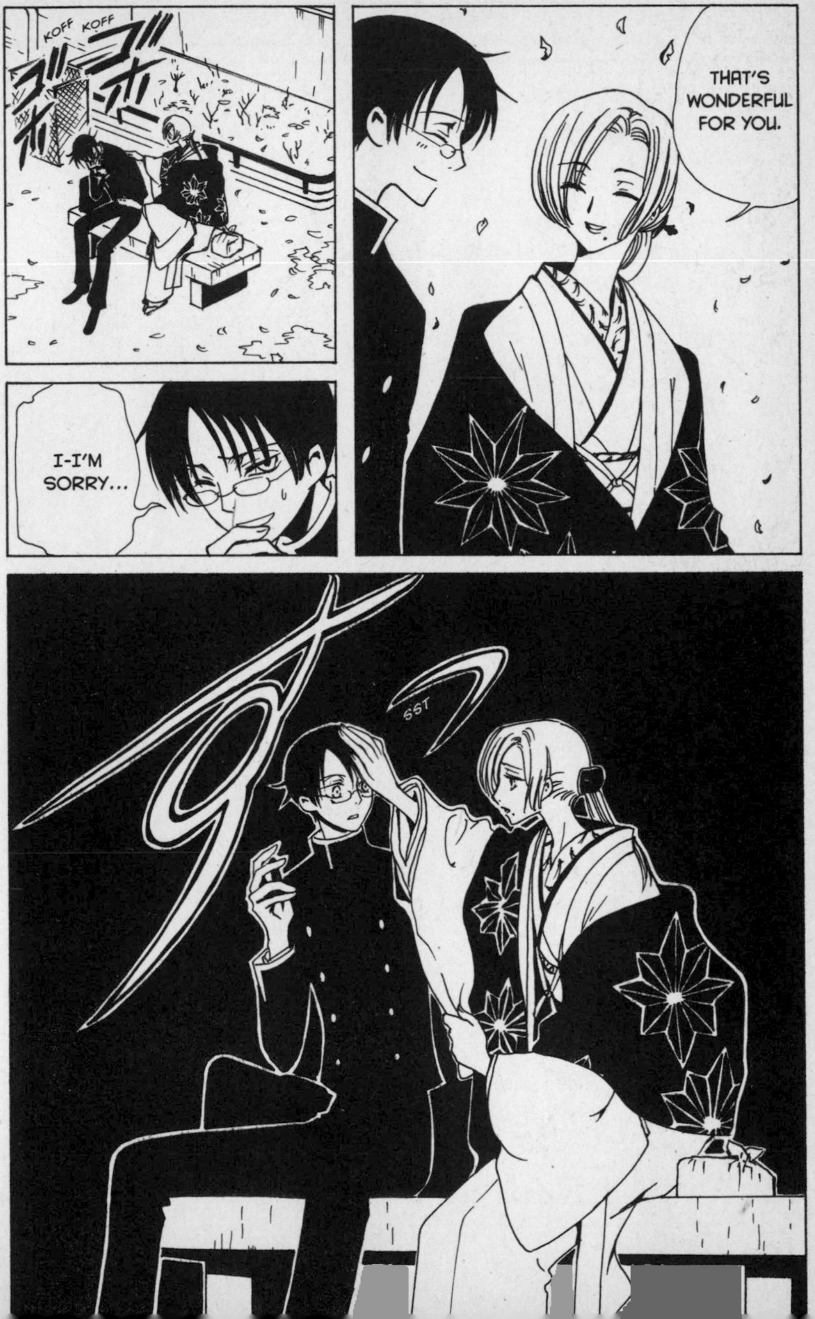
THAT'S WONDERFUL FOR YOU.
KOFF KOFF
I-I'M SORRY...
SST

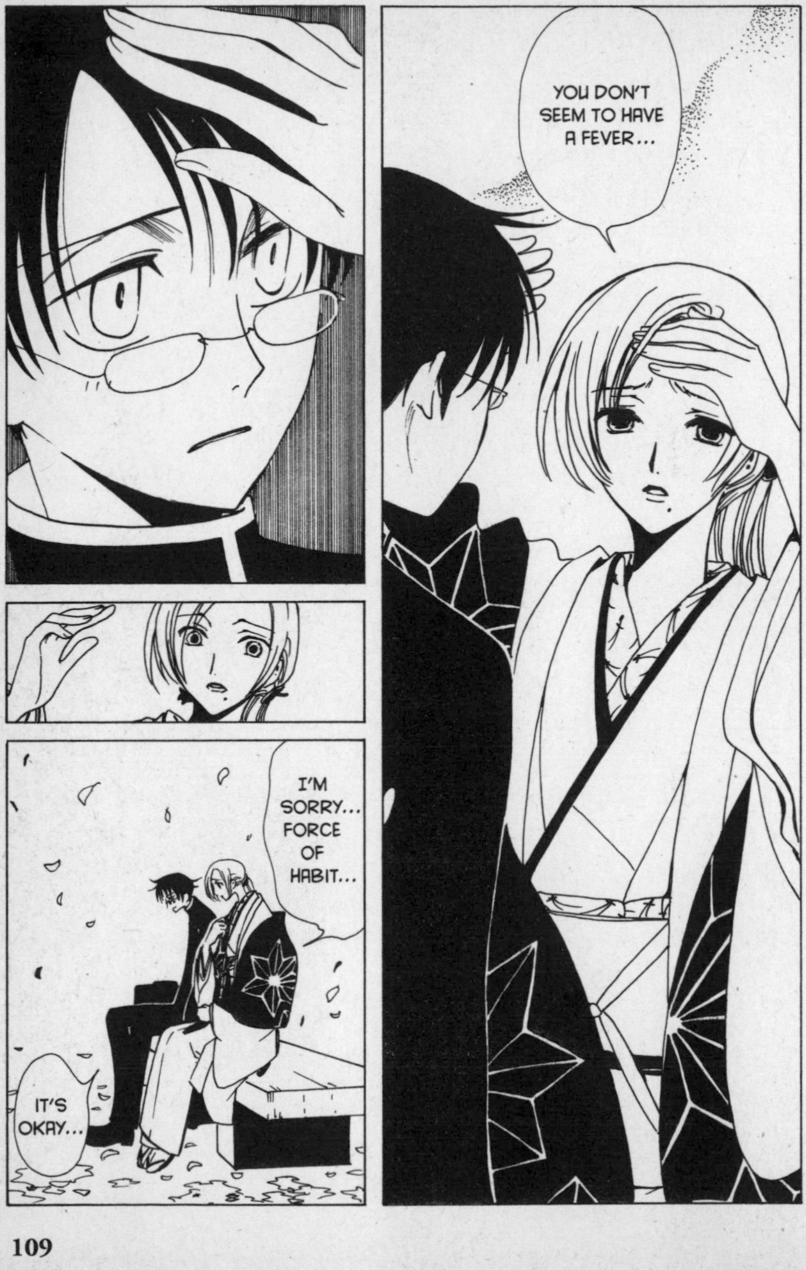
YOU DON'T SEEM TO HAVE A FEVER...
I'M SORRY... FORCE OF HABIT...
IT'S OKAY...

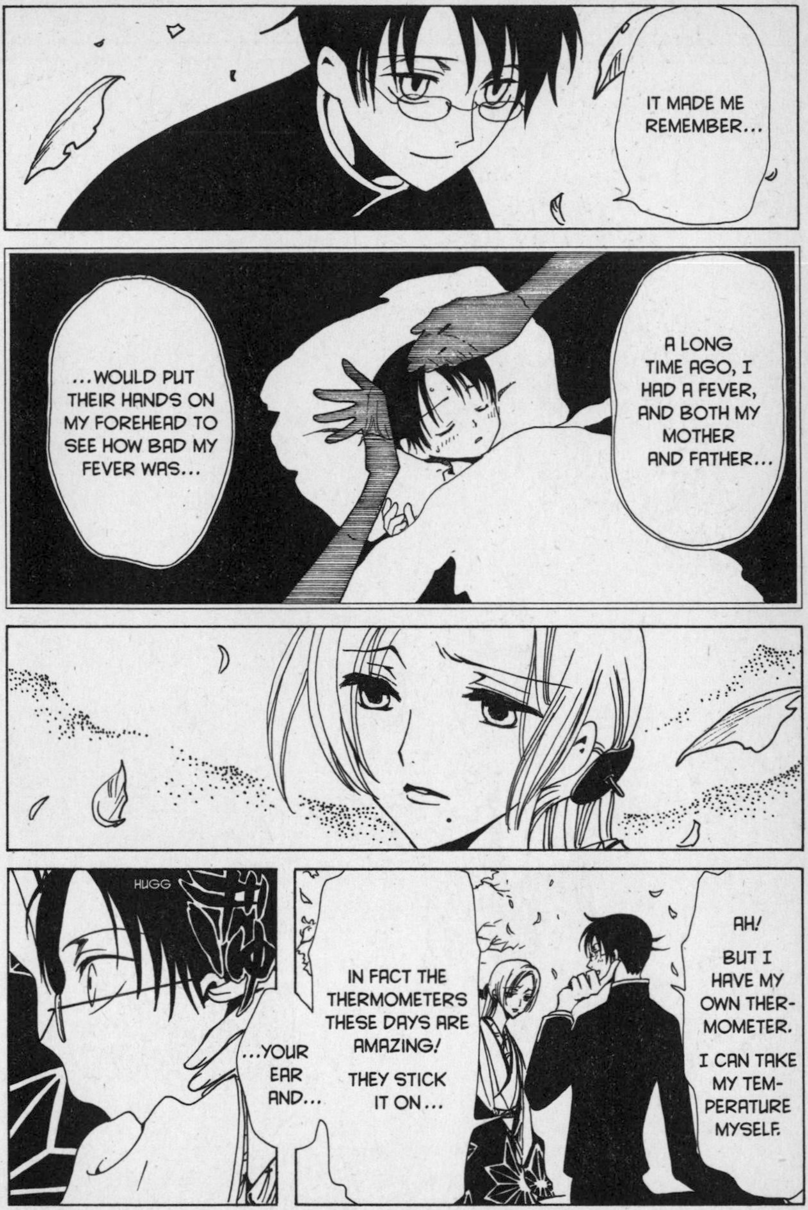
IT MADE ME REMEMBER...
A LONG TIME AGO, I HAD A FEVER, AND BOTH MY MOTHER AND FATHER...
...WOULD PUT THEIR HANDS ON MY FOREHEAD TO SEE HOW BAD MY FEVER WAS...
AH!
BUT I HAVE MY OWN THER-MOMETER.
I CAN TAKE MY TEM-PERATURE MYSELF.
IN FACT THE THERMOMETERS THESE DAYS ARE AMAZING!
THEY STICK IT ON...
...YOUR EAR AND...
HUGG

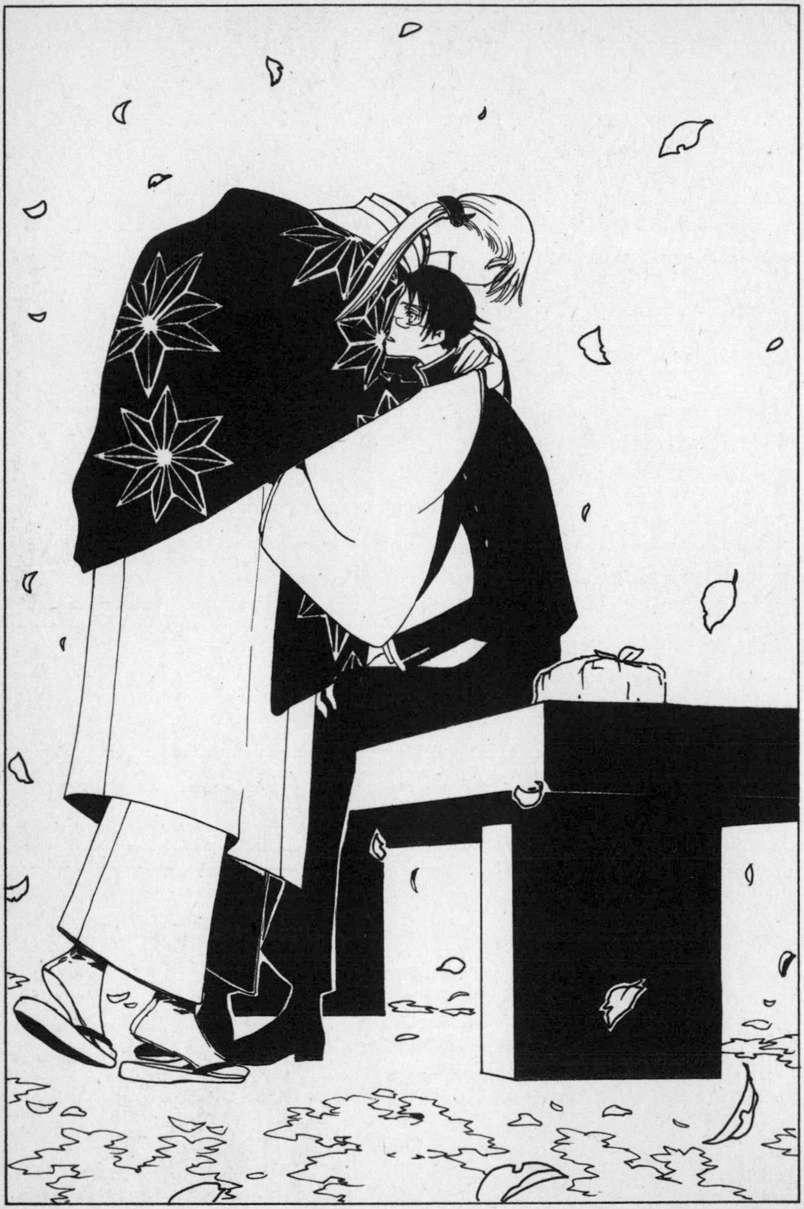

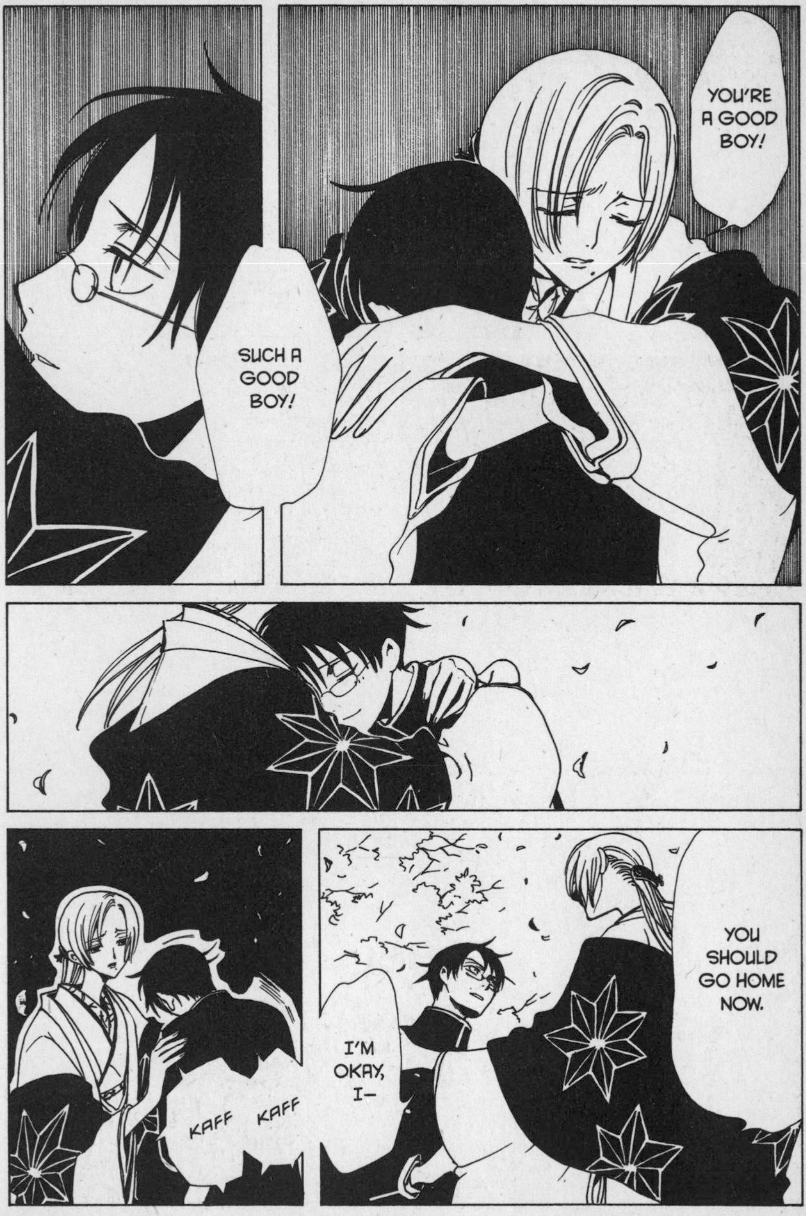
YOU'RE A GOOD BOY!
SUCH A GOOD BOY!
YOU SHOULD GO HOME NOW.
I'M OKAY, I–
KAFF KAFF

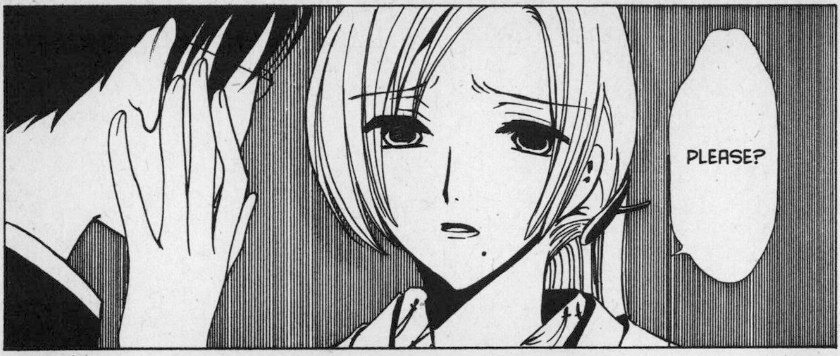
PLEASE?

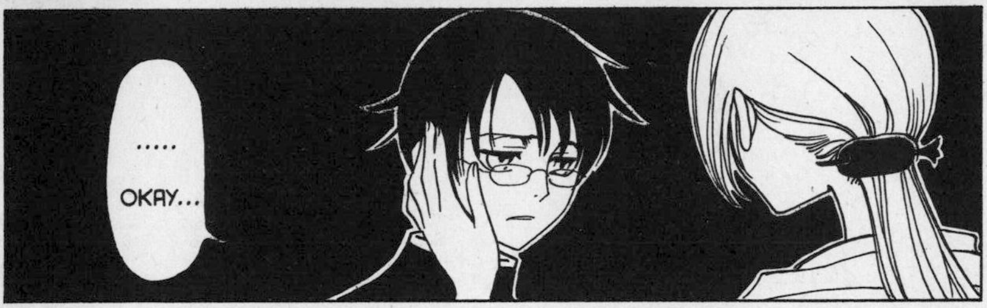
.....
OKAY...

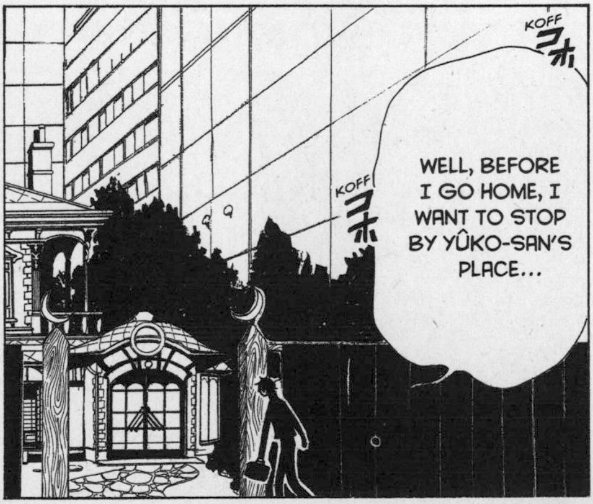
KOFF
KOFF
WELL, BEFORE I GO HOME, I WANT TO STOP BY YÛKO-SAN'S PLACE...

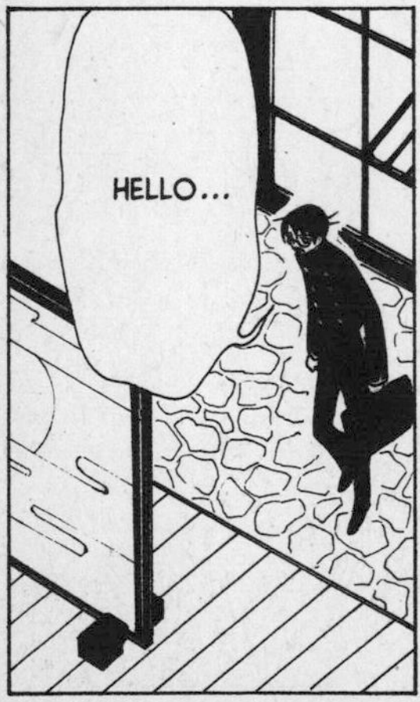
HELLO...

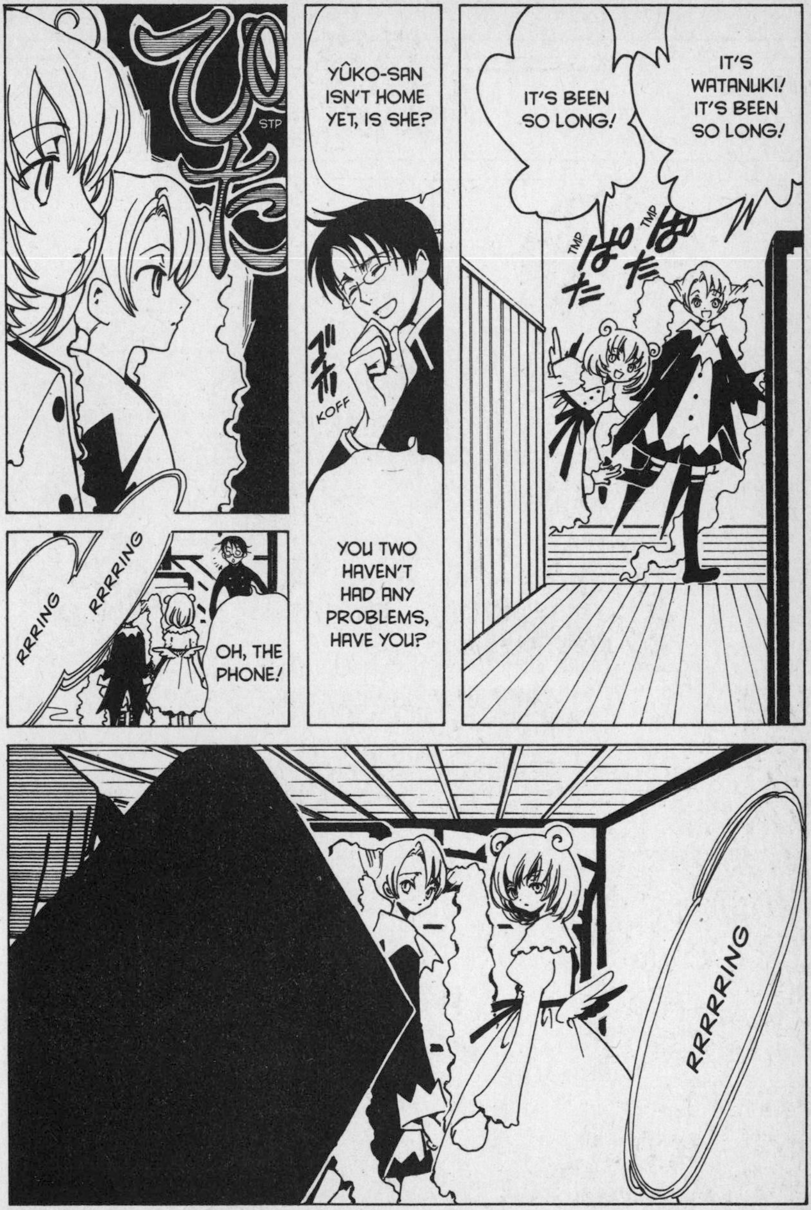
IT'S WATANUKI! IT'S BEEN SO LONG!
IT'S BEEN SO LONG!
ぱた TMP
ぱた TMP
YÛKO-SAN ISN'T HOME YET, IS SHE?
ゴホ
KOFF
ぴた
STP
YOU TWO HAVEN'T HAD ANY PROBLEMS, HAVE YOU?
RRRRING
RRRING
OH, THE PHONE!
RRRRRING

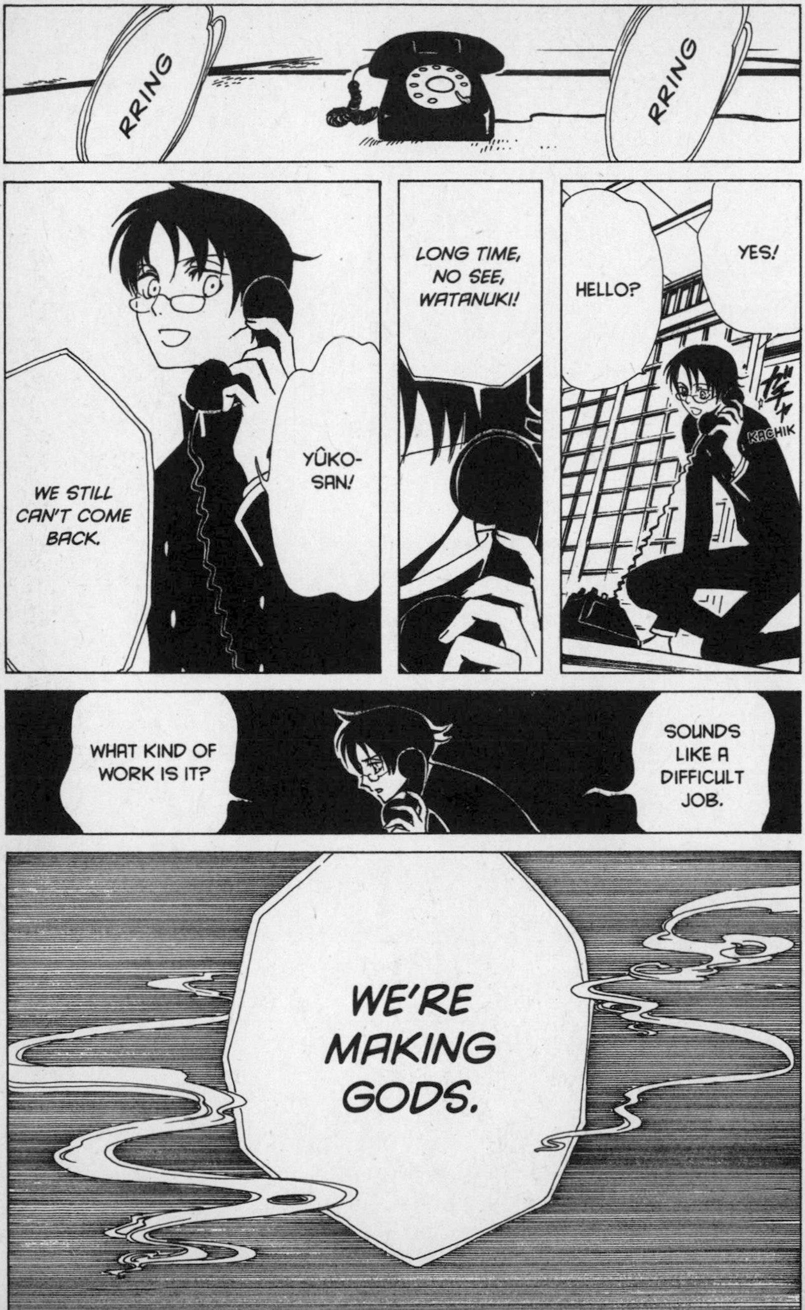

RRING
RRING
YES!
HELLO?
KACHIK
LONG TIME, NO SEE, WATANUKI!
YÛKO-SAN!
WE STILL CAN'T COME BACK.
SOUNDS LIKE A DIFFICULT JOB.
WHAT KIND OF WORK IS IT?
WE'RE MAKING GODS.

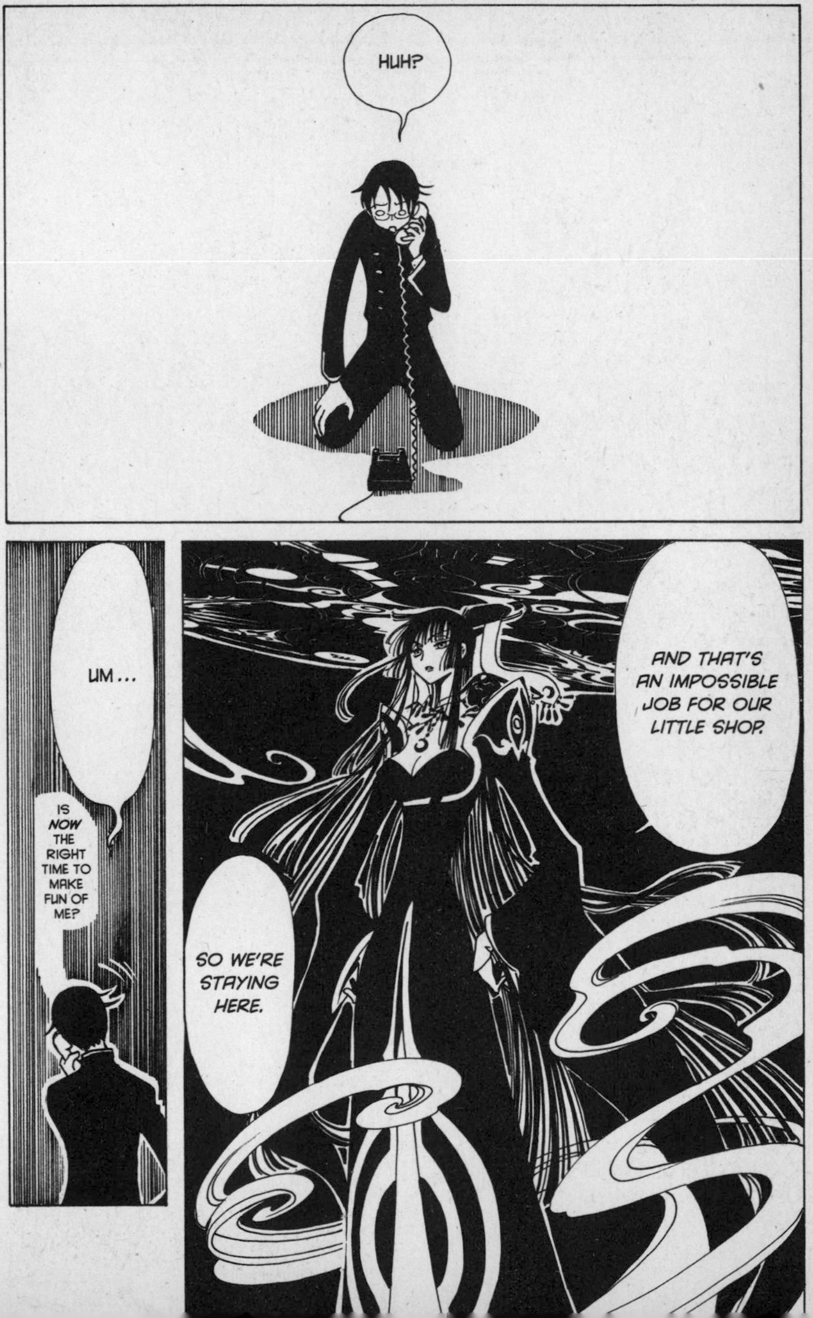
HUH?
AND THAT'S AN IMPOSSIBLE JOB FOR OUR LITTLE SHOP.
SO WE'RE STAYING HERE.
UM...
IS *NOW* THE RIGHT TIME TO MAKE FUN OF ME?

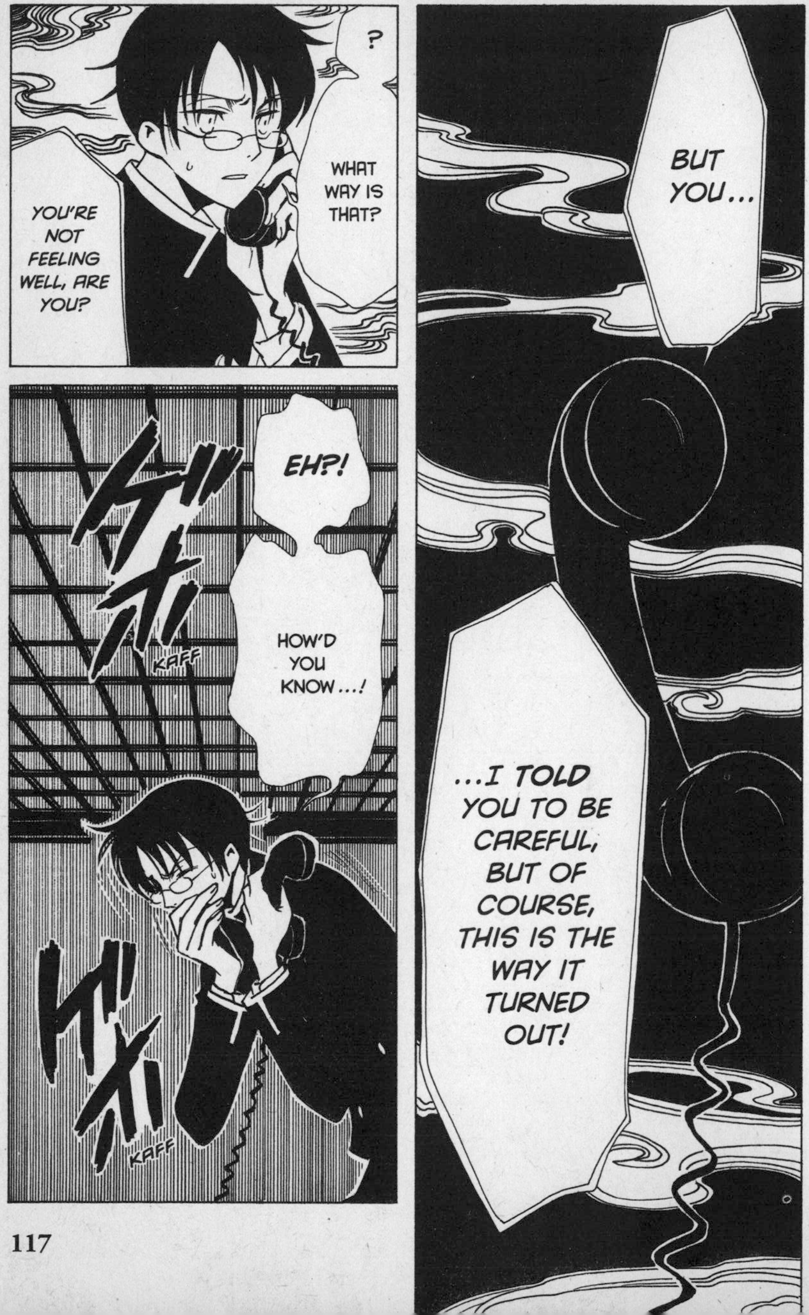
BUT YOU...
...I TOLD YOU TO BE CAREFUL, BUT OF COURSE, THIS IS THE WAY IT TURNED OUT!
?
WHAT WAY IS THAT?
YOU'RE NOT FEELING WELL, ARE YOU?
EH?!
HOW'D YOU KNOW...!
KAFF
KAFF

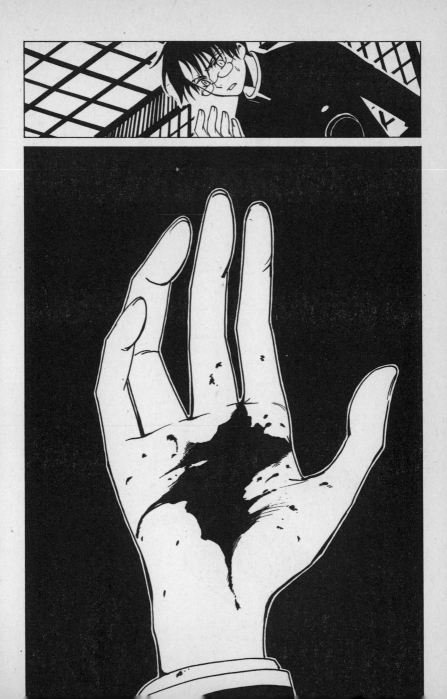

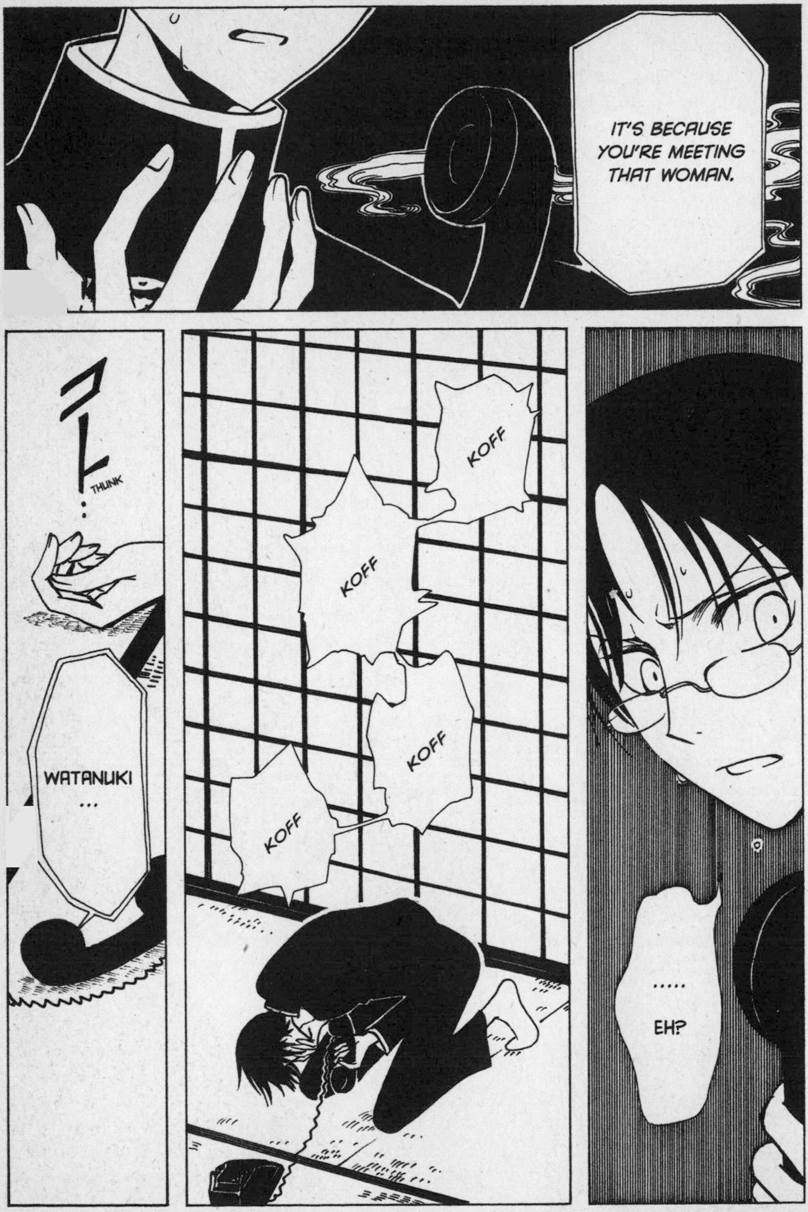
IT'S BECAUSE YOU'RE MEETING THAT WOMAN.
.....
EH?
KOFF
KOFF
KOFF
KOFF
THUNK
WATANUKI ...

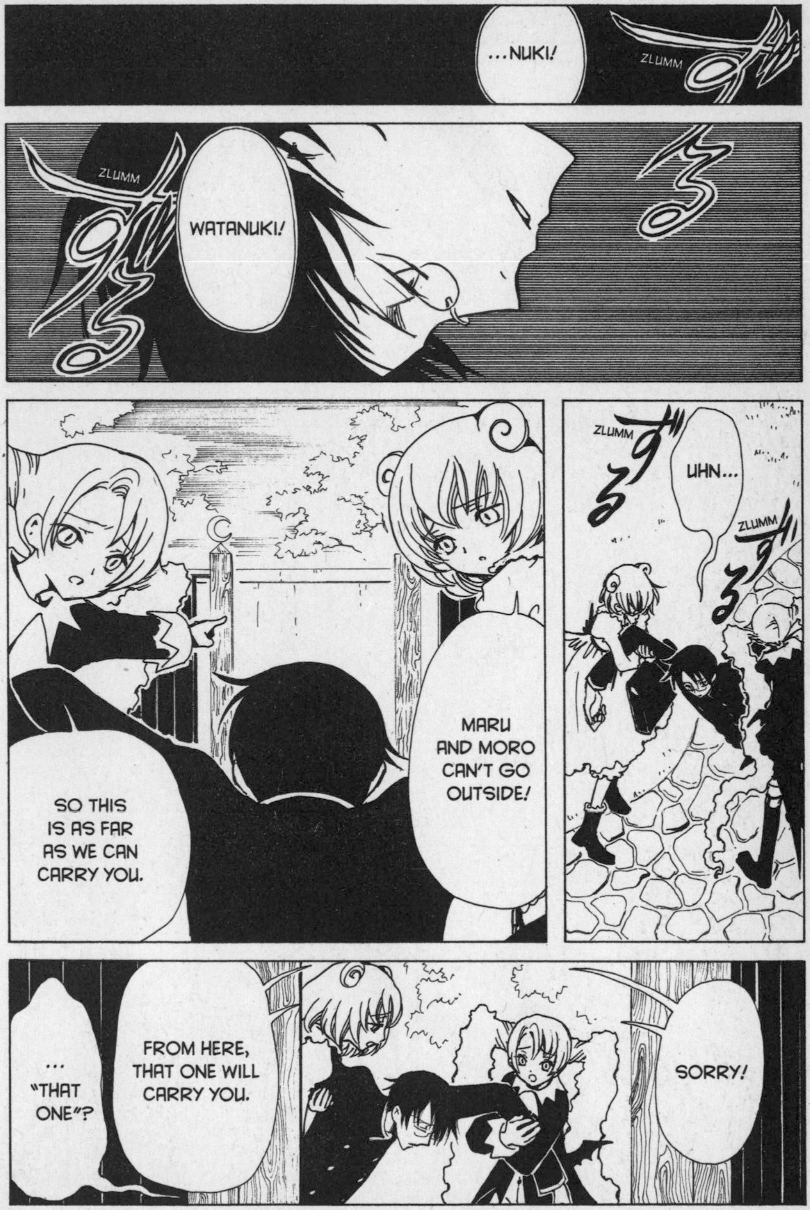
ZLUMM
...NUKI!
WATANUKI!
ZLUMM
ZLUMM
UHN...
ZLUMM
MARU AND MORO CAN'T GO OUTSIDE!
SO THIS IS AS FAR AS WE CAN CARRY YOU.
SORRY!
FROM HERE, THAT ONE WILL CARRY YOU.
... "THAT ONE"?

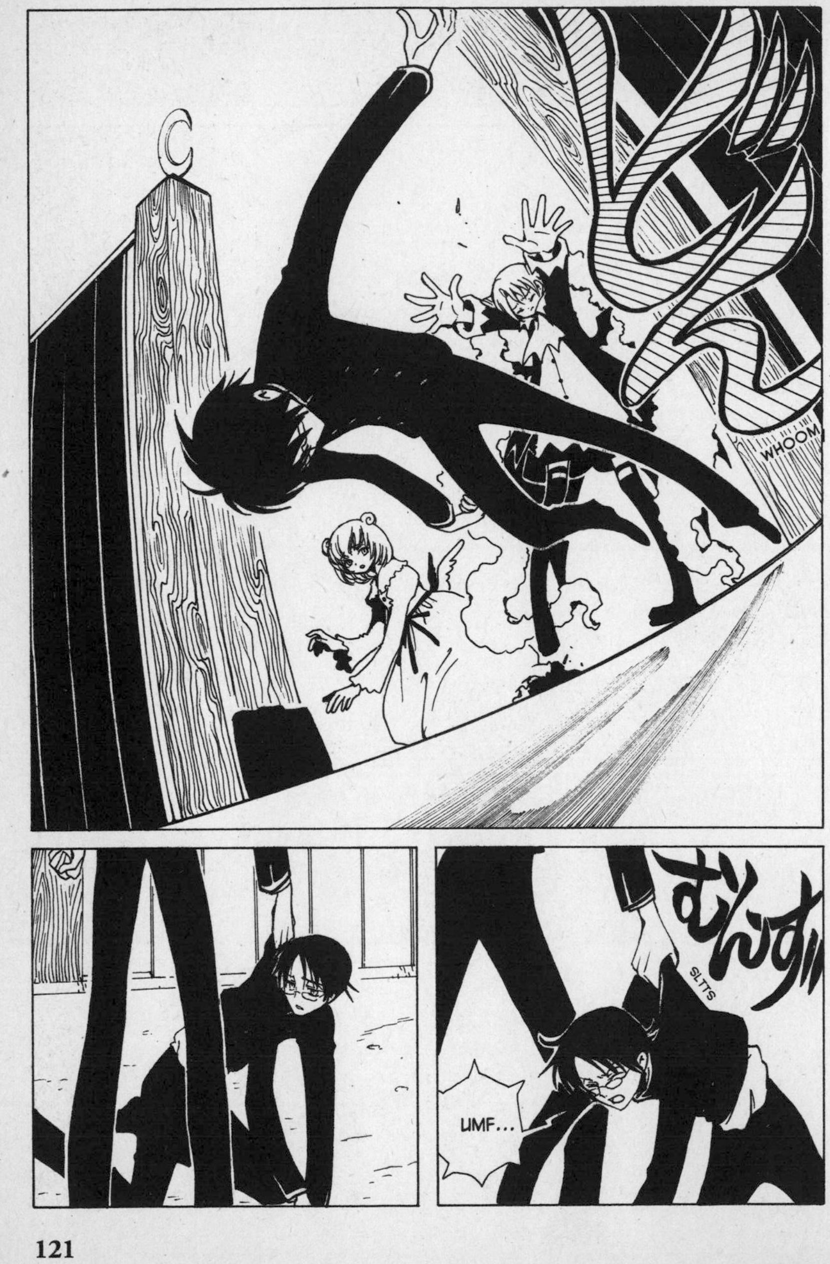
WHOOM
むんず
SLTTS
UMF...

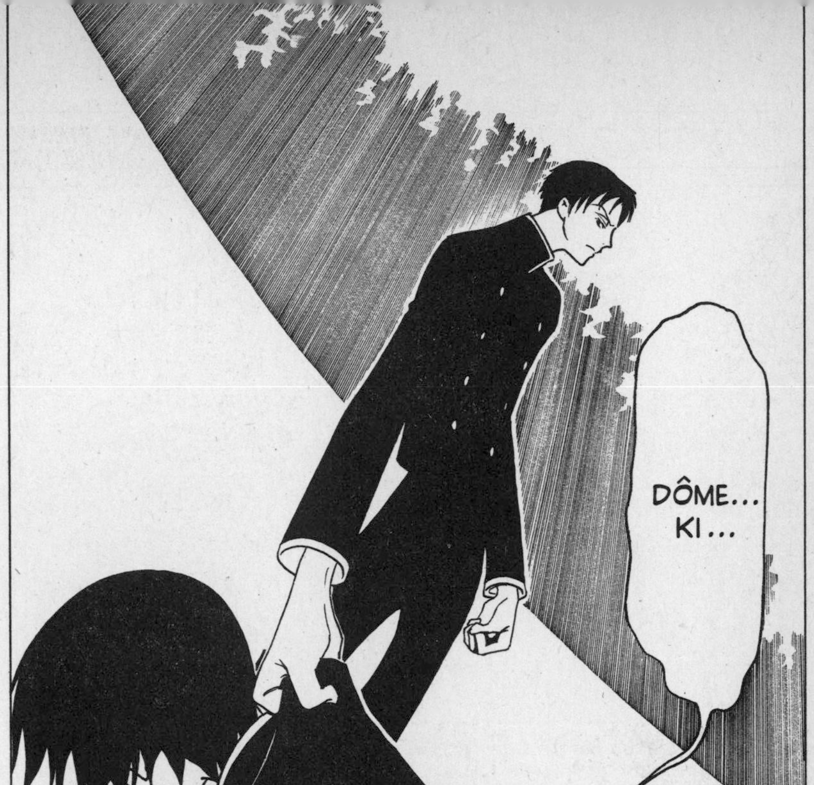
DÔME...
KI...

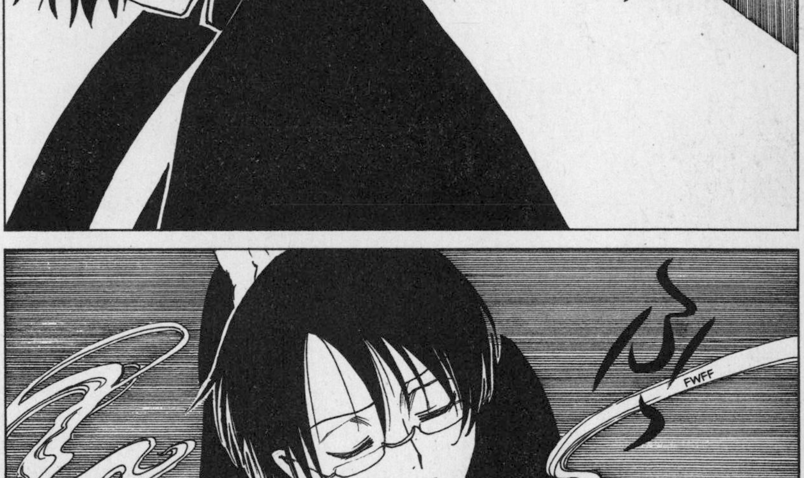
FWFF

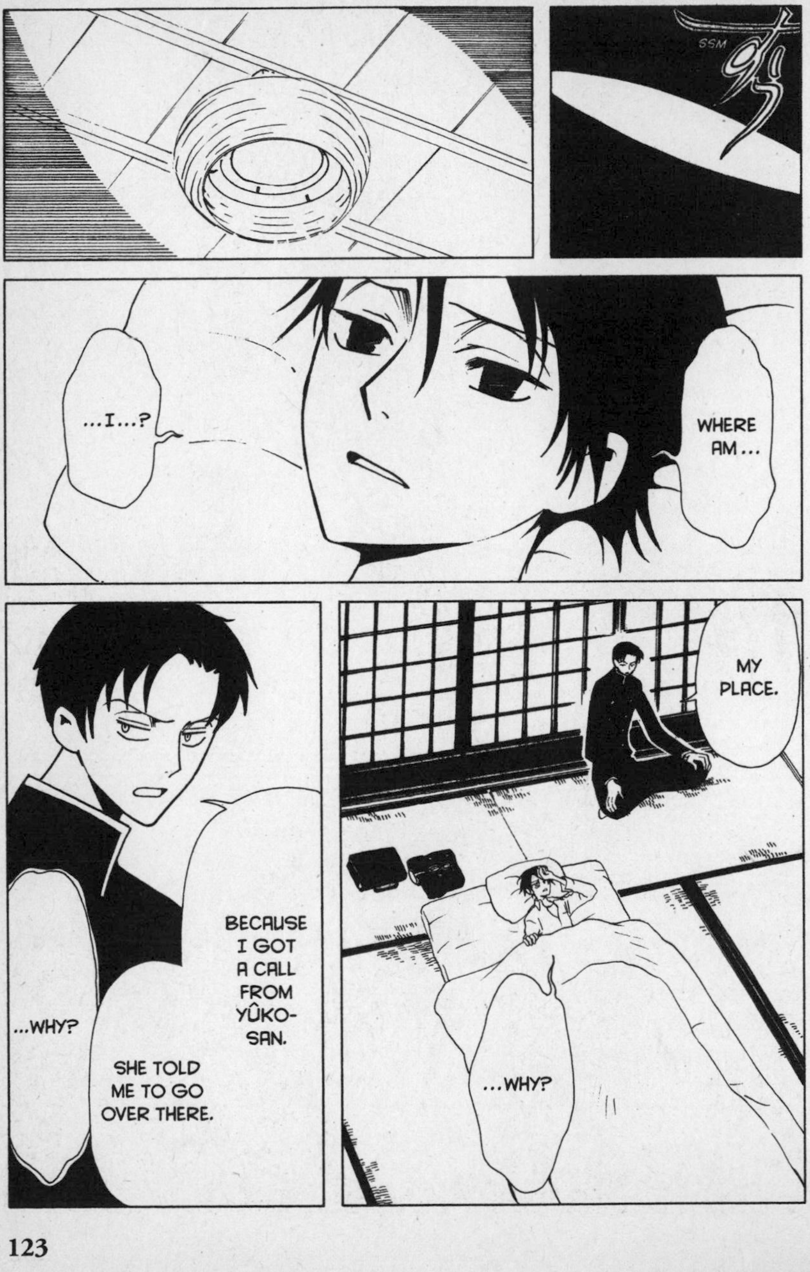
SSM
WHERE AM...
...I...?
MY PLACE.
...WHY?
BECAUSE I GOT A CALL FROM YÛKO-SAN.
SHE TOLD ME TO GO OVER THERE.
...WHY?

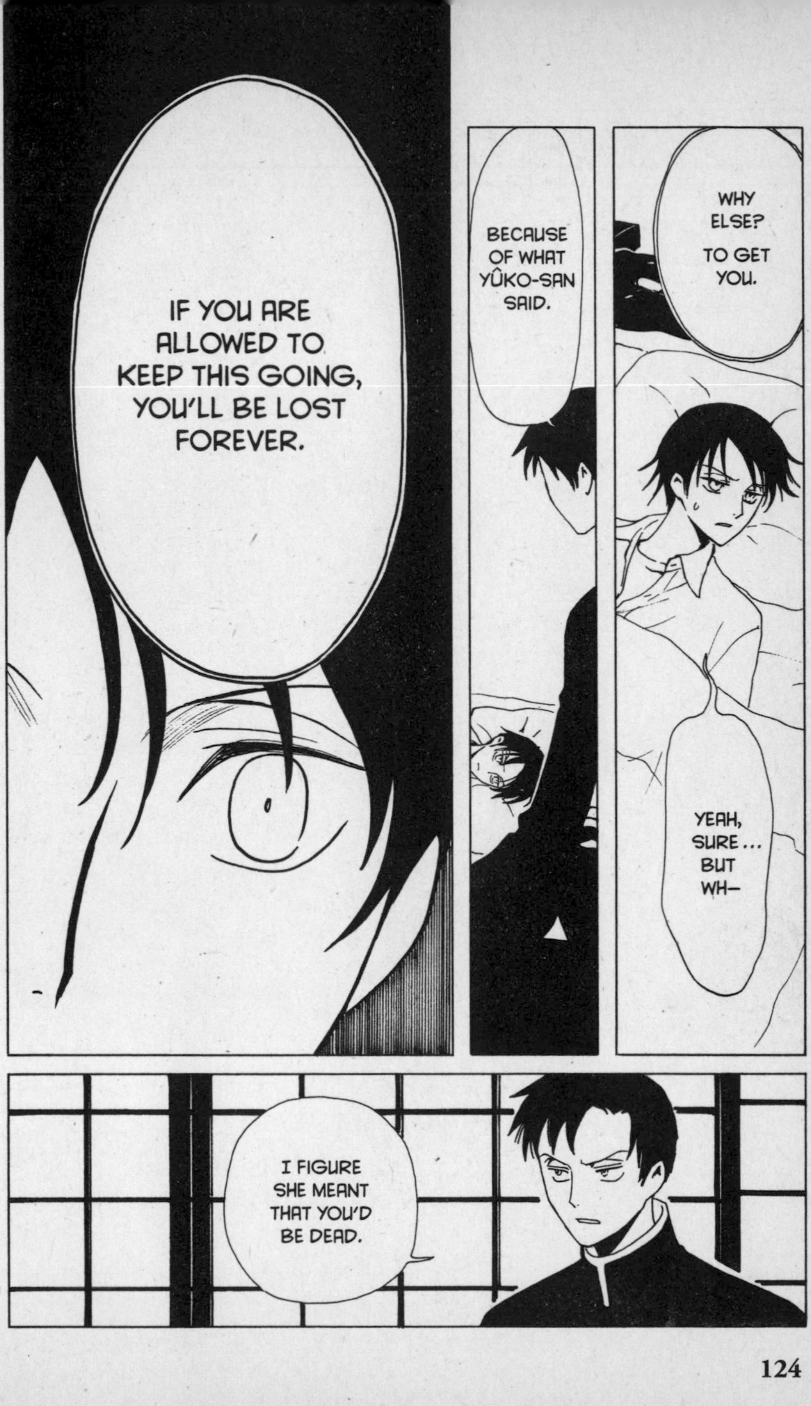
WHY ELSE? TO GET YOU.
YEAH, SURE... BUT WH—
BECAUSE OF WHAT YÛKO-SAN SAID.
IF YOU ARE ALLOWED TO KEEP THIS GOING, YOU'LL BE LOST FOREVER.
I FIGURE SHE MEANT THAT YOU'D BE DEAD.

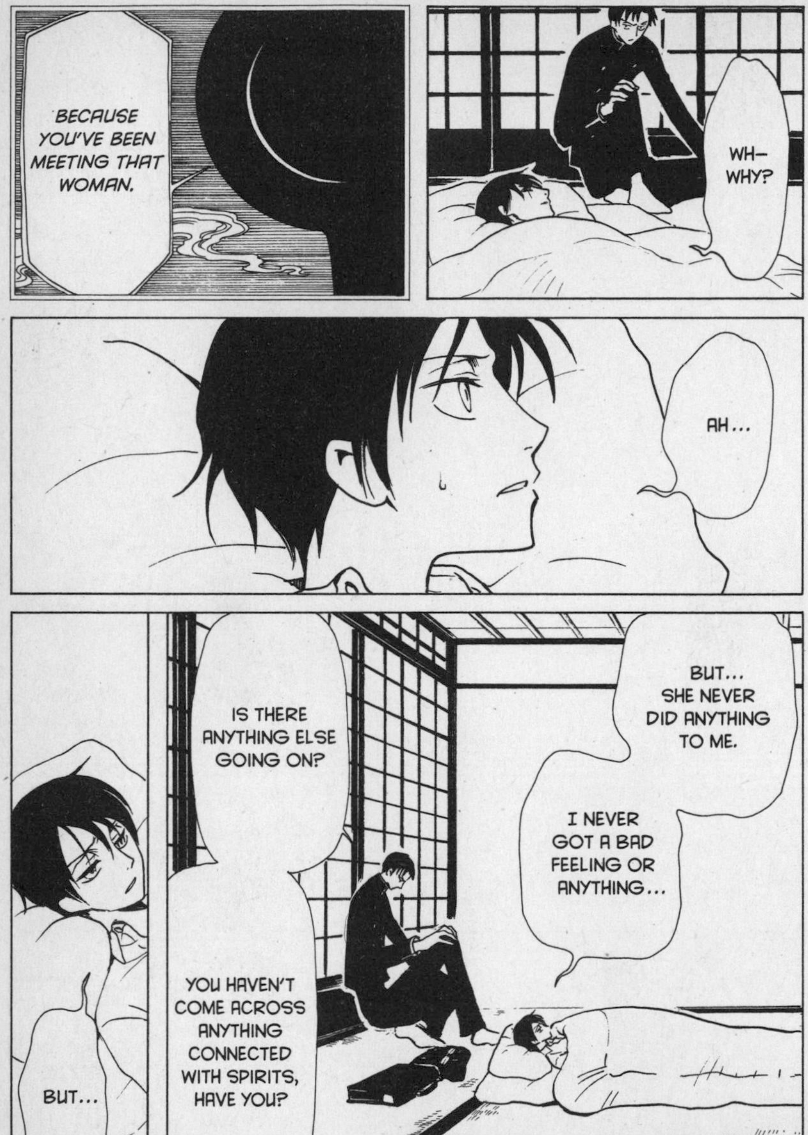
WH— WHY?
BECAUSE YOU'VE BEEN MEETING THAT WOMAN.
AH...
BUT... SHE NEVER DID ANYTHING TO ME.
I NEVER GOT A BAD FEELING OR ANYTHING...
IS THERE ANYTHING ELSE GOING ON?
YOU HAVEN'T COME ACROSS ANYTHING CONNECTED WITH SPIRITS, HAVE YOU?
BUT...

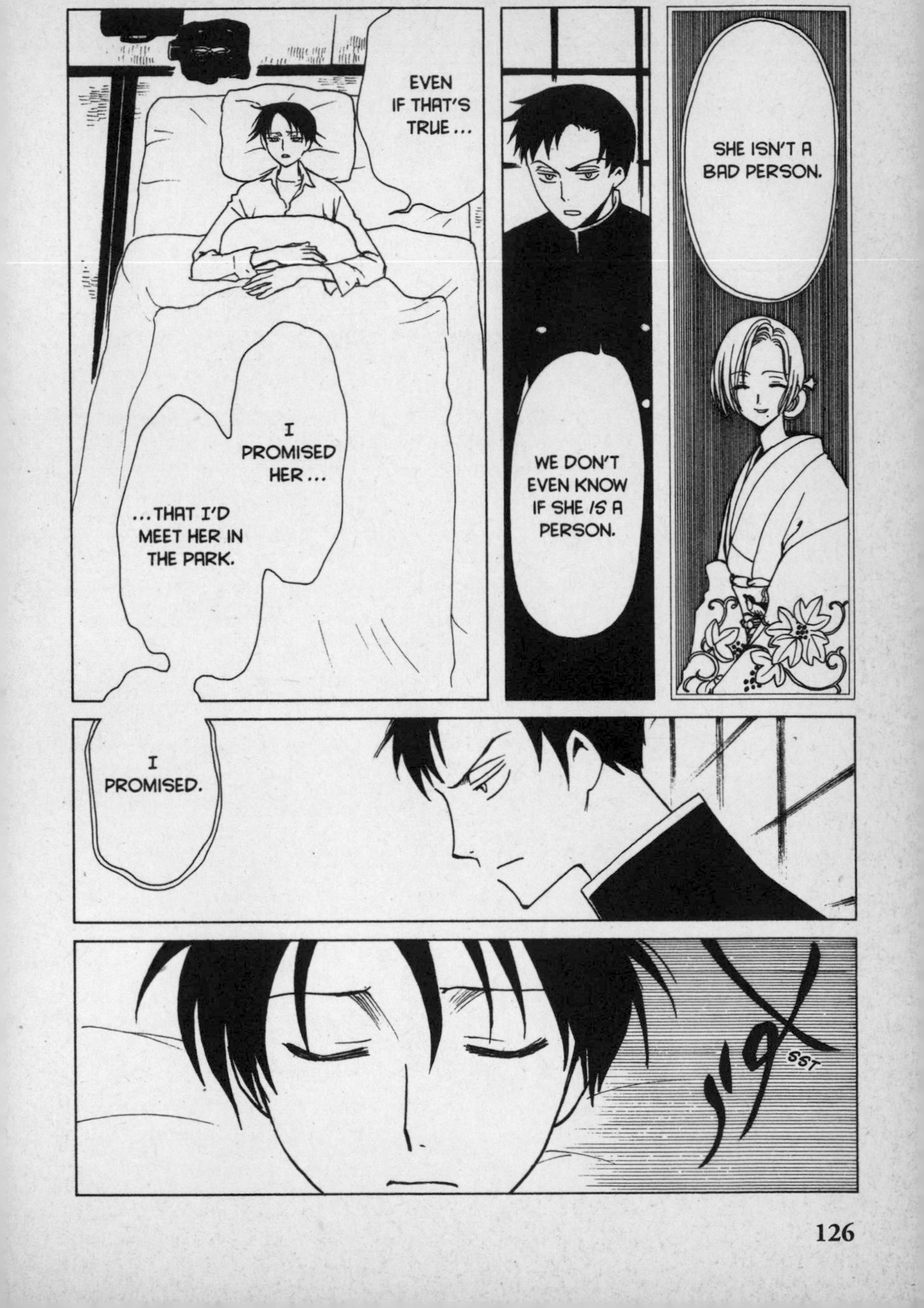
SHE ISN'T A BAD PERSON.
WE DON'T EVEN KNOW IF SHE IS A PERSON.
EVEN IF THAT'S TRUE...
I PROMISED HER...
...THAT I'D MEET HER IN THE PARK.
I PROMISED.
SST

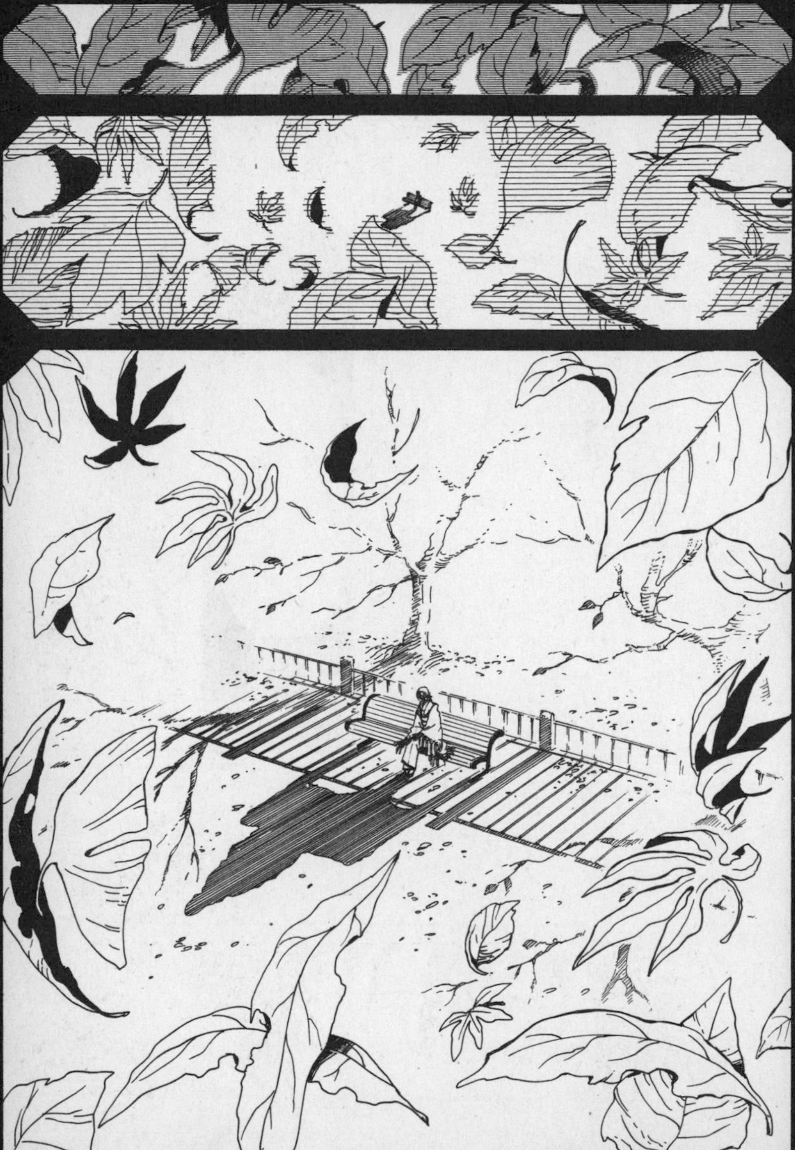

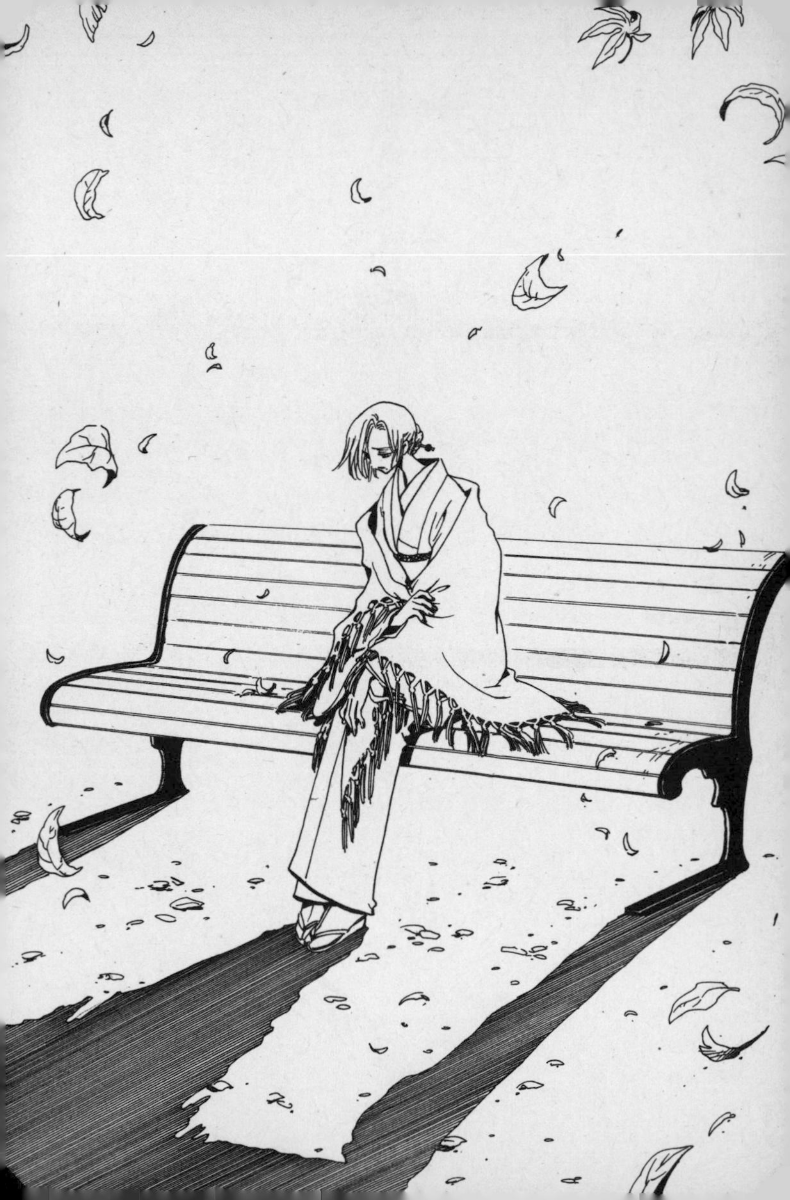

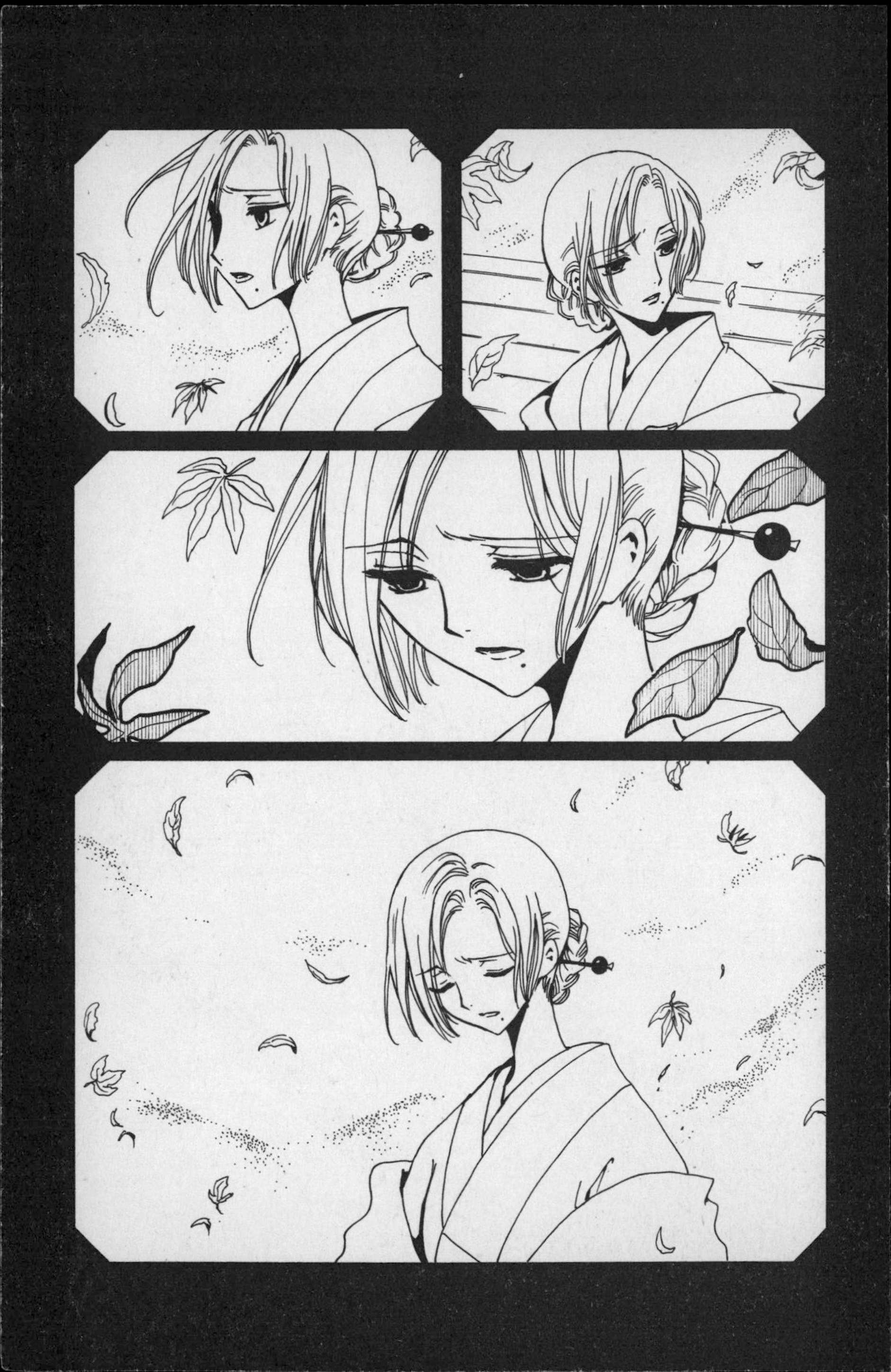

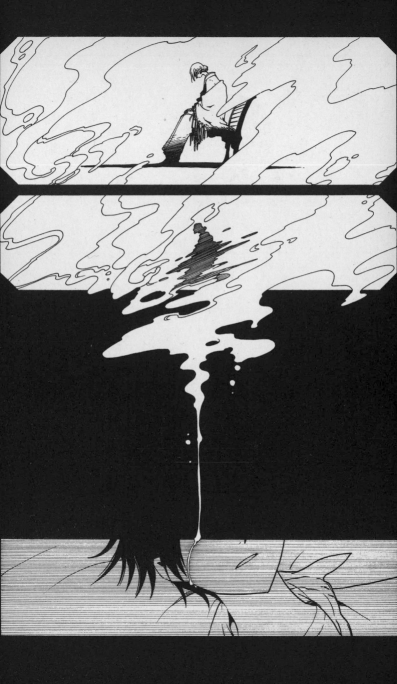

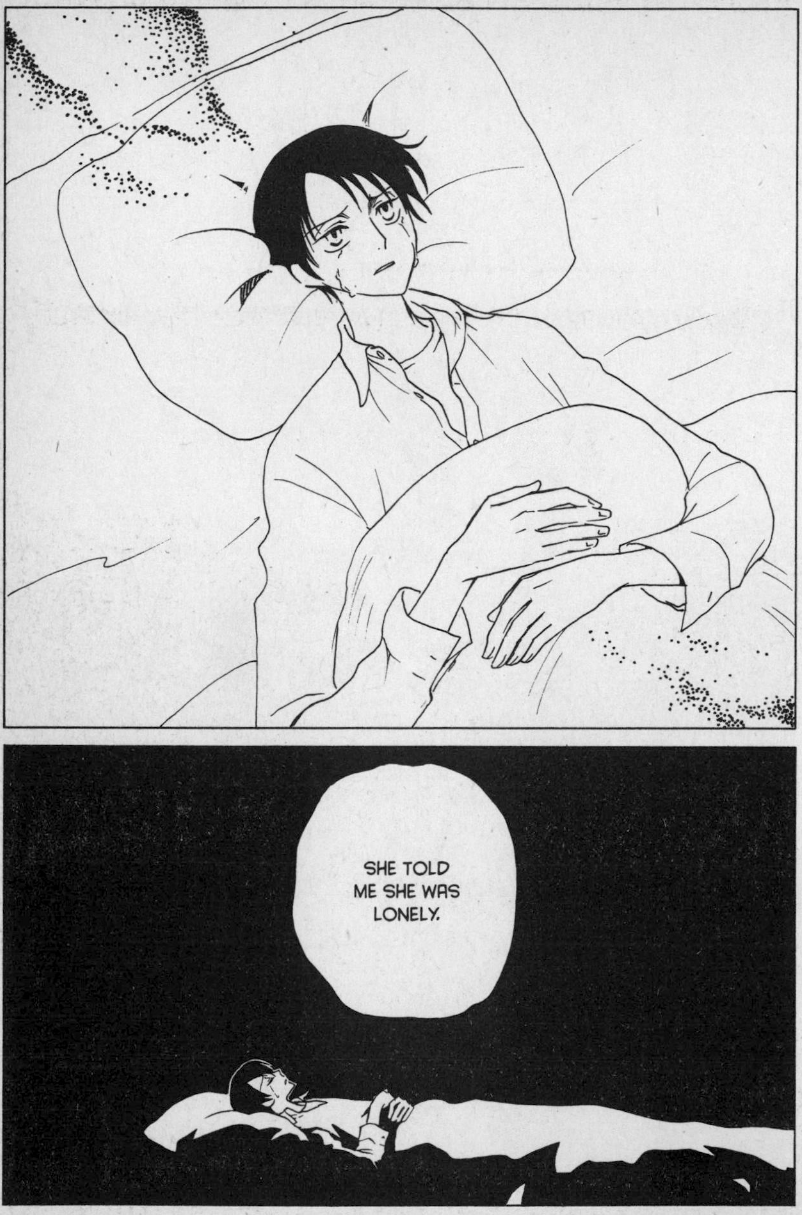
SHE TOLD ME SHE WAS LONELY.

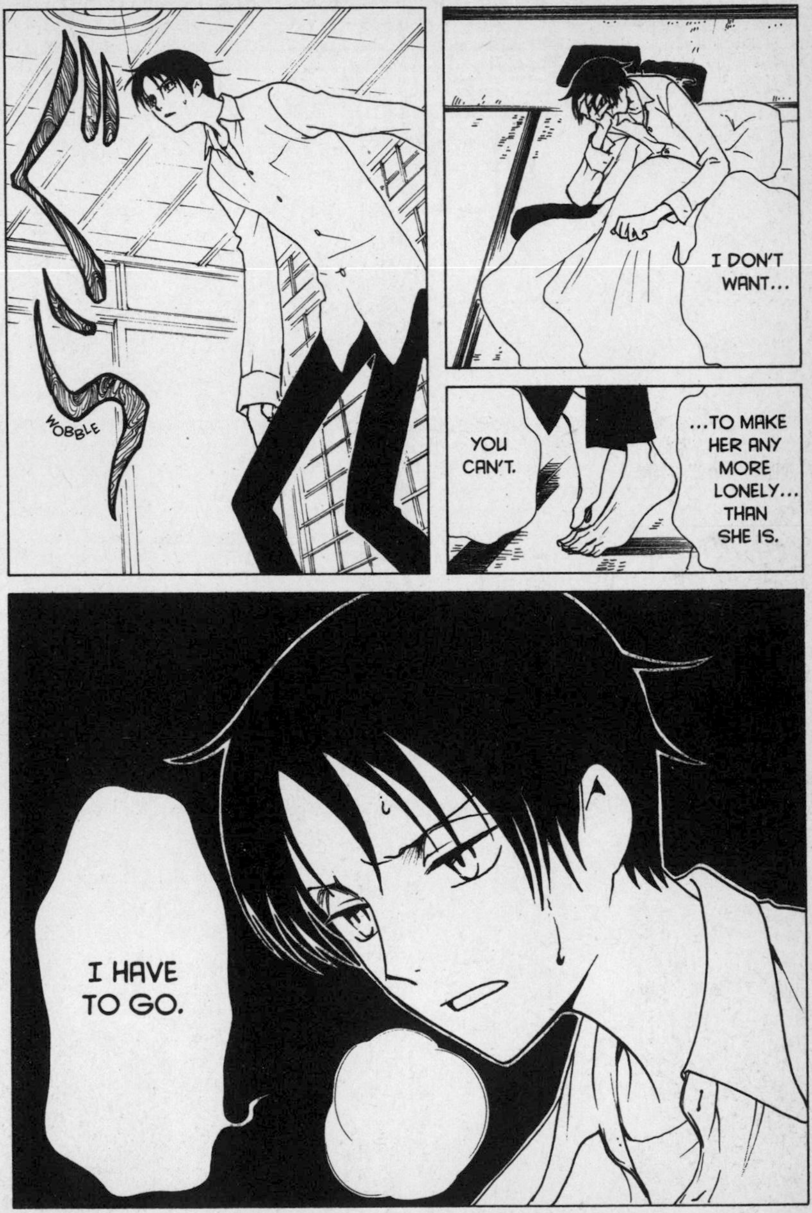
I DON'T WANT...
...TO MAKE HER ANY MORE LONELY... THAN SHE IS.
YOU CAN'T.
WOBBLE
I HAVE TO GO.

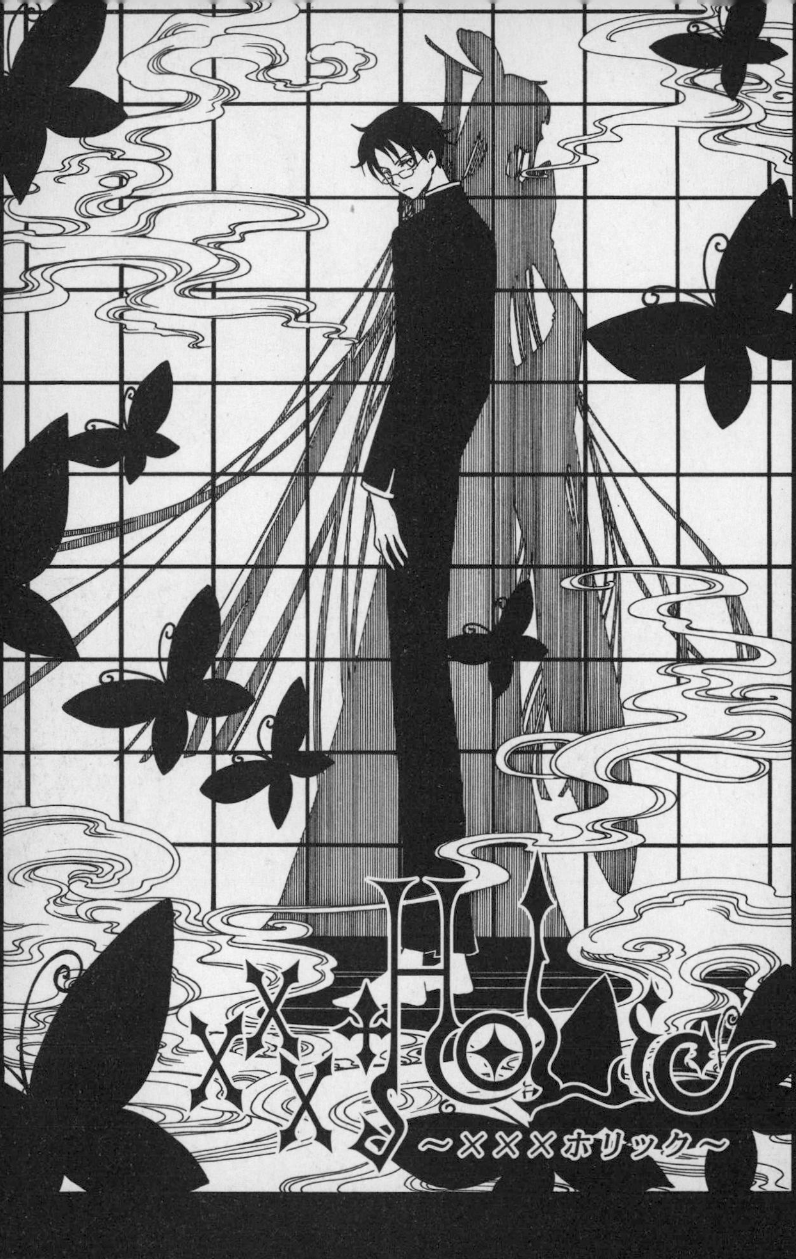
xxxHOLiC
〜×××ホリック〜

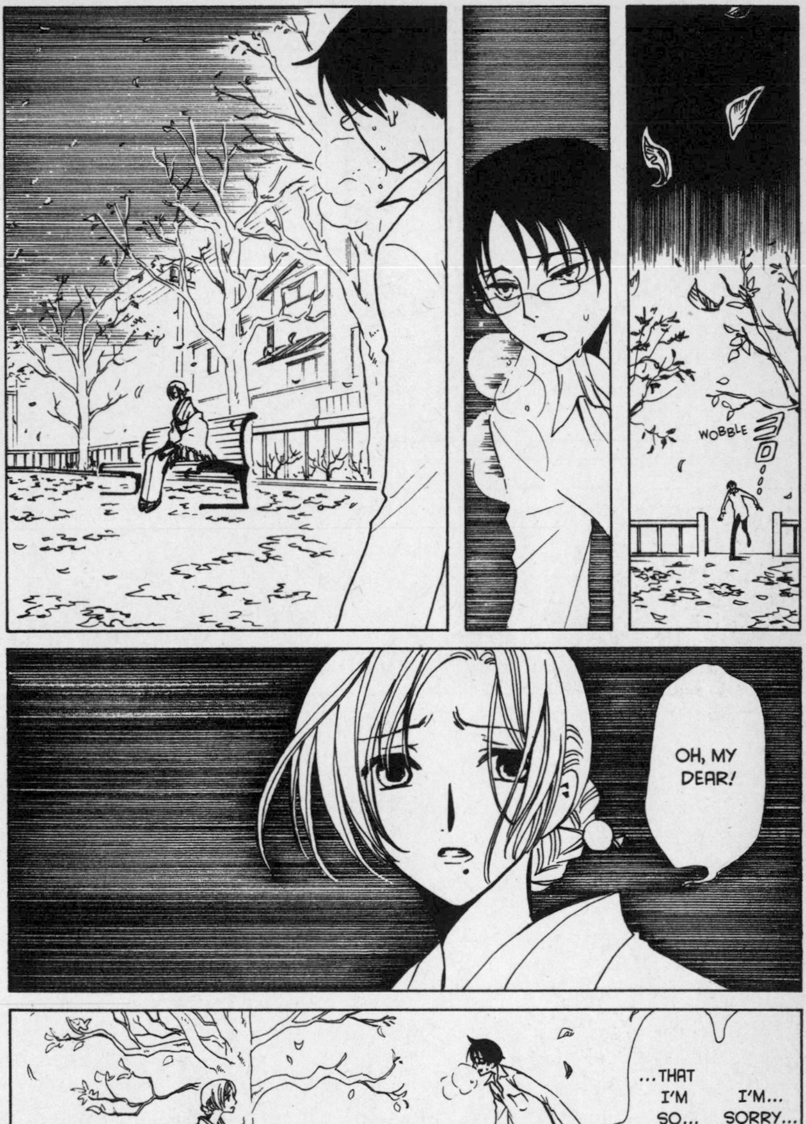
WOBBLE
ヨロ
OH, MY DEAR!
I'M... SORRY...
...THAT I'M SO... LATE...

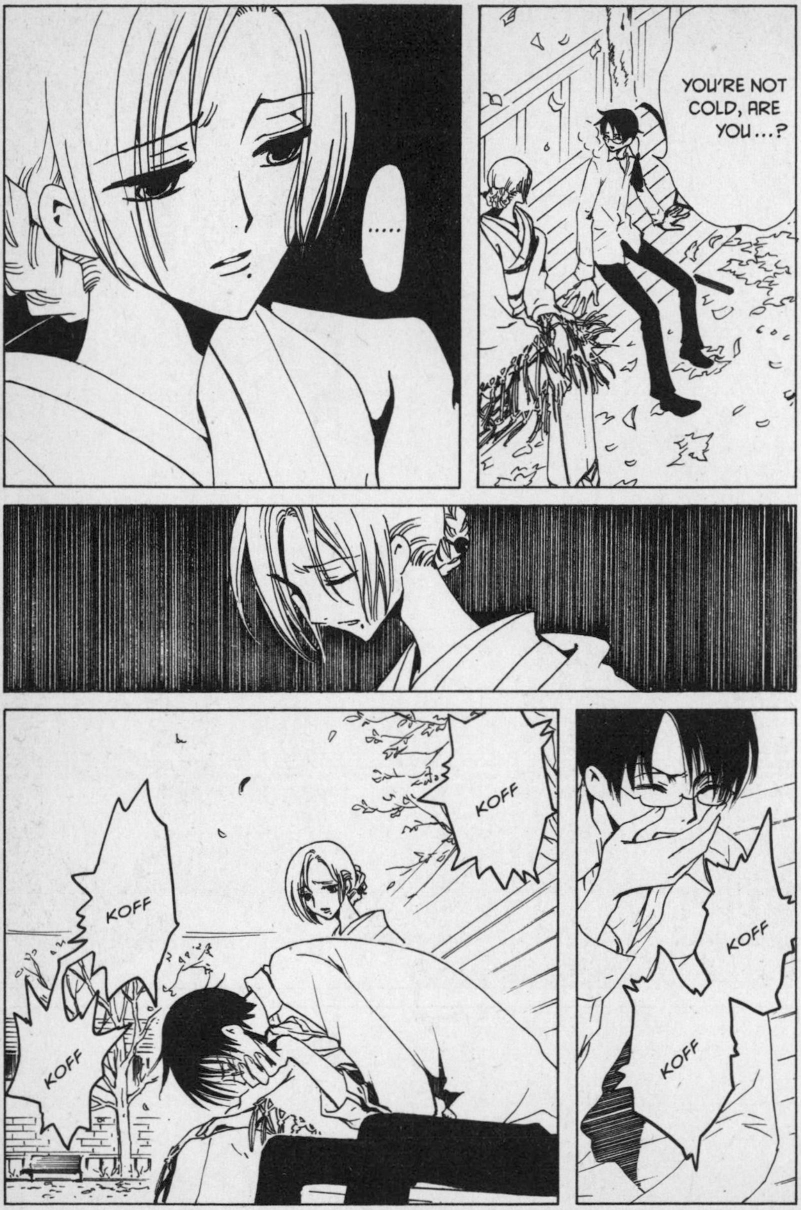

YOU'RE NOT COLD, ARE YOU...?
.....
KOFF
KOFF
KOFF
KOFF
KOFF

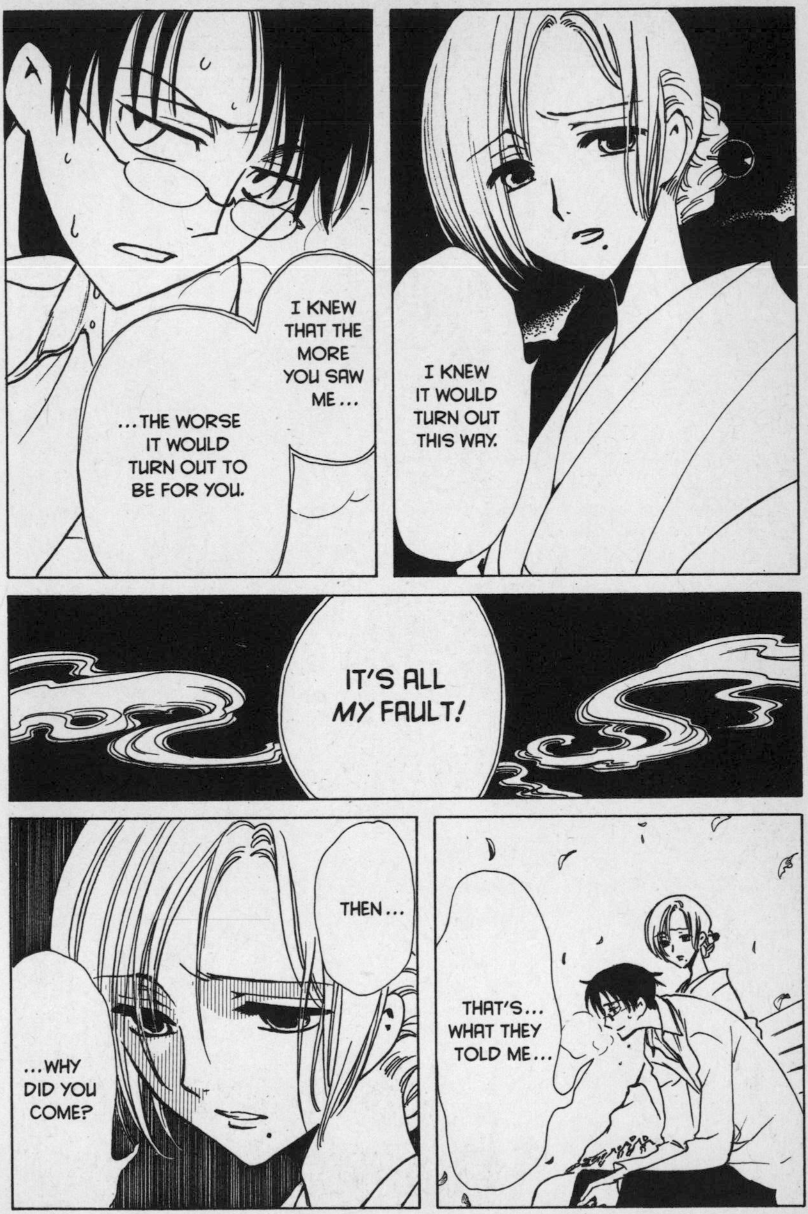
I KNEW IT WOULD TURN OUT THIS WAY.
I KNEW THAT THE MORE YOU SAW ME...
...THE WORSE IT WOULD TURN OUT TO BE FOR YOU.
IT'S ALL *MY* FAULT!
THAT'S... WHAT THEY TOLD ME...
THEN...
...WHY DID YOU COME?

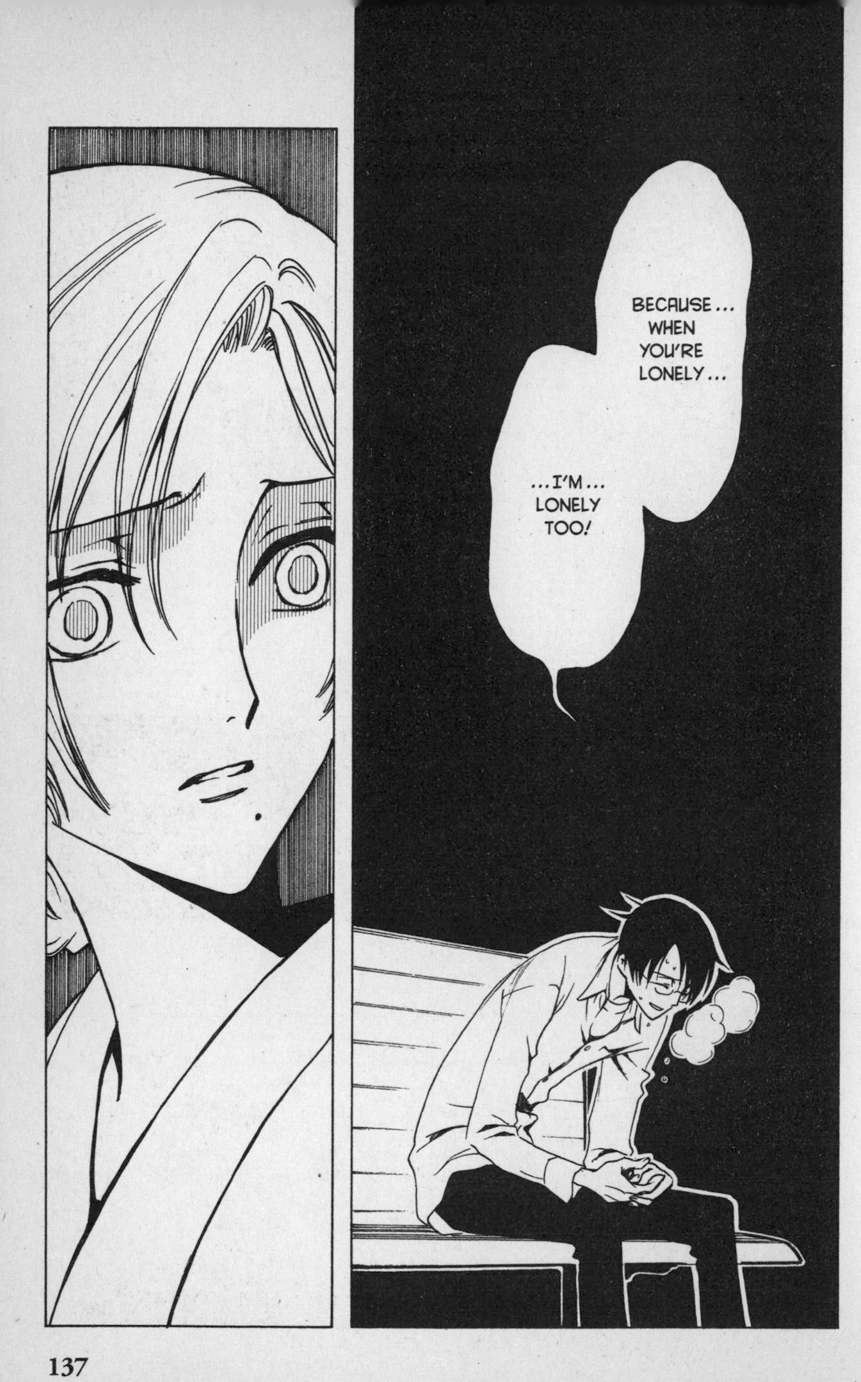
BECAUSE... WHEN YOU'RE LONELY...
...I'M... LONELY TOO!

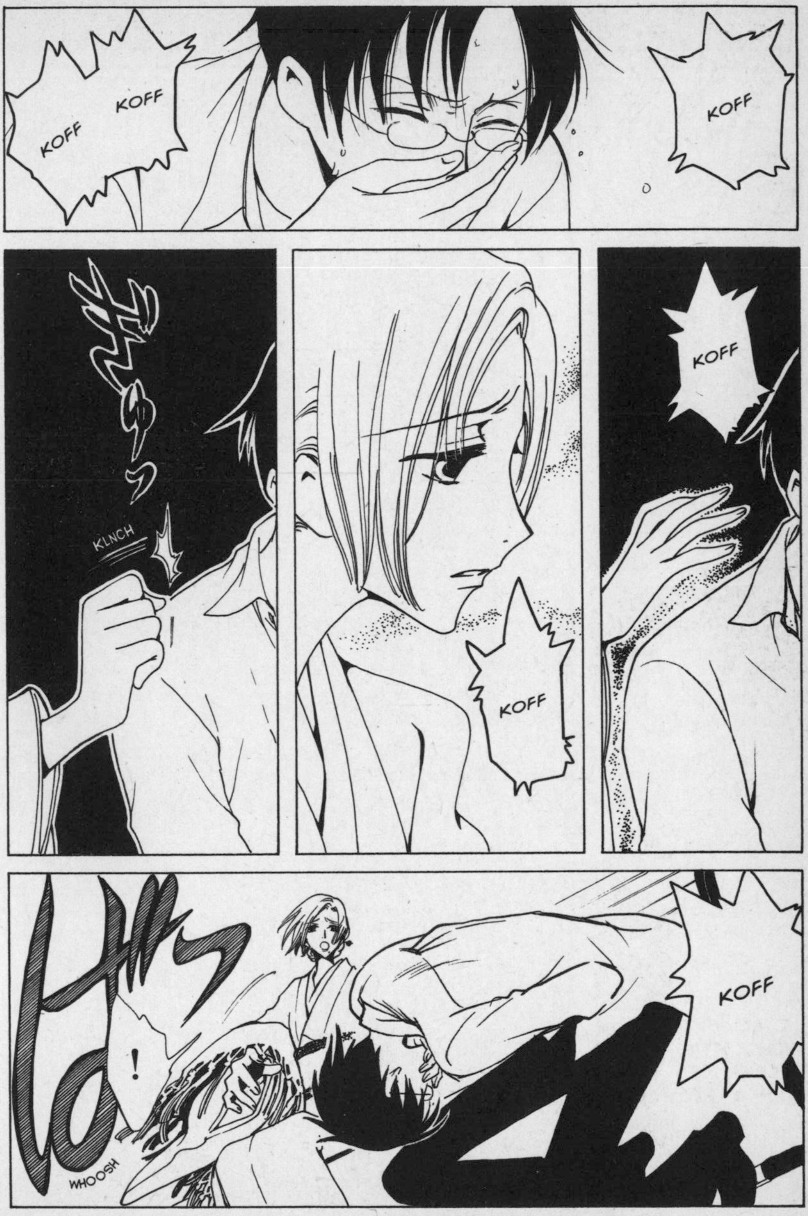
KOFF
KOFF
KOFF
KOFF
KOFF
KLNCH
KOFF
!
WHOOSH

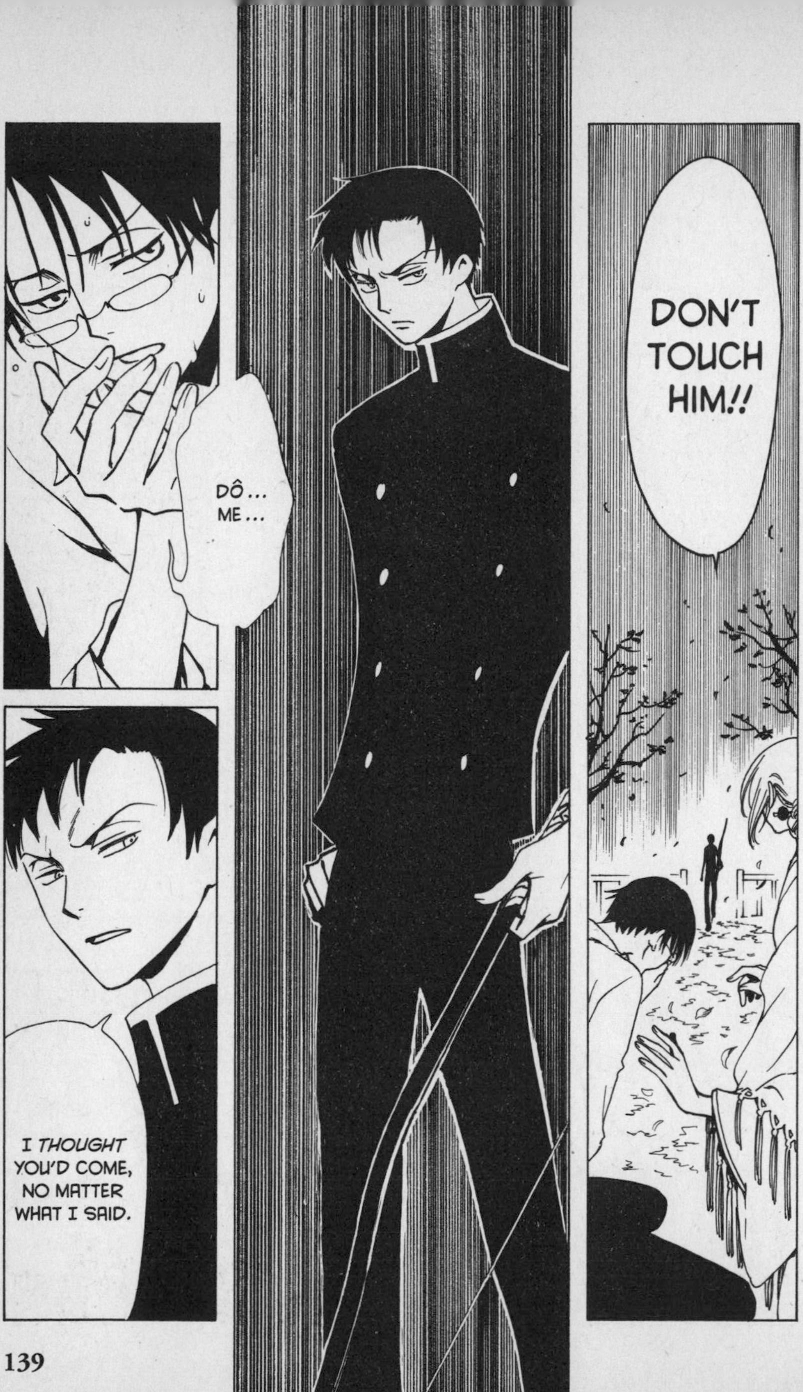
DON'T TOUCH HIM!!
DÔ... ME...
I *THOUGHT* YOU'D COME, NO MATTER WHAT I SAID.

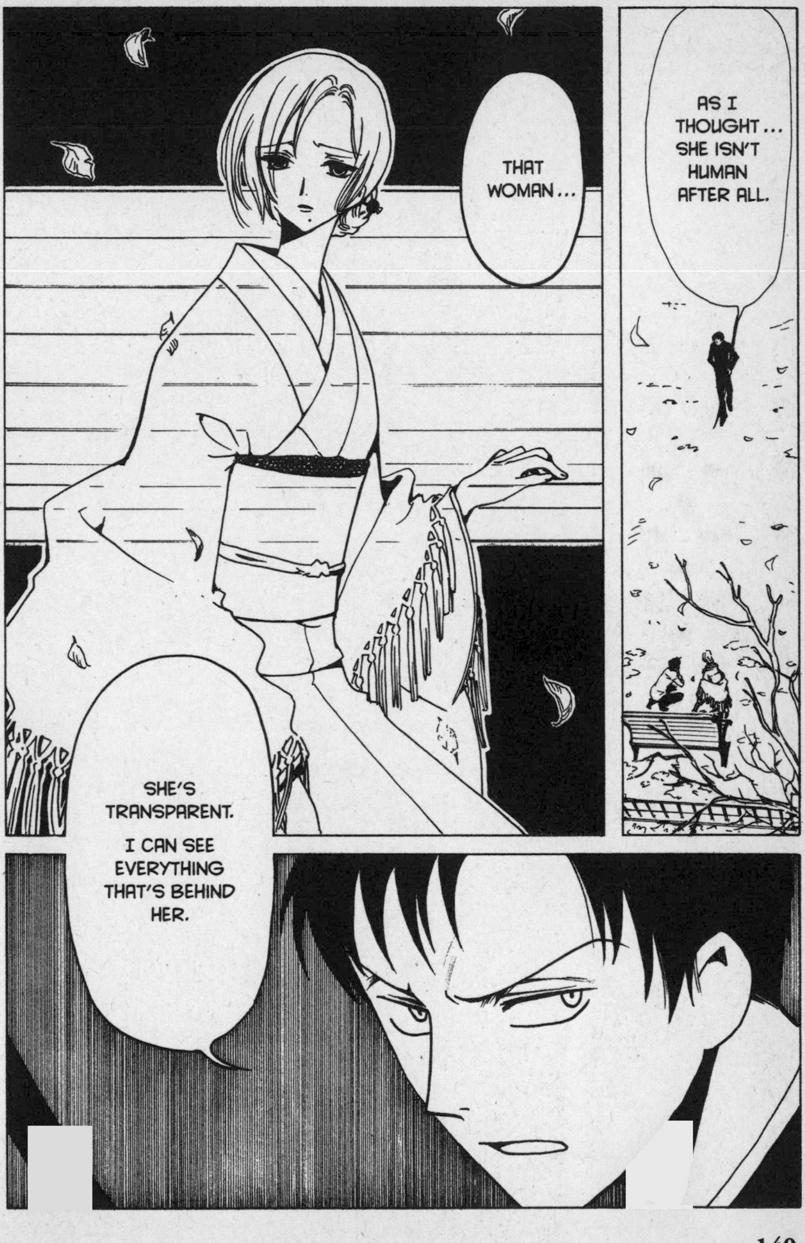
AS I THOUGHT... SHE ISN'T HUMAN AFTER ALL.
THAT WOMAN...
SHE'S TRANSPARENT.
I CAN SEE EVERYTHING THAT'S BEHIND HER.

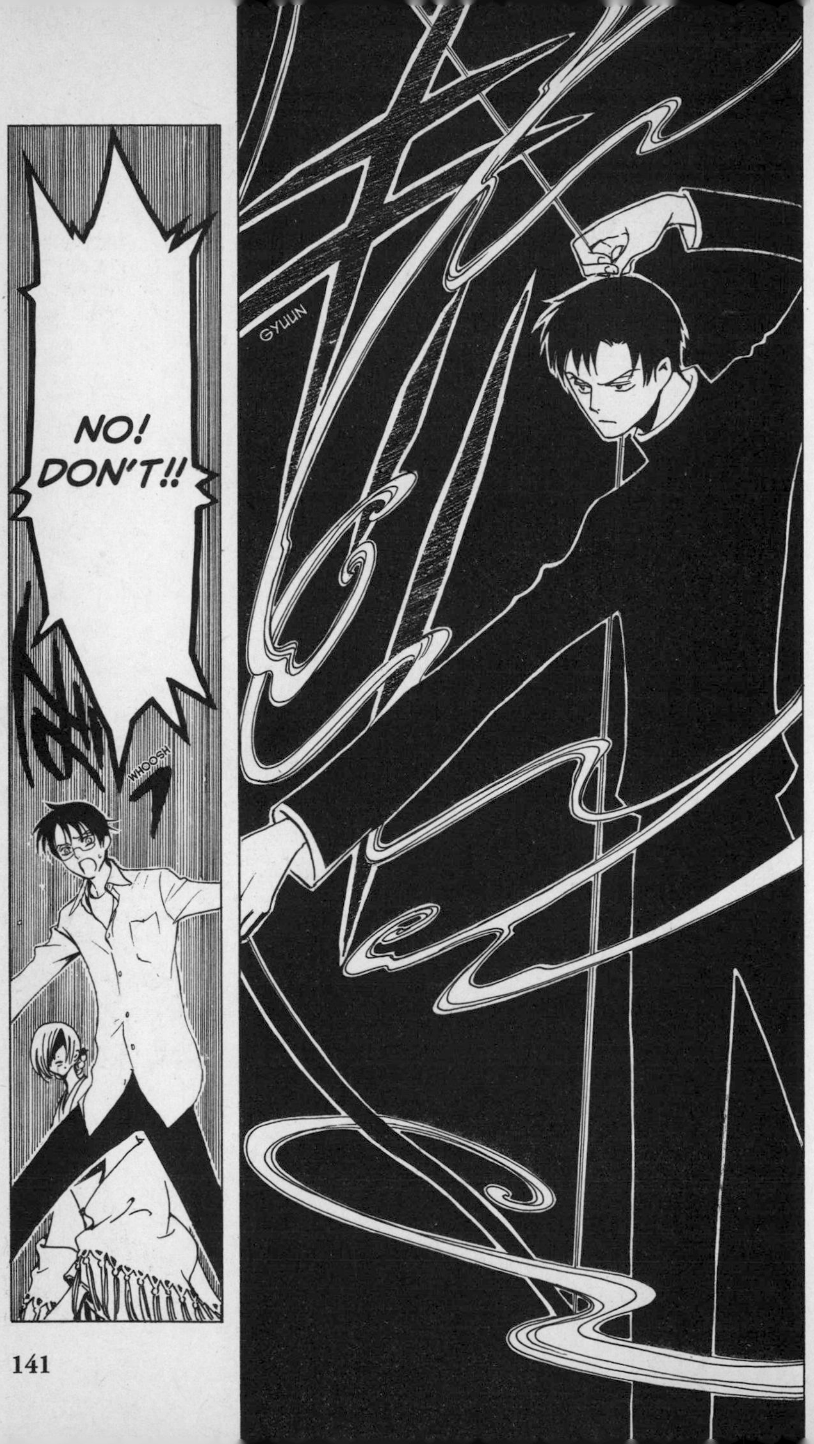
GYUUN
NO! DON'T!!
WHOOSH

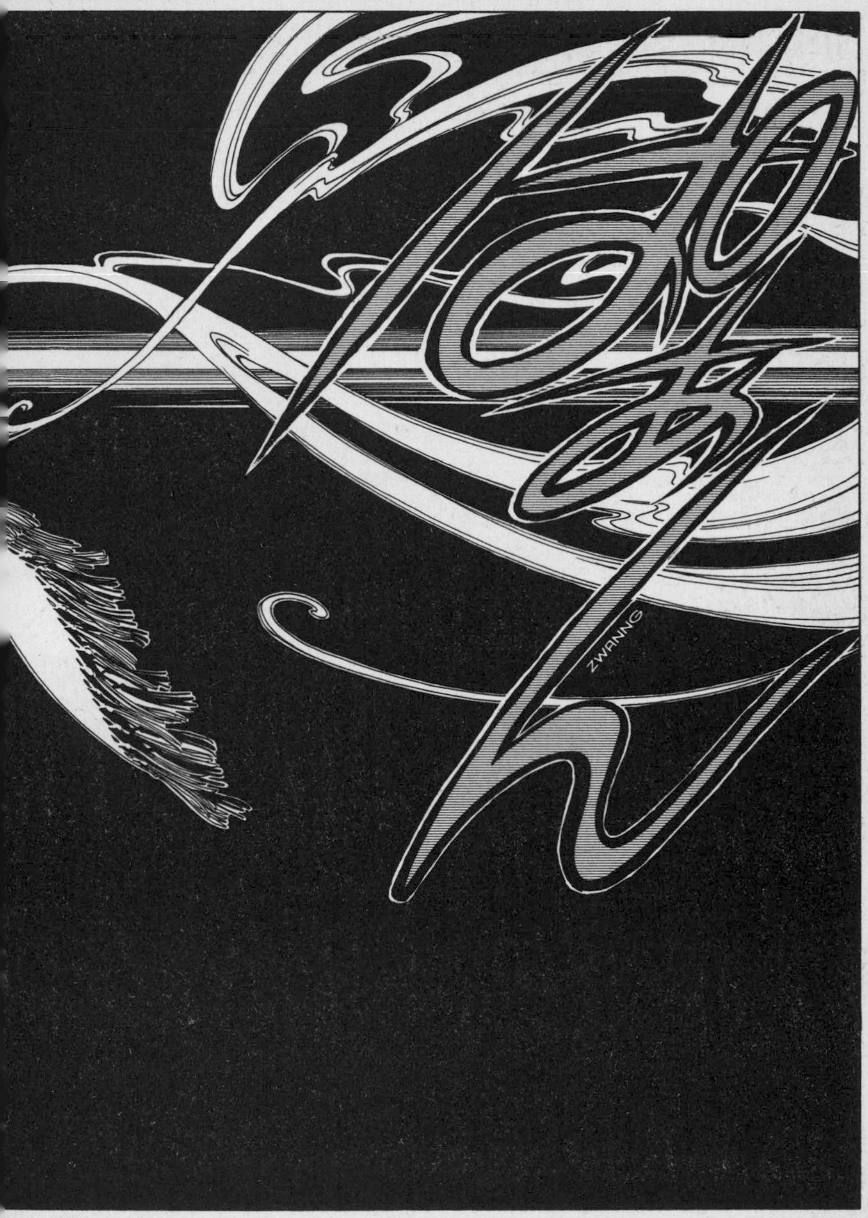
ZWANNG

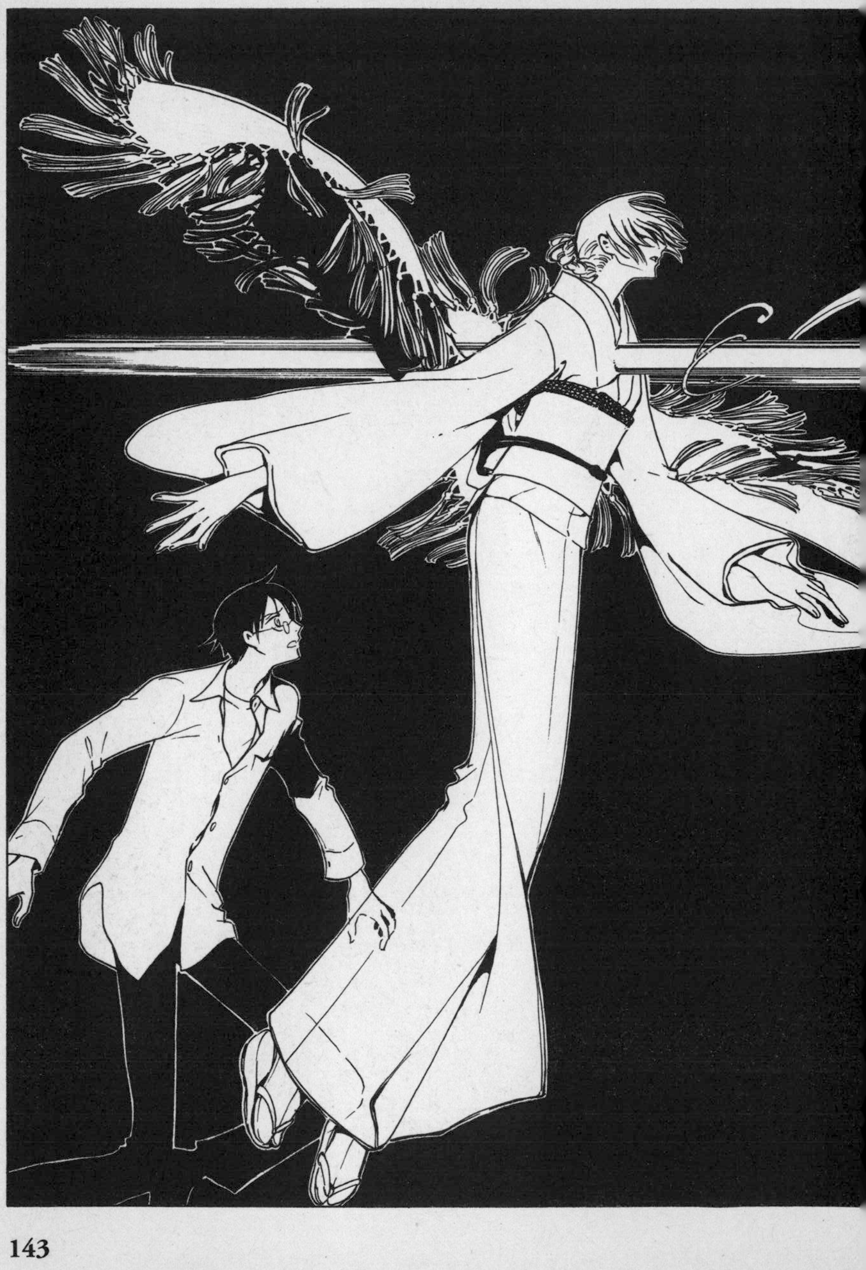

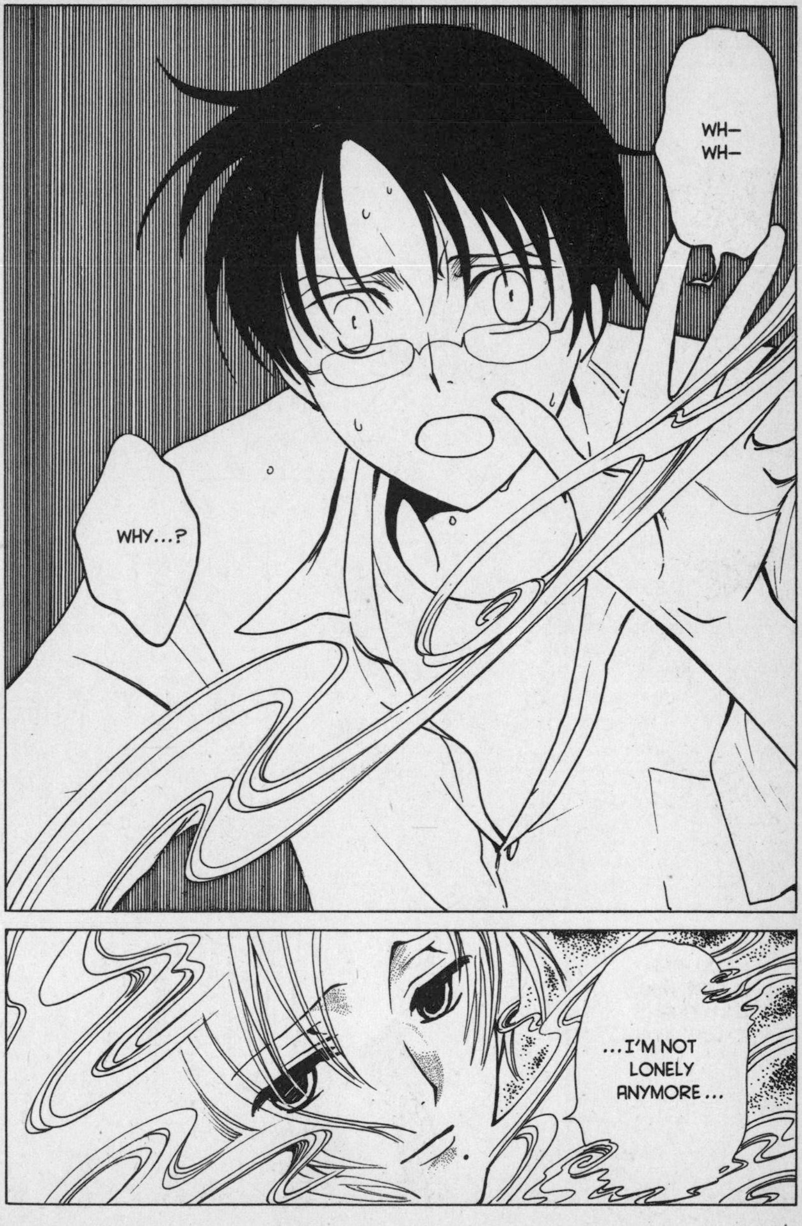
WH-
WH-
WHY...?
...I'M NOT LONELY ANYMORE...

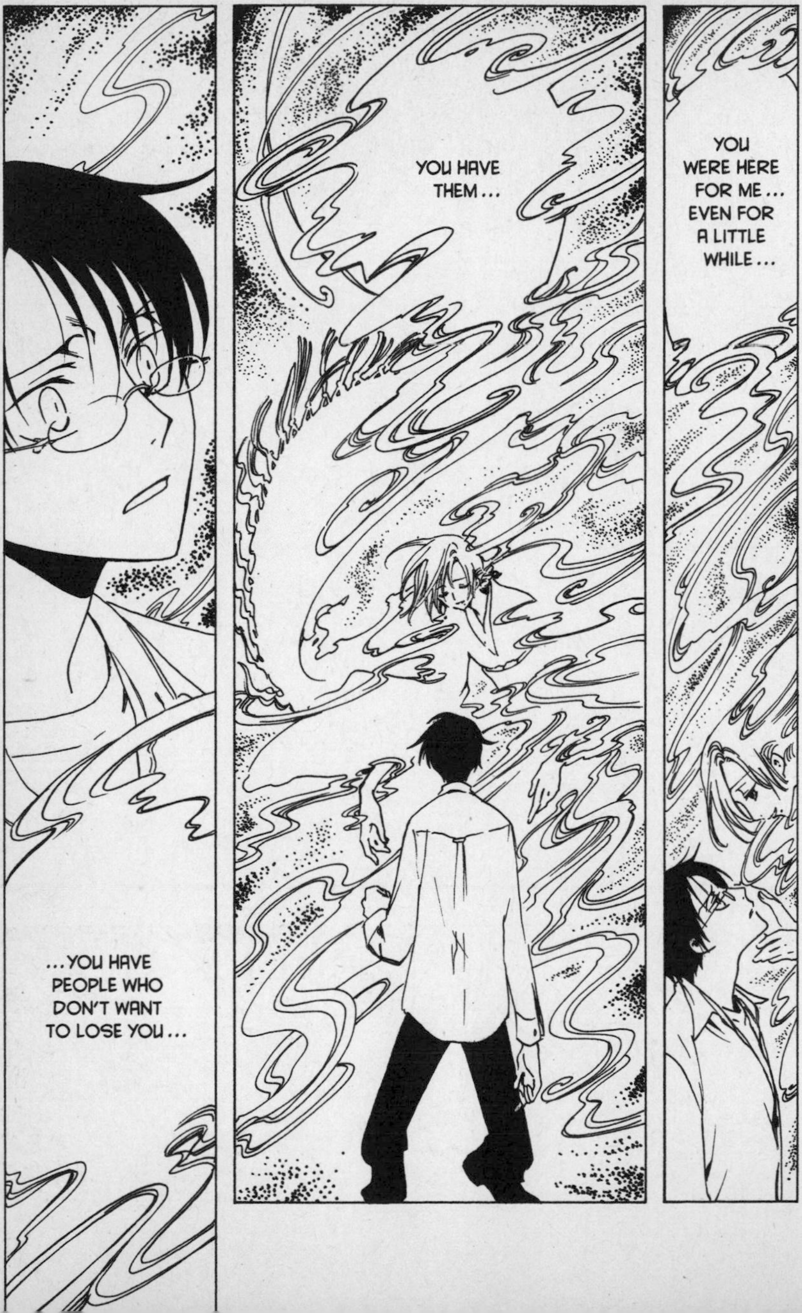
YOU WERE HERE FOR ME... EVEN FOR A LITTLE WHILE...
YOU HAVE THEM...
...YOU HAVE PEOPLE WHO DON'T WANT TO LOSE YOU...

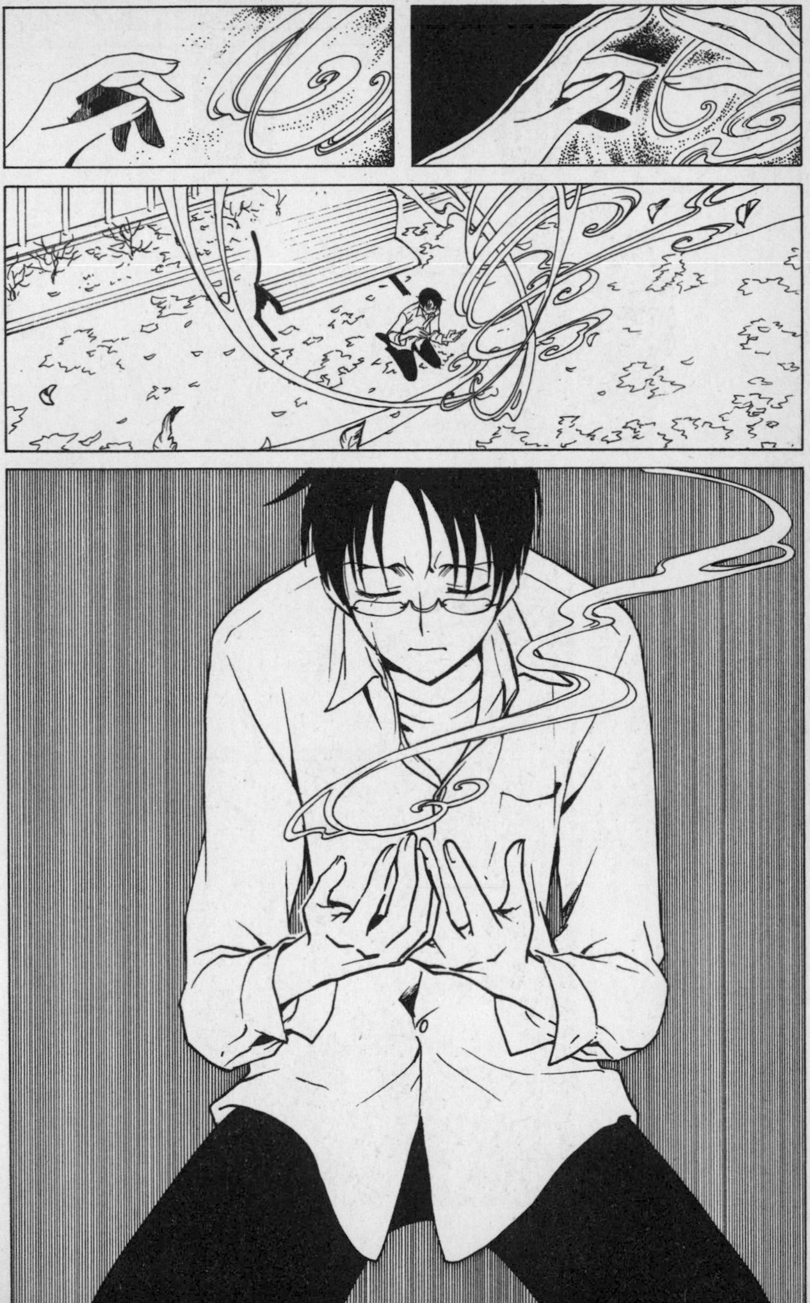

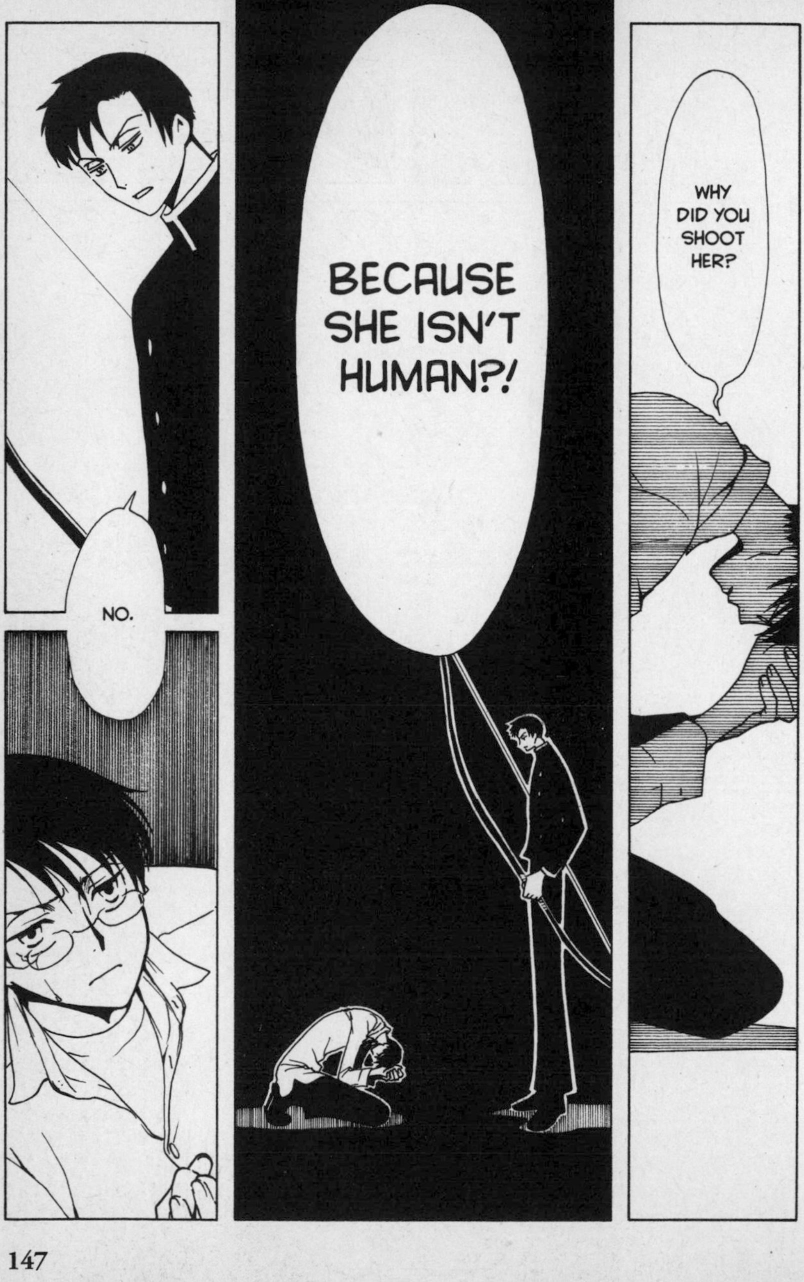
WHY DID YOU SHOOT HER?
BECAUSE SHE ISN'T HUMAN?!
NO.

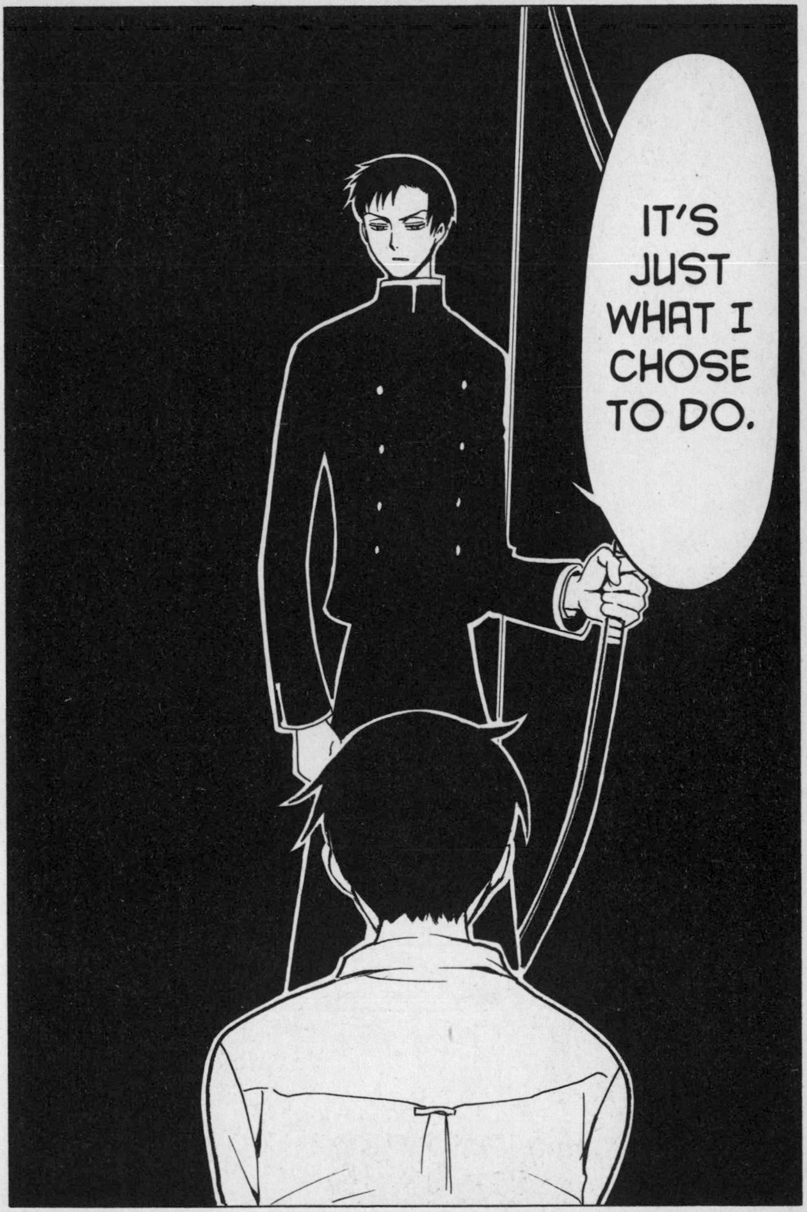
IT'S JUST WHAT I CHOSE TO DO.

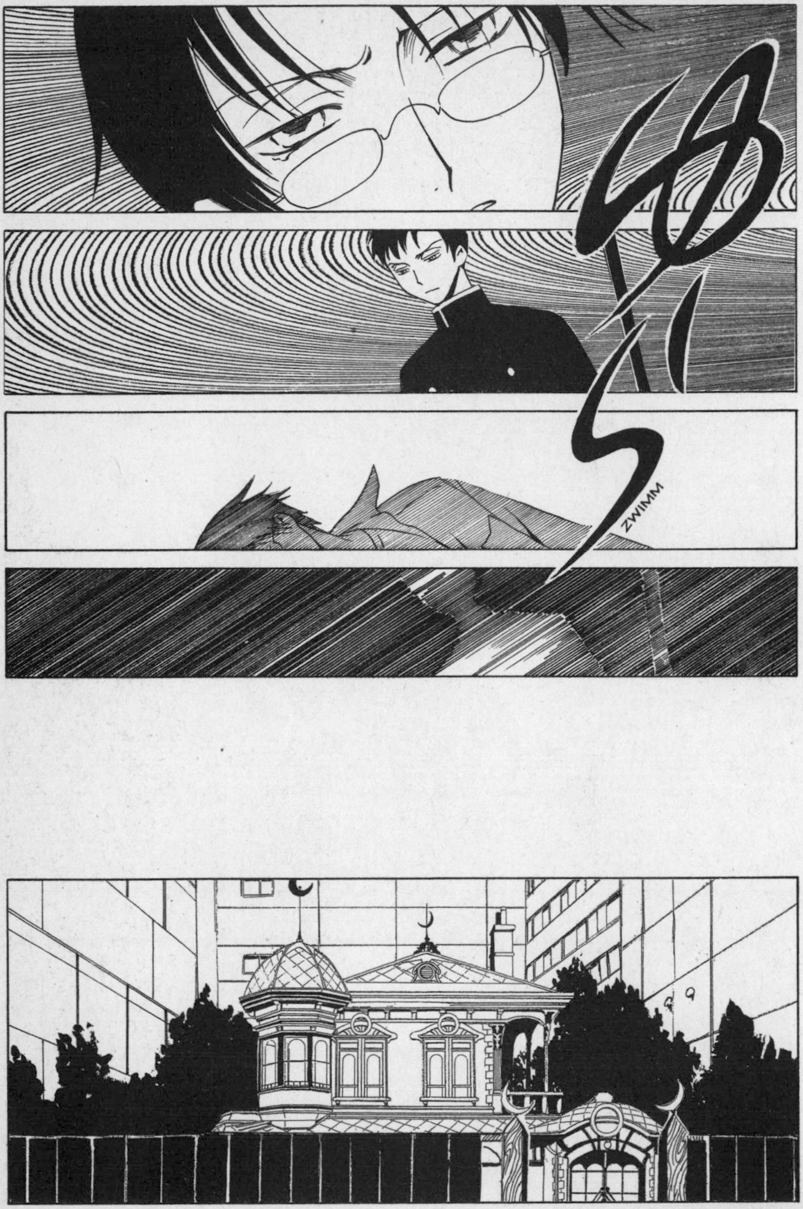
ZWIMM

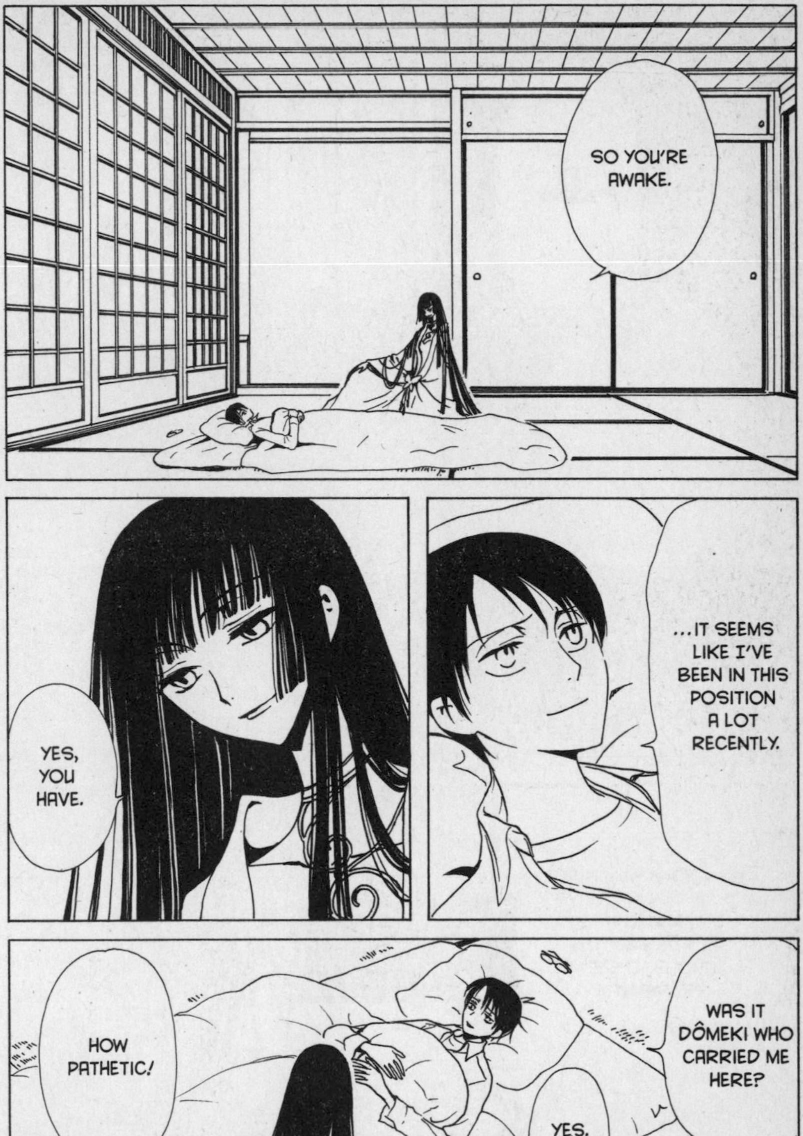
SO YOU'RE AWAKE.
...IT SEEMS LIKE I'VE BEEN IN THIS POSITION A LOT RECENTLY.
YES, YOU HAVE.
WAS IT DÔMEKI WHO CARRIED ME HERE?
YES.
HOW PATHETIC!

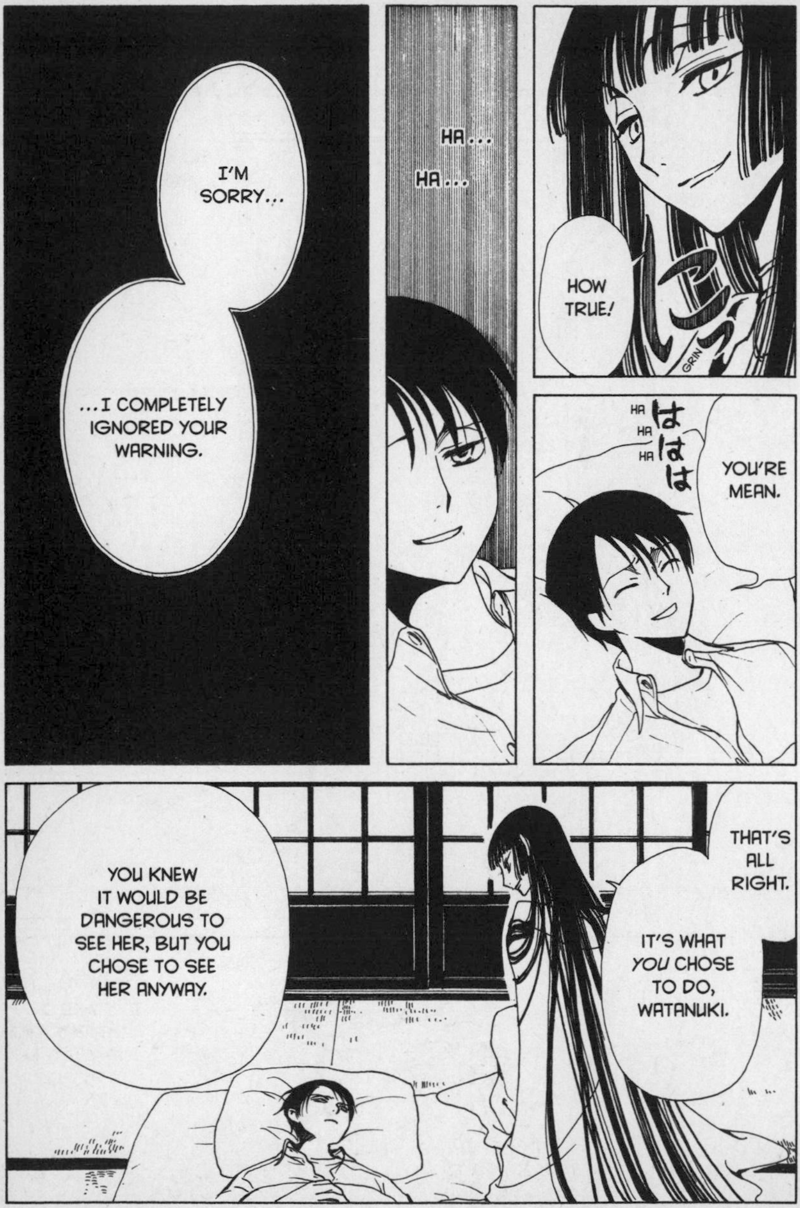
HOW TRUE!
GRIN
HA HA HA
ははは
YOU'RE MEAN.
HA...
HA...
I'M SORRY...
...I COMPLETELY IGNORED YOUR WARNING.
THAT'S ALL RIGHT.
IT'S WHAT *YOU* CHOSE TO DO, WATANUKI.
YOU KNEW IT WOULD BE DANGEROUS TO SEE HER, BUT YOU CHOSE TO SEE HER ANYWAY.

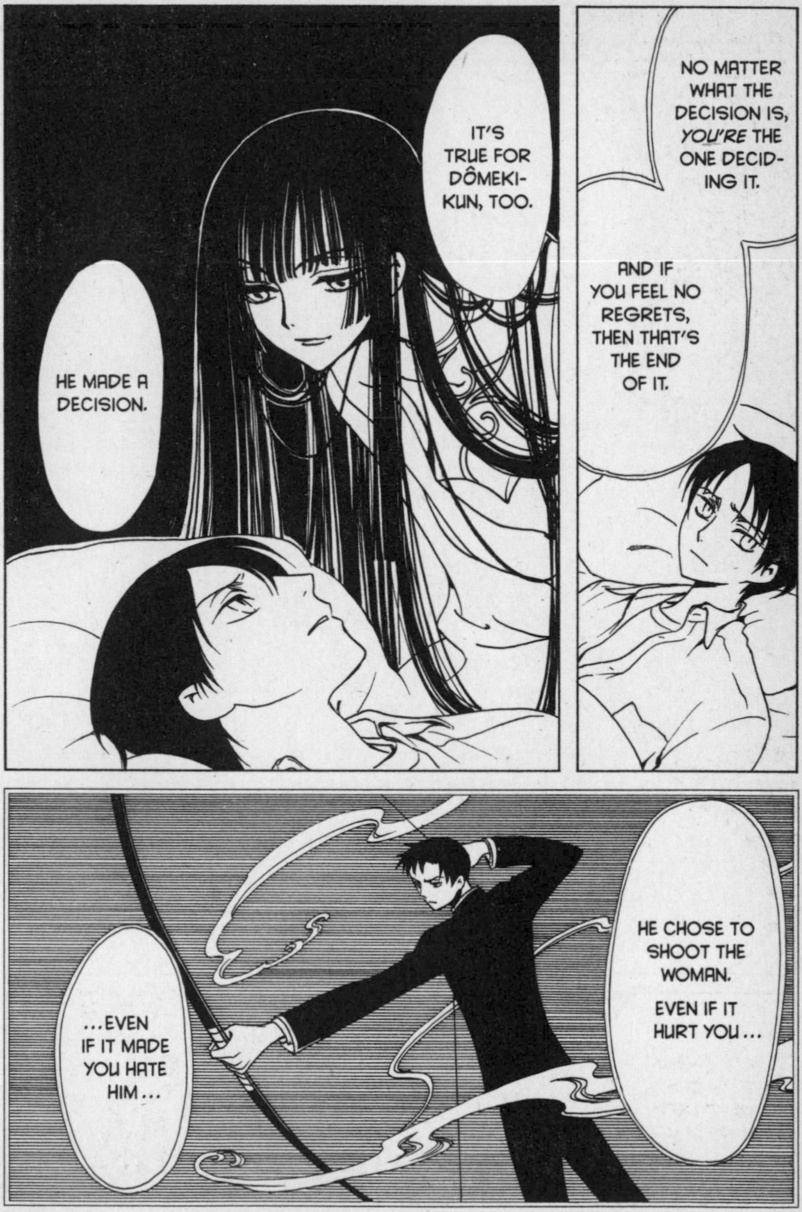
NO MATTER WHAT THE DECISION IS, *YOU'RE* THE ONE DECIDING IT.
AND IF YOU FEEL NO REGRETS, THEN THAT'S THE END OF IT.
IT'S TRUE FOR DÔMEKI-KUN, TOO.
HE MADE A DECISION.
HE CHOSE TO SHOOT THE WOMAN.
EVEN IF IT HURT YOU...
...EVEN IF IT MADE YOU HATE HIM...

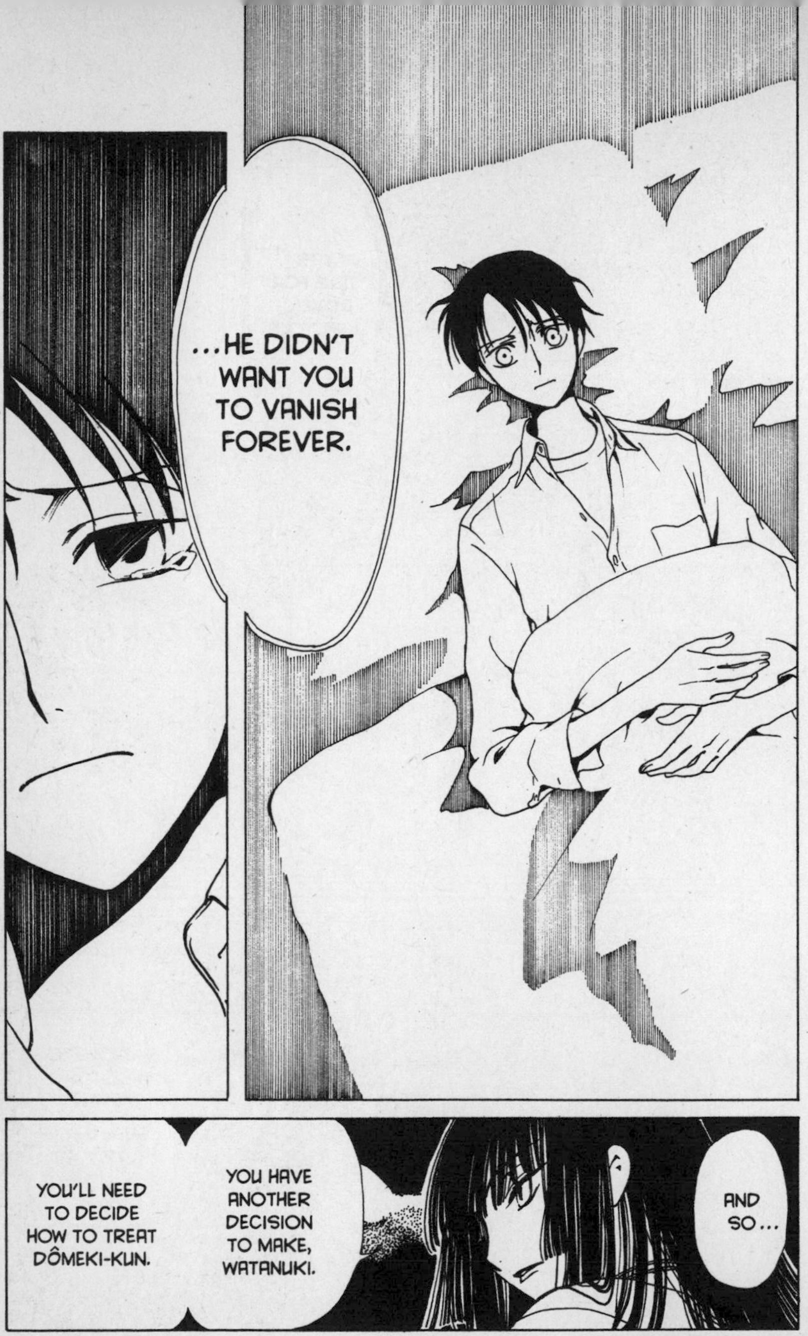
...HE DIDN'T WANT YOU TO VANISH FOREVER.
AND SO...
YOU HAVE ANOTHER DECISION TO MAKE, WATANUKI.
YOU'LL NEED TO DECIDE HOW TO TREAT DÔMEKI-KUN.

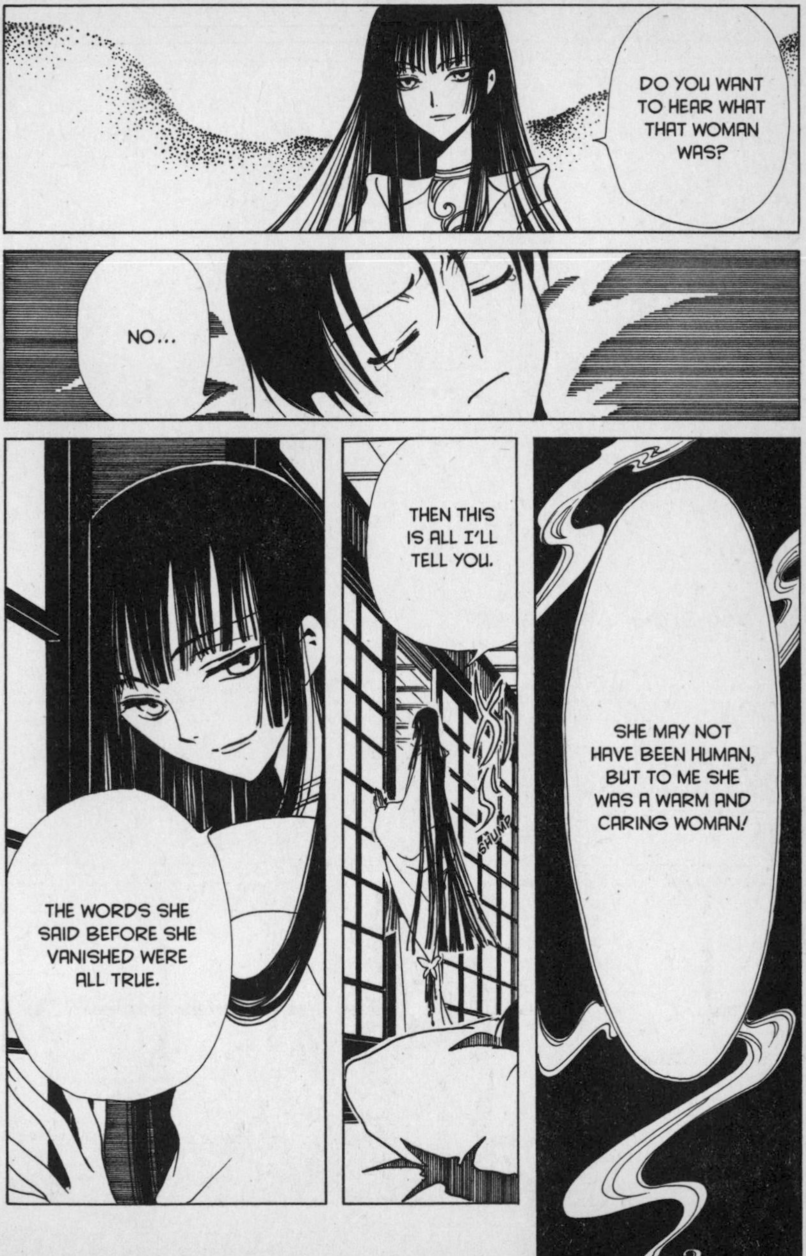
DO YOU WANT TO HEAR WHAT THAT WOMAN WAS?
NO...
SHE MAY NOT HAVE BEEN HUMAN, BUT TO ME SHE WAS A WARM AND CARING WOMAN!
THEN THIS IS ALL I'LL TELL YOU.
SHUMP
THE WORDS SHE SAID BEFORE SHE VANISHED WERE ALL TRUE.

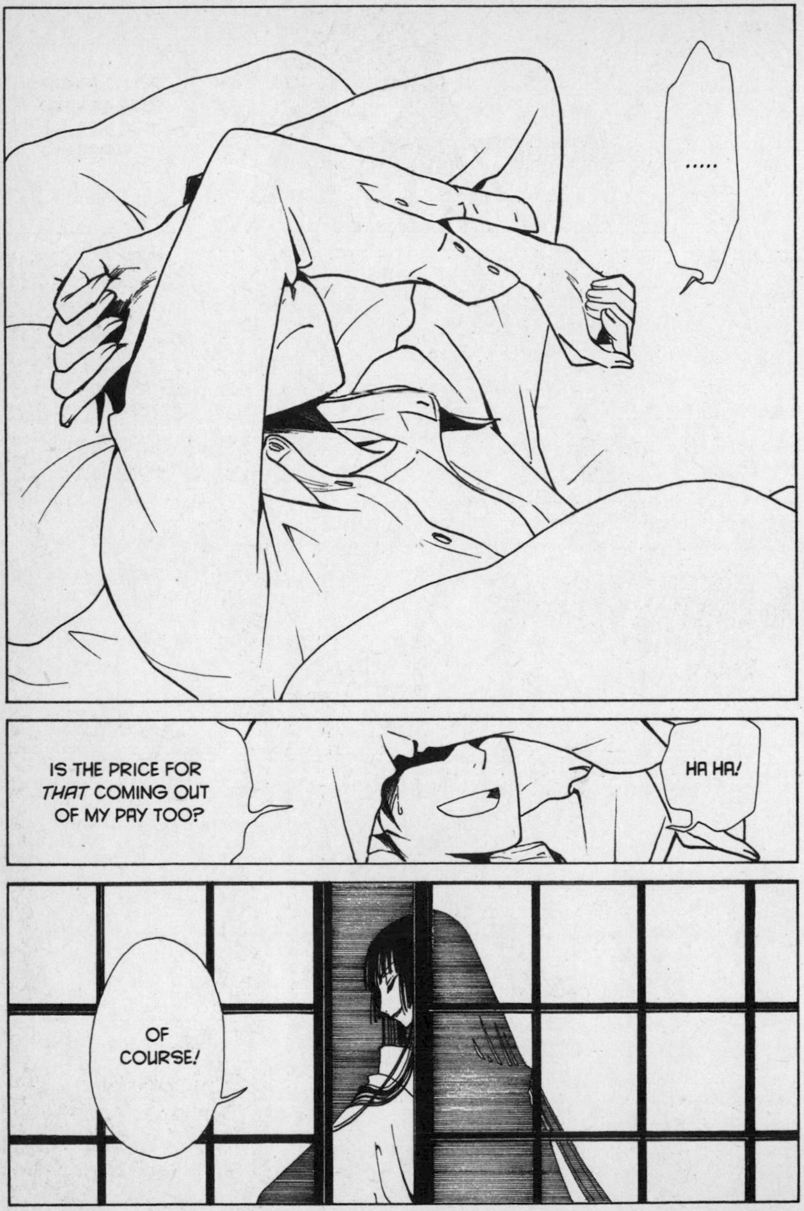
.....
HA HA!
IS THE PRICE FOR *THAT* COMING OUT OF MY PAY TOO?
OF COURSE!

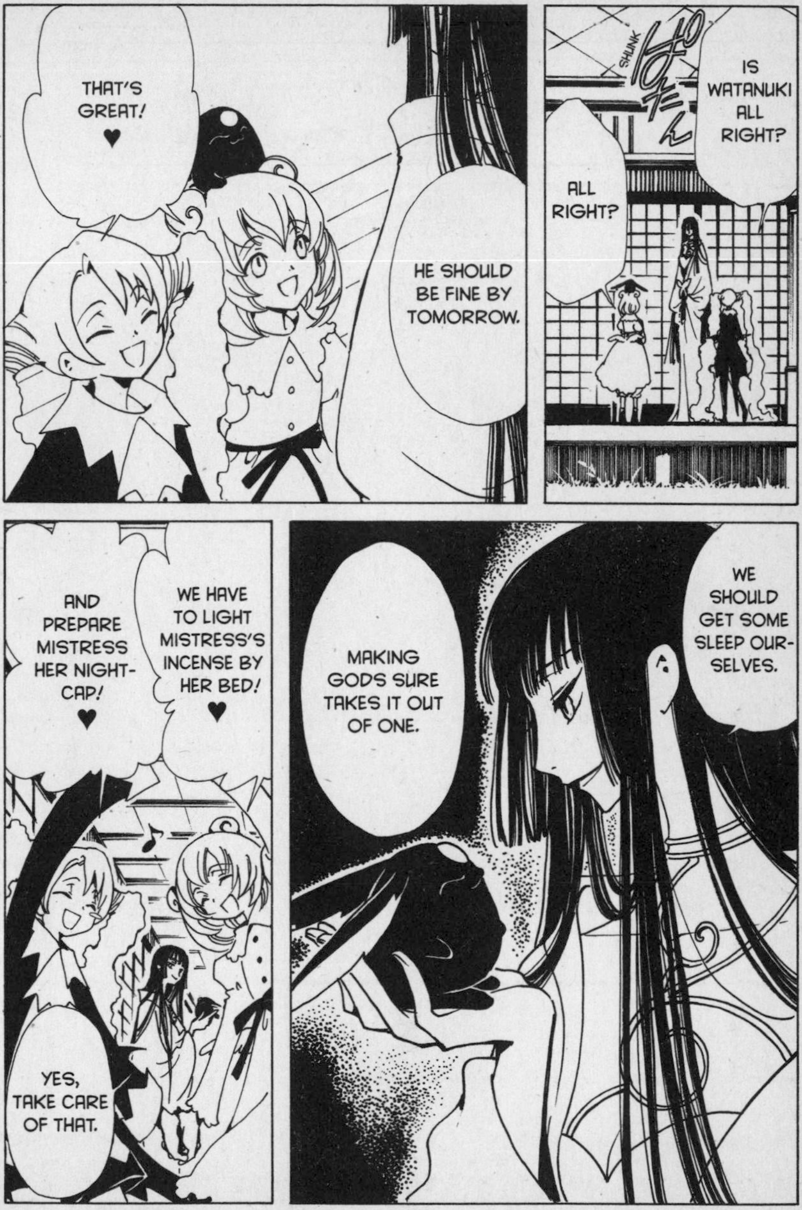
IS WATANUKI ALL RIGHT?
SHUNK
ぱたん
ALL RIGHT?
HE SHOULD BE FINE BY TOMORROW.
THAT'S GREAT! ♥
WE SHOULD GET SOME SLEEP OURSELVES.
MAKING GODS SURE TAKES IT OUT OF ONE.
WE HAVE TO LIGHT MISTRESS'S INCENSE BY HER BED! ♥
AND PREPARE MISTRESS HER NIGHT-CAP! ♥
YES, TAKE CARE OF THAT.

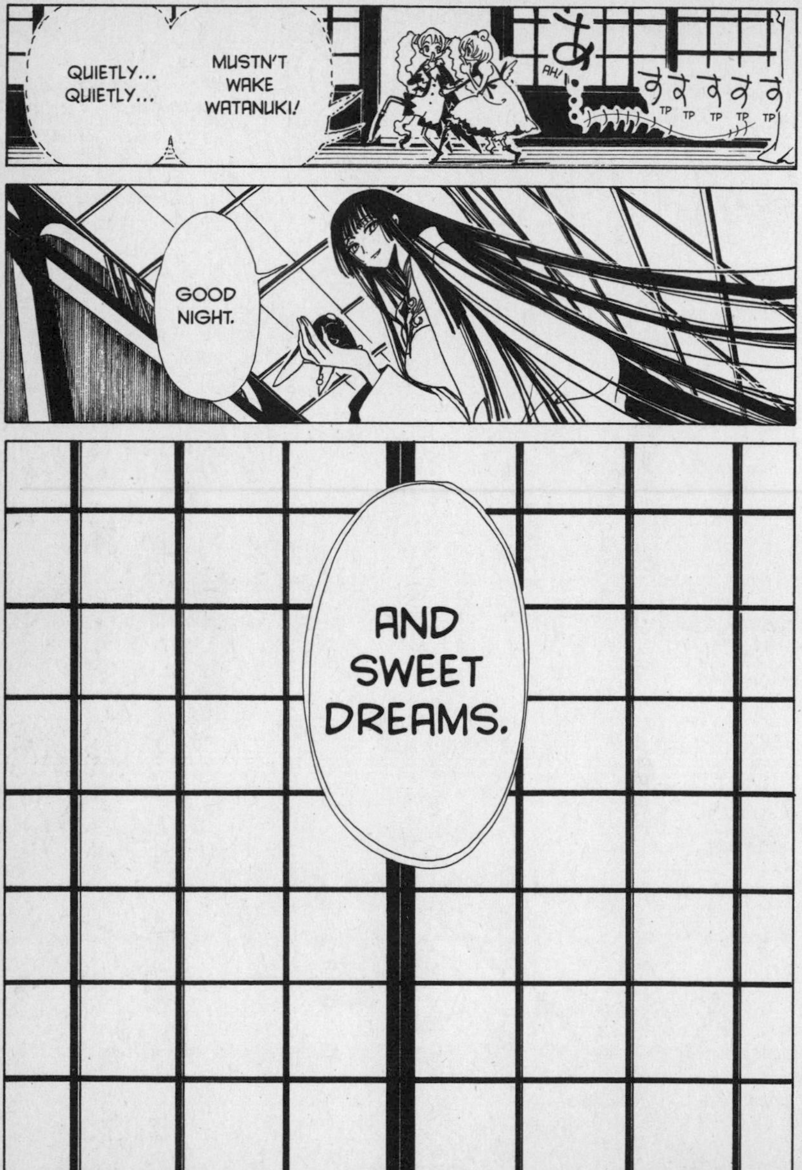
あ
AH!
すすすすす
TP TP TP TP TP
MUSTN'T WAKE WATANUKI!
QUIETLY... QUIETLY...
GOOD NIGHT.
AND SWEET DREAMS.

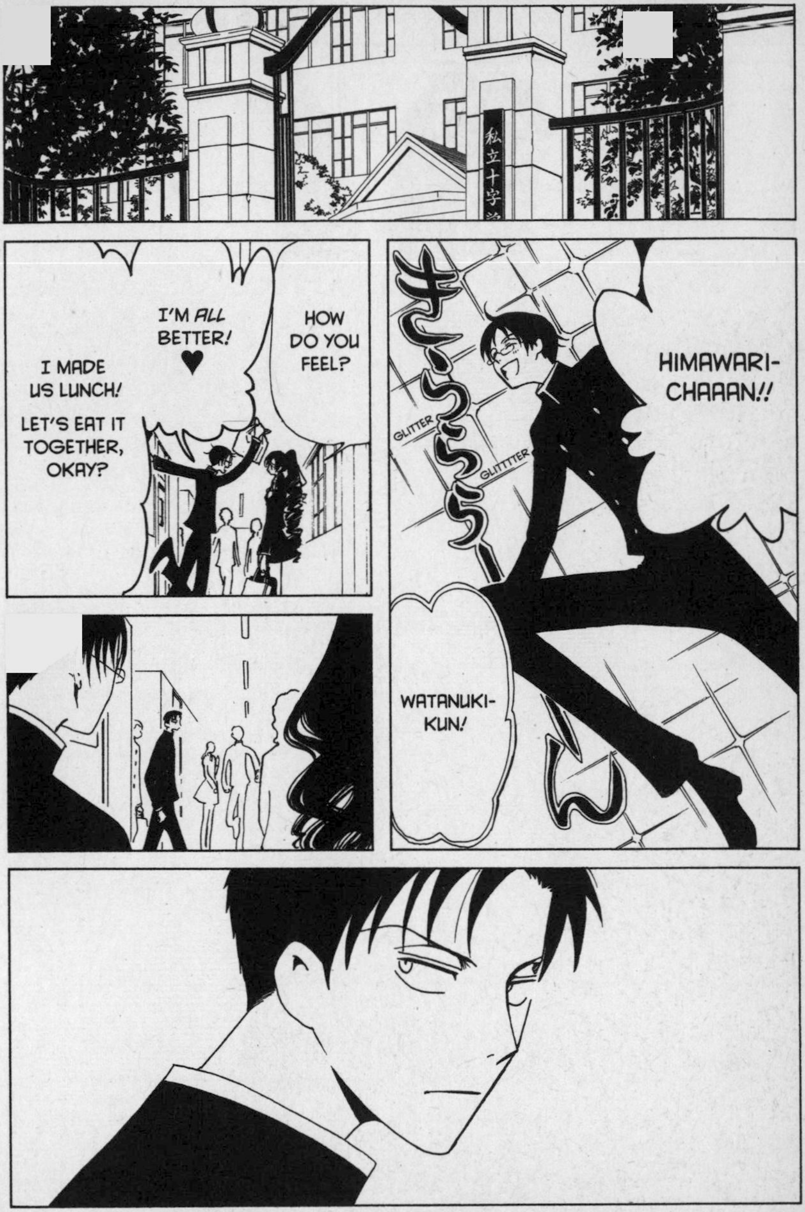
私立十字
HIMAWARI-CHAAAN!!
きららら～ん
GLITTER
GLITTTER
WATANUKI-KUN!
HOW DO YOU FEEL?
I'M ALL BETTER! ♥
I MADE US LUNCH!
LET'S EAT IT TOGETHER, OKAY?

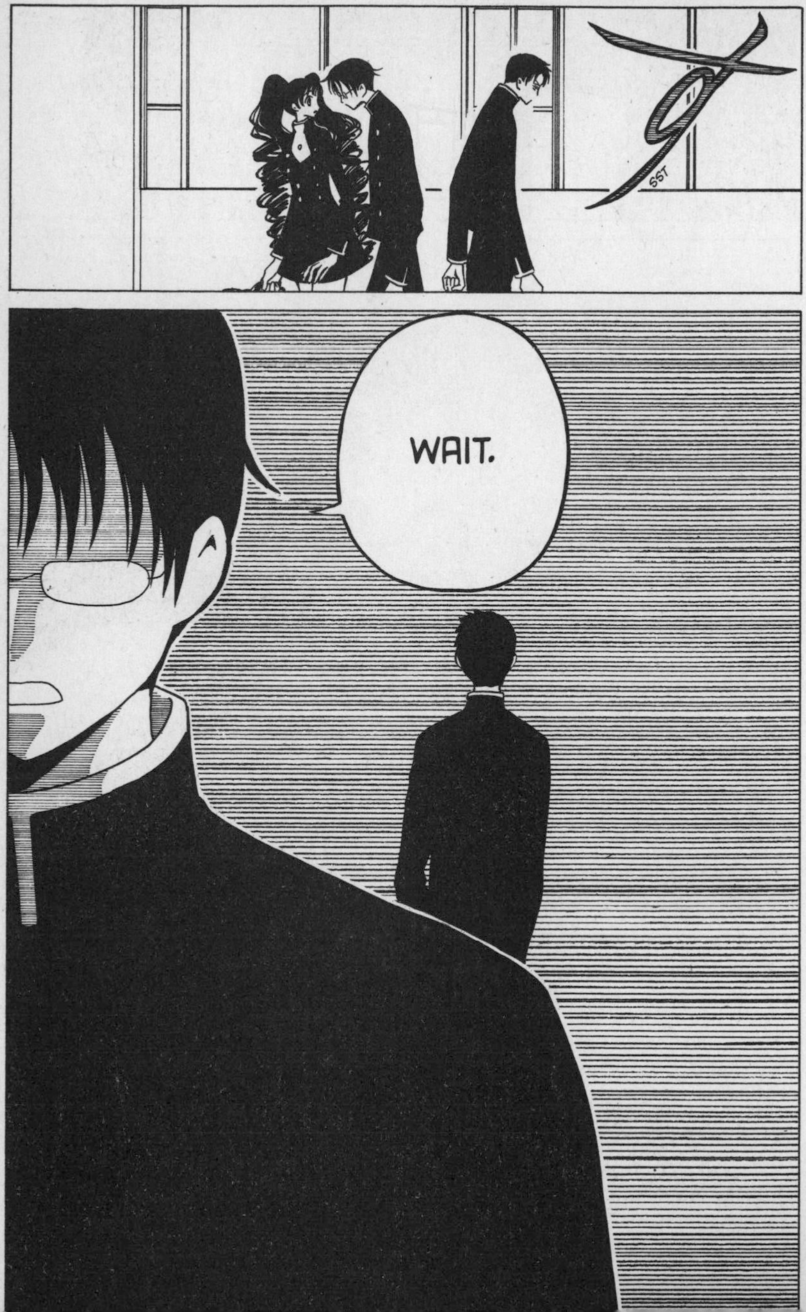
す
SST
WAIT.

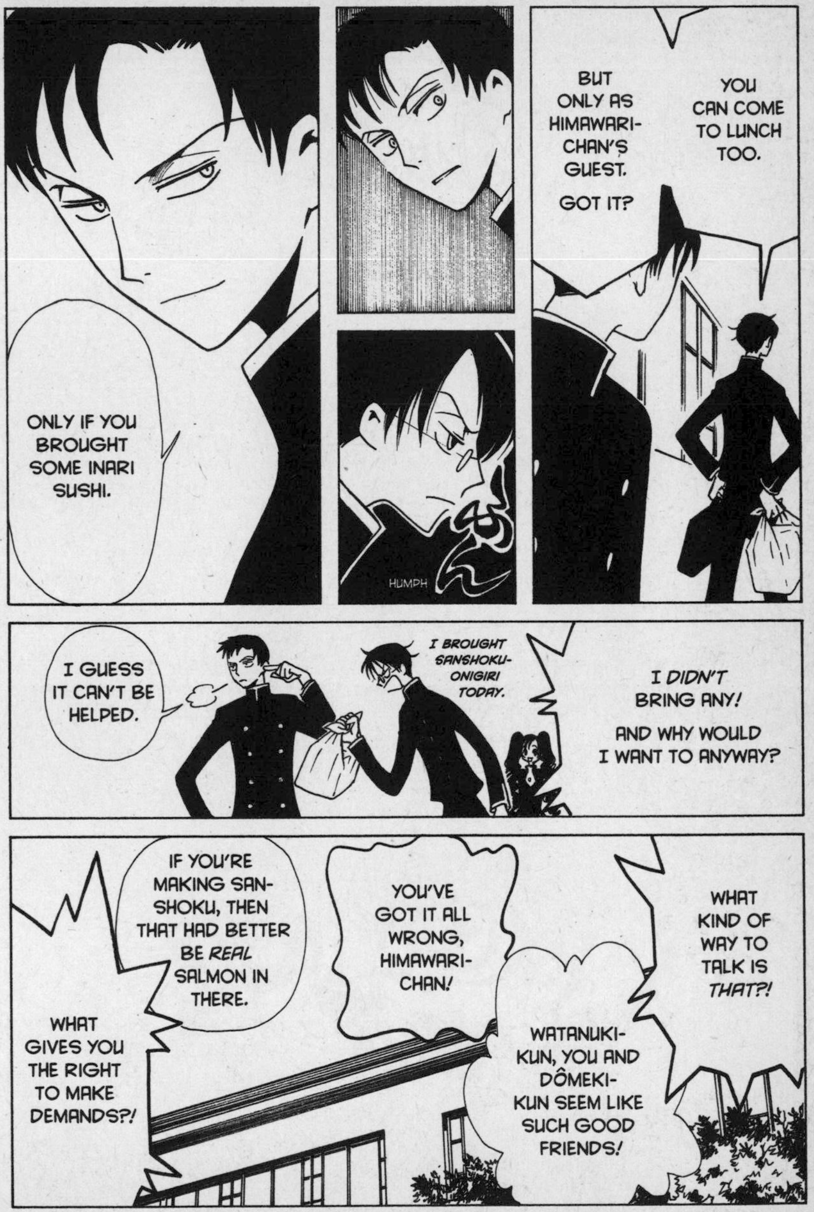
YOU CAN COME TO LUNCH TOO.
BUT ONLY AS HIMAWARI-CHAN'S GUEST.
GOT IT?
HUMPH
ONLY IF YOU BROUGHT SOME INARI SUSHI.
I *DIDN'T* BRING ANY!
AND WHY WOULD I WANT TO ANYWAY?
I BROUGHT SANSHOKU-ONIGIRI TODAY.
I GUESS IT CAN'T BE HELPED.
WHAT KIND OF WAY TO TALK IS *THAT?!*
YOU'VE GOT IT ALL WRONG, HIMAWARI-CHAN!
IF YOU'RE MAKING SAN-SHOKU, THEN THAT HAD BETTER BE *REAL* SALMON IN THERE.
WATANUKI-KUN, YOU AND DÔMEKI-KUN SEEM LIKE SUCH GOOD FRIENDS!
WHAT GIVES YOU THE RIGHT TO MAKE DEMANDS?!

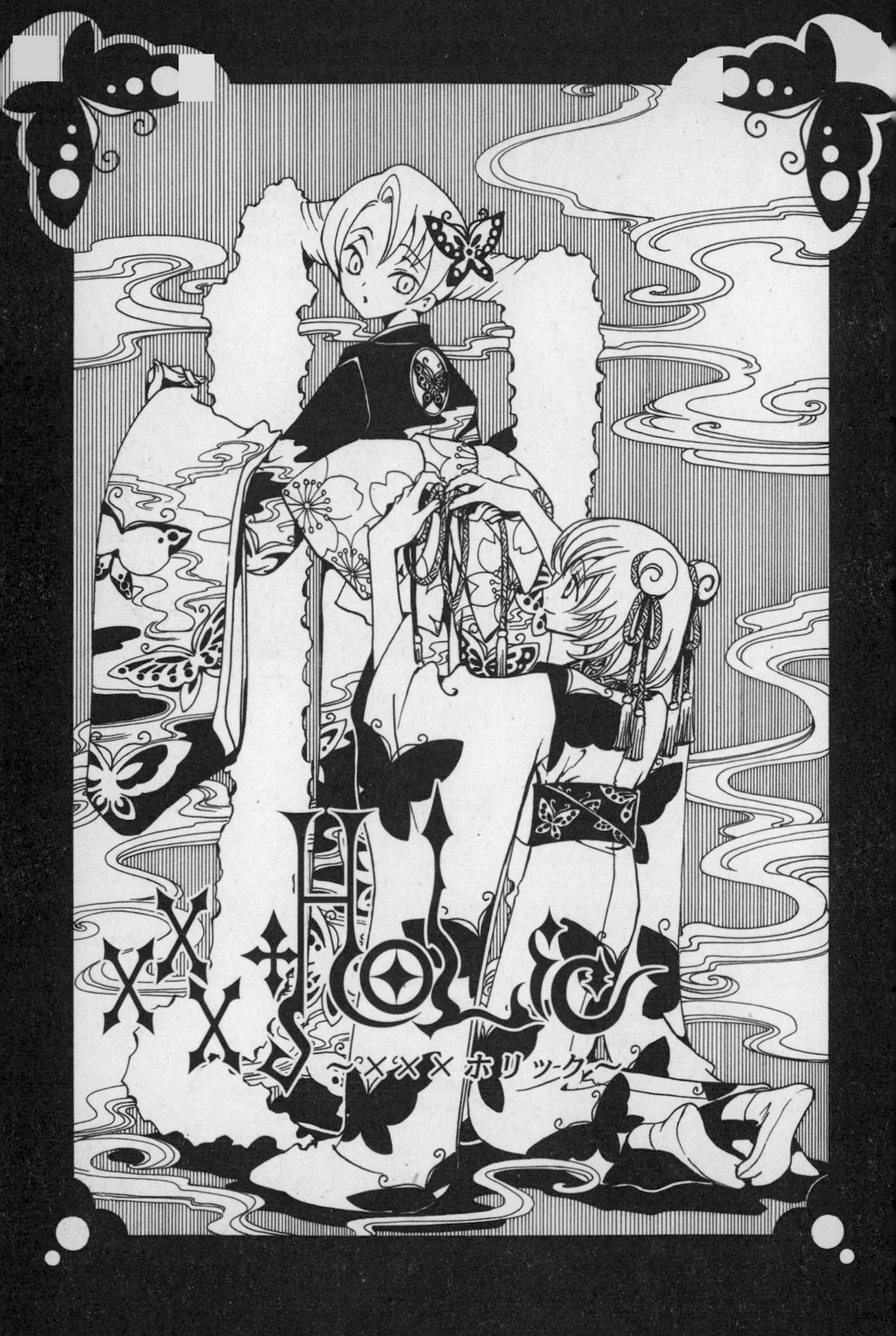
xxxHOLiC
〜×××ホリック〜

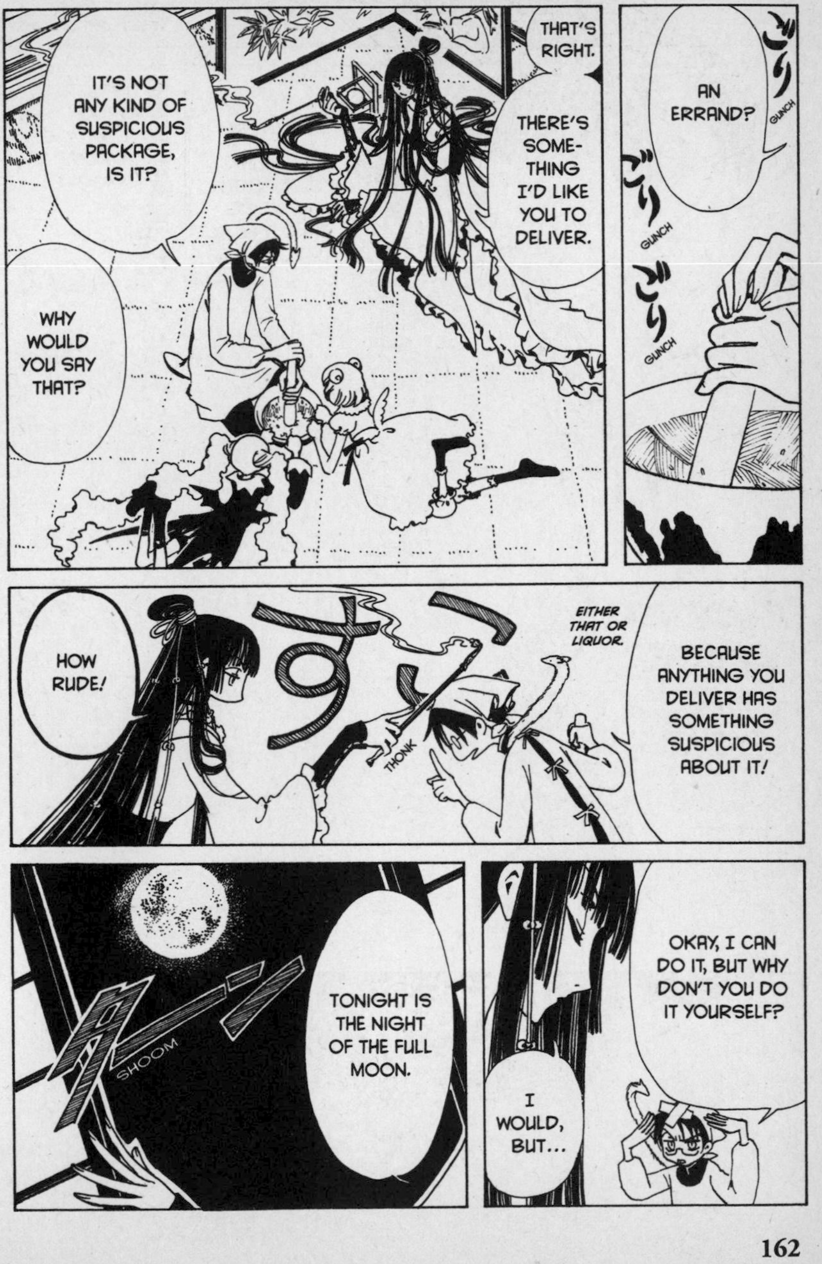
AN ERRAND?
ごり
GUNCH
ごり
GUNCH
ごり
GUNCH
THAT'S RIGHT.
THERE'S SOME-THING I'D LIKE YOU TO DELIVER.
IT'S NOT ANY KIND OF SUSPICIOUS PACKAGE, IS IT?
WHY WOULD YOU SAY THAT?
BECAUSE ANYTHING YOU DELIVER HAS SOMETHING SUSPICIOUS ABOUT IT!
EITHER THAT OR LIQUOR.
THONK
HOW RUDE!
OKAY, I CAN DO IT, BUT WHY DON'T YOU DO IT YOURSELF?
I WOULD, BUT...
TONIGHT IS THE NIGHT OF THE FULL MOON.
SHOOM

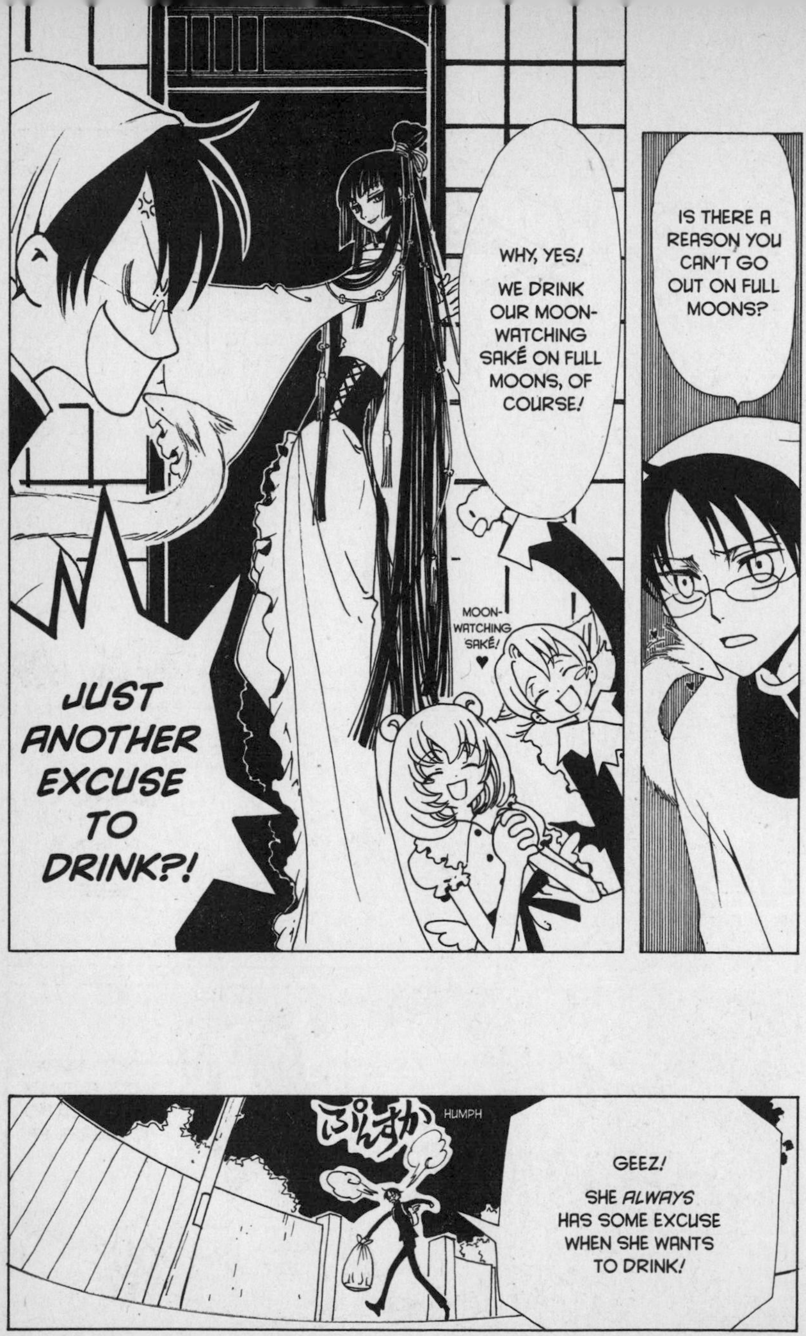
IS THERE A REASON YOU CAN'T GO OUT ON FULL MOONS?
WHY, YES!
WE DRINK OUR MOON-WATCHING SAKÉ ON FULL MOONS, OF COURSE!
MOON-WATCHING SAKÉ! ♥
JUST ANOTHER EXCUSE TO DRINK?!
ぷんすか
HUMPH
GEEZ!
SHE *ALWAYS* HAS SOME EXCUSE WHEN SHE WANTS TO DRINK!

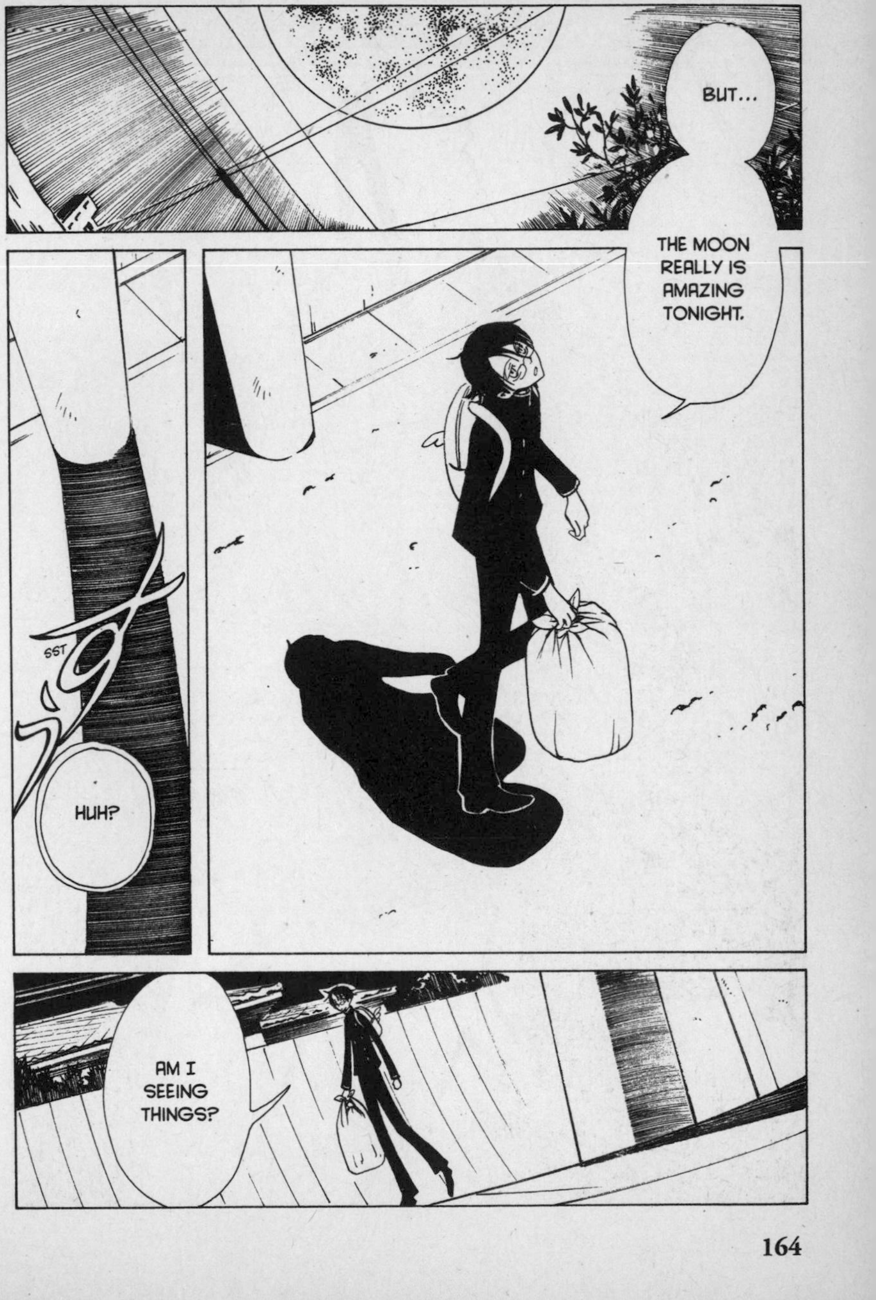
BUT...
THE MOON REALLY IS AMAZING TONIGHT.
SST
HUH?
AM I SEEING THINGS?

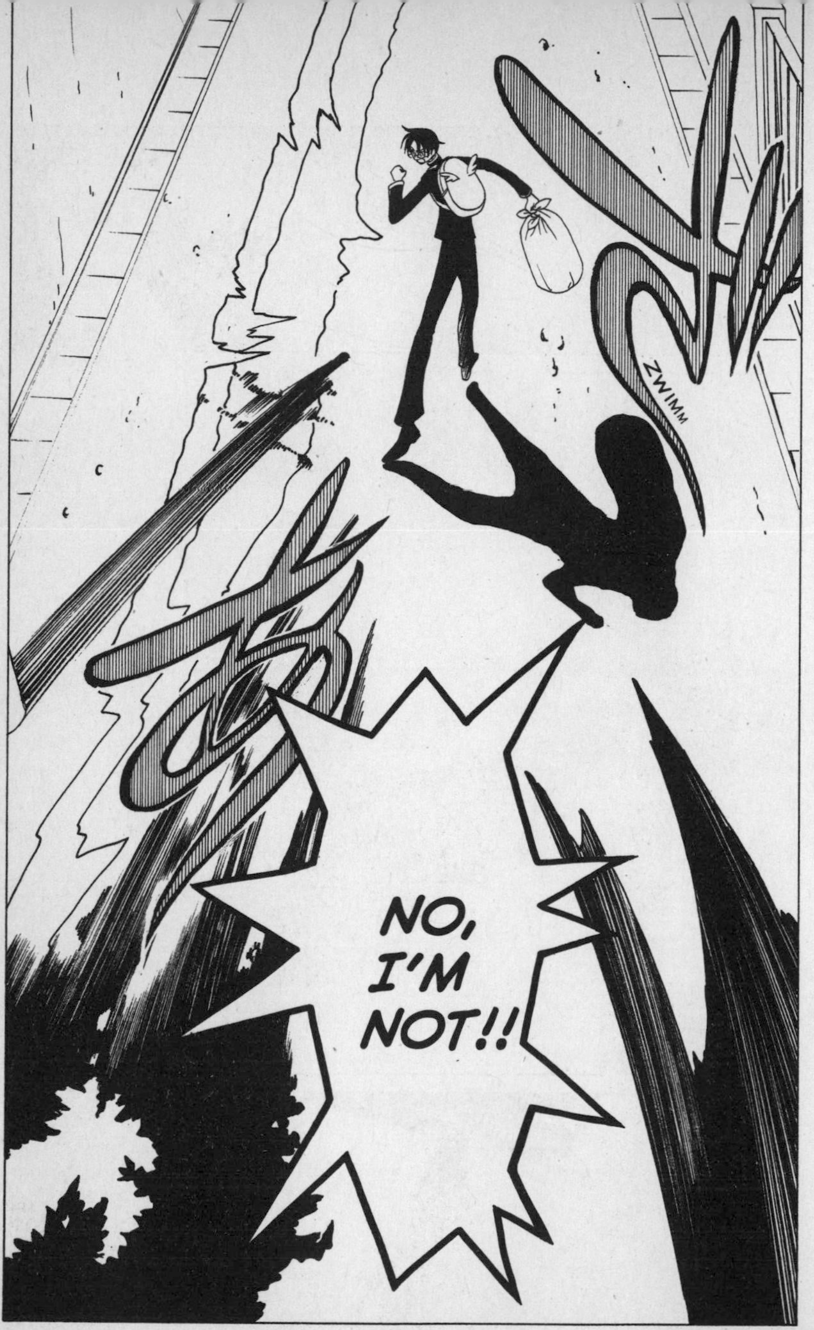
ZWIMM
NO, I'M NOT!!

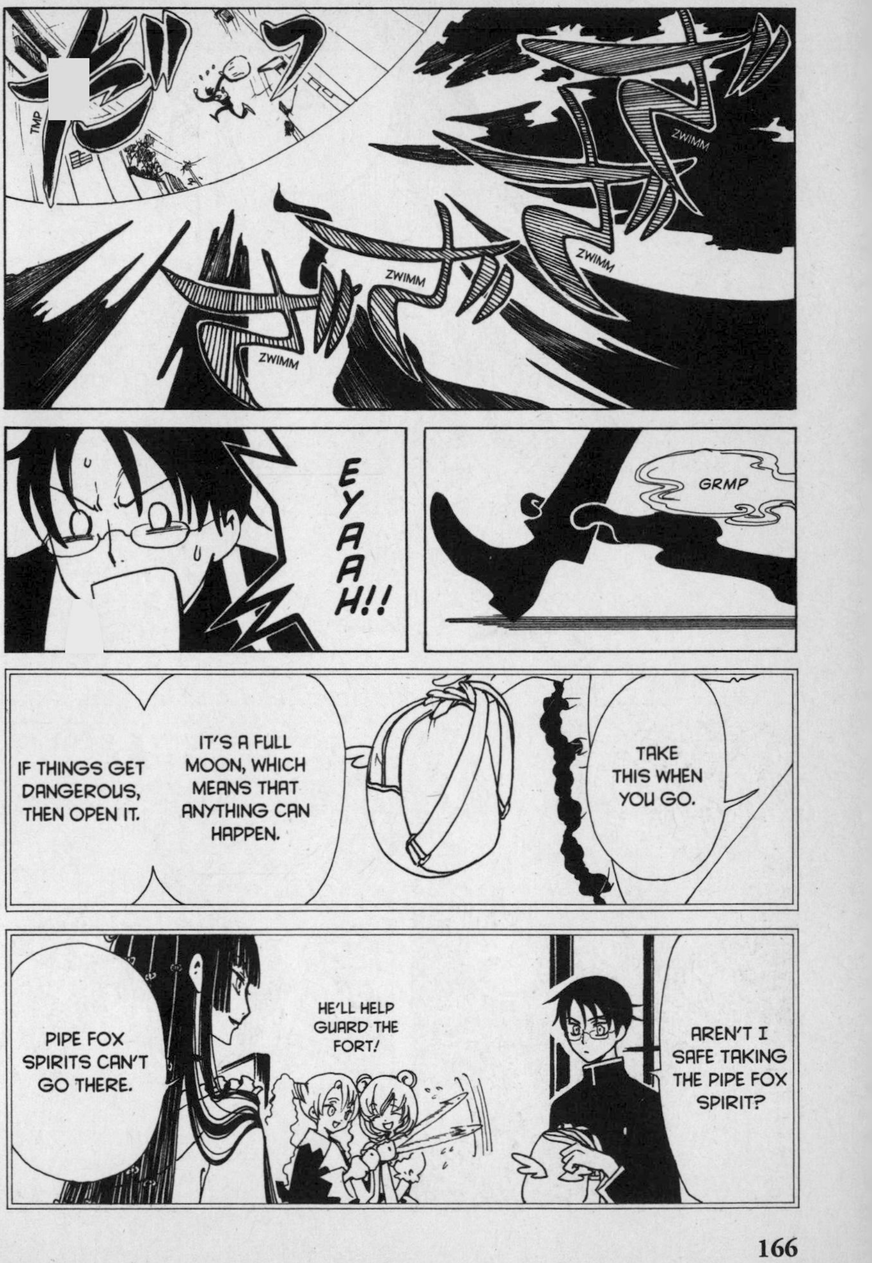
TMP
ZWIMM
ZWIMM
ZWIMM
ZWIMM
GRMP
EYAAAH!!
TAKE THIS WHEN YOU GO.
IT'S A FULL MOON, WHICH MEANS THAT ANYTHING CAN HAPPEN.
IF THINGS GET DANGEROUS, THEN OPEN IT.
AREN'T I SAFE TAKING THE PIPE FOX SPIRIT?
HE'LL HELP GUARD THE FORT!
PIPE FOX SPIRITS CAN'T GO THERE.

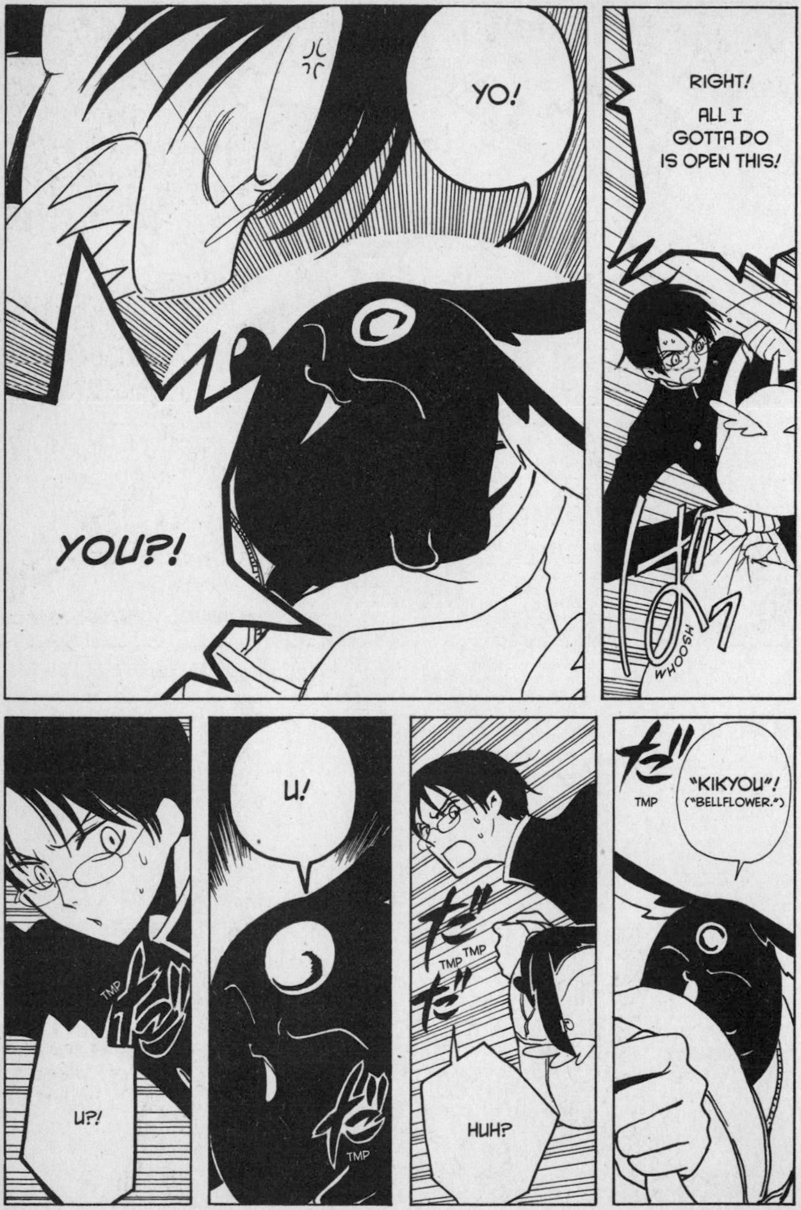
RIGHT!
ALL I GOTTA DO IS OPEN THIS!
WHOOSH
YO!
YOU?!
"KIKYOU"! ("BELLFLOWER.")
TMP
TMP TMP
HUH?
U!
TMP
TMP
U?!

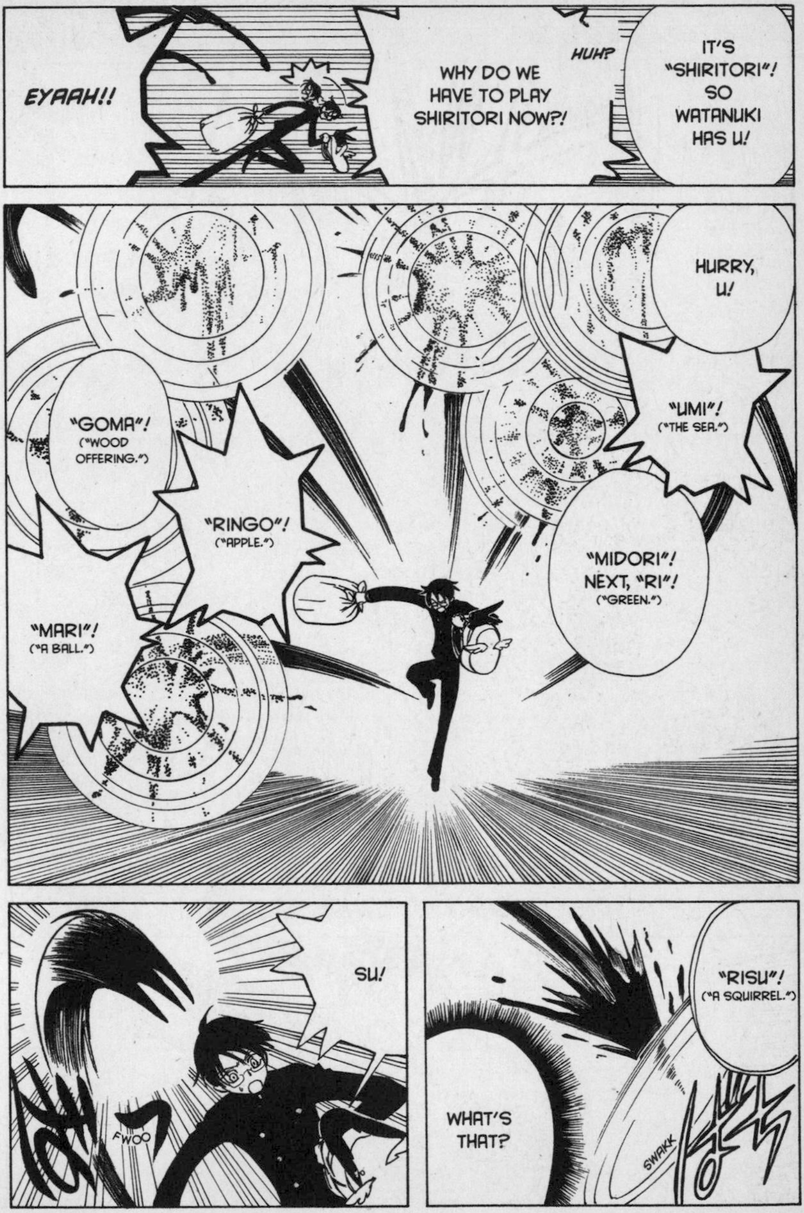
IT'S "SHIRITORI"! SO WATANUKI HAS U!
HUH?
WHY DO WE HAVE TO PLAY SHIRITORI NOW?!
EYAAH!!
HURRY, U!
"UMI"! ("THE SEA.")
"MIDORI"! NEXT, "RI"! ("GREEN.")
"RINGO"! ("APPLE.")
"GOMA"! ("WOOD OFFERING.")
"MARI"! ("A BALL.")
"RISU"! ("A SQUIRREL.")
SWAKK
WHAT'S THAT?
SU!
FWOO

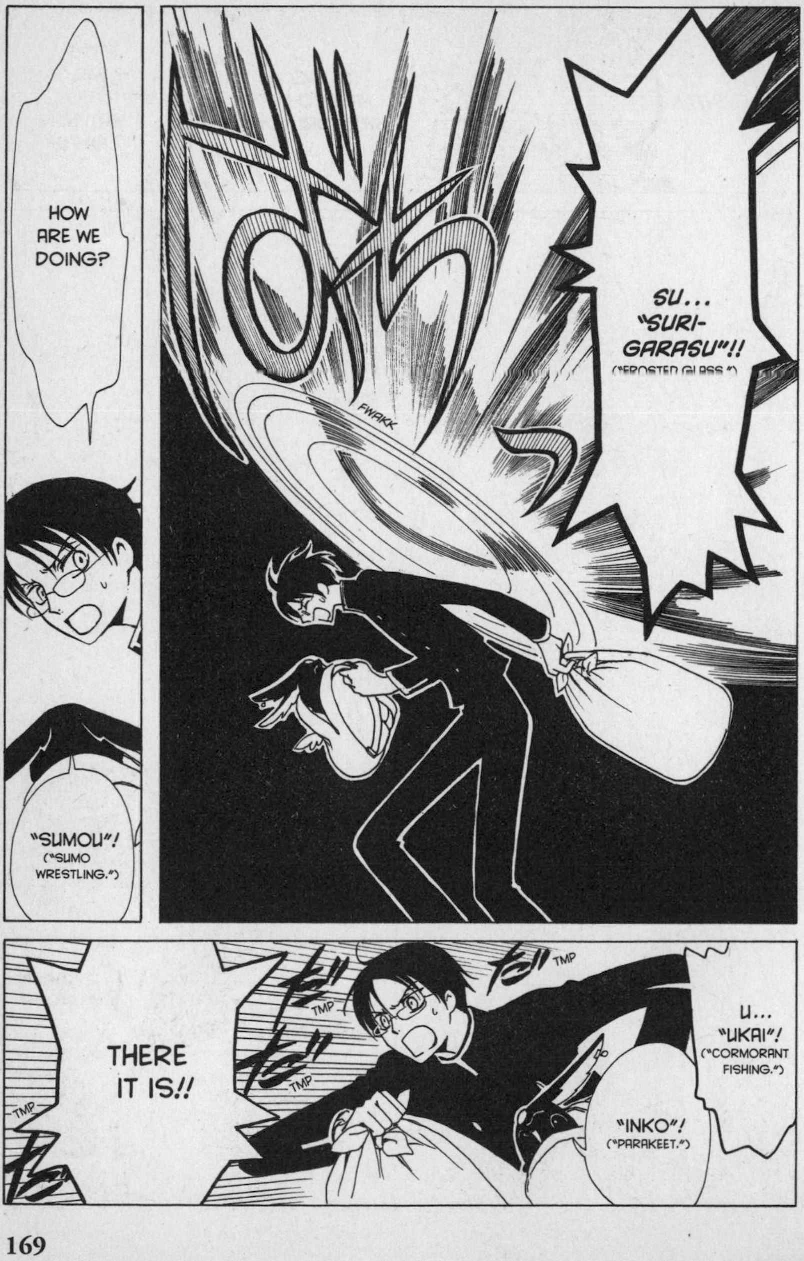
SU... "SURI-GARASU"!!
("FROSTED GLASS.")
FWAKK
HOW ARE WE DOING?
"SUMOU"!
("SUMO WRESTLING.")
U... "UKAI"!
("CORMORANT FISHING.")
"INKO"!
("PARAKEET.")
TMP
TMP
TMP
TMP
THERE IT IS!!

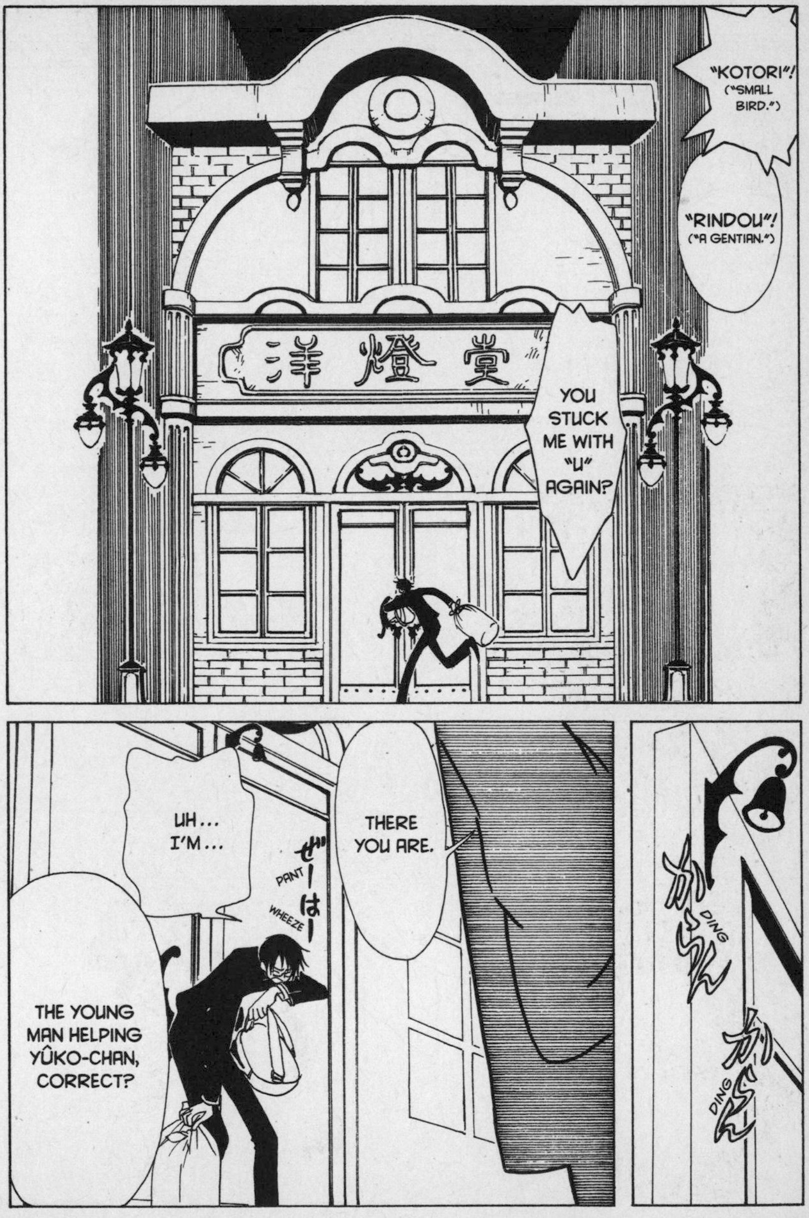
"KOTORI"!
("SMALL BIRD.")
"RINDOU"!
("A GENTIAN.")
洋燈堂
YOU STUCK ME WITH "U" AGAIN?
DING
DING
THERE YOU ARE.
UH... I'M...
PANT
WHEEZE
THE YOUNG MAN HELPING YÛKO-CHAN, CORRECT?

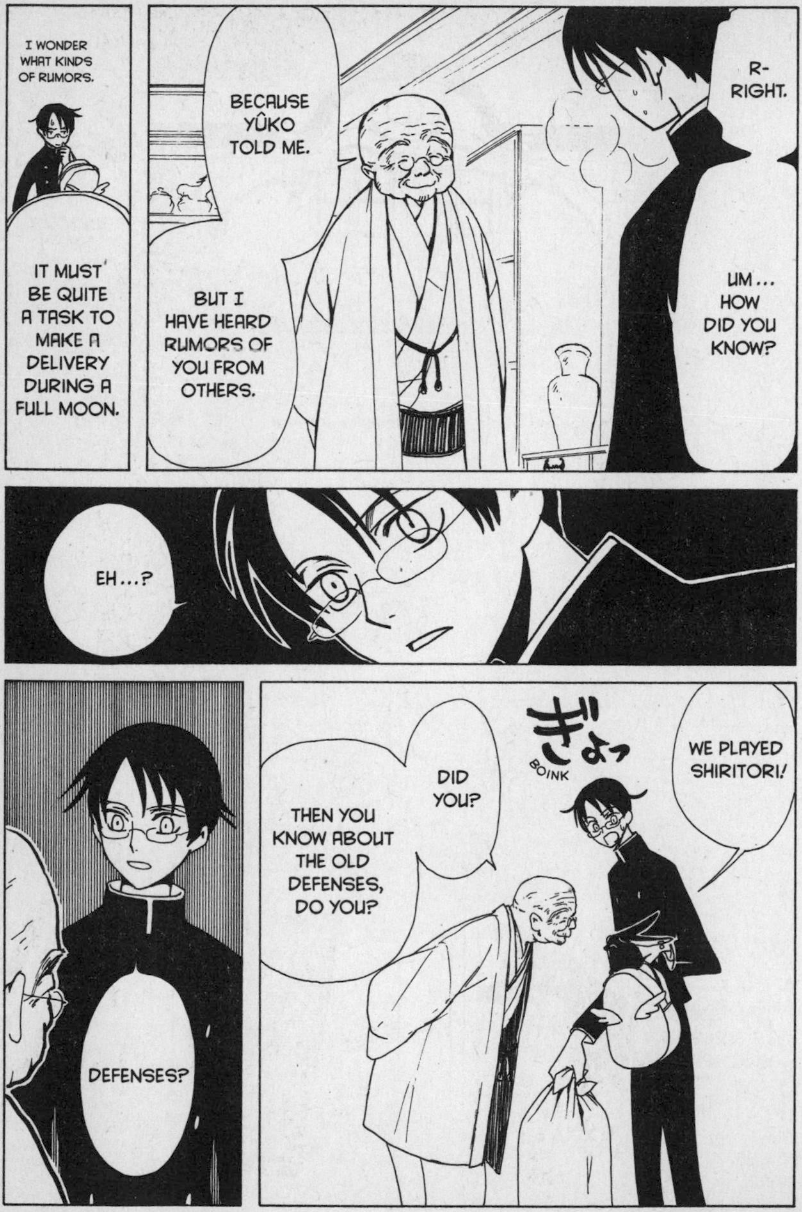
R-RIGHT.
UM... HOW DID YOU KNOW?
BECAUSE YÛKO TOLD ME.
BUT I HAVE HEARD RUMORS OF YOU FROM OTHERS.
I WONDER WHAT KINDS OF RUMORS.
IT MUST BE QUITE A TASK TO MAKE A DELIVERY DURING A FULL MOON.
EH...?
WE PLAYED SHIRITORI!
ぎょっ
BOINK
DID YOU?
THEN YOU KNOW ABOUT THE OLD DEFENSES, DO YOU?
DEFENSES?

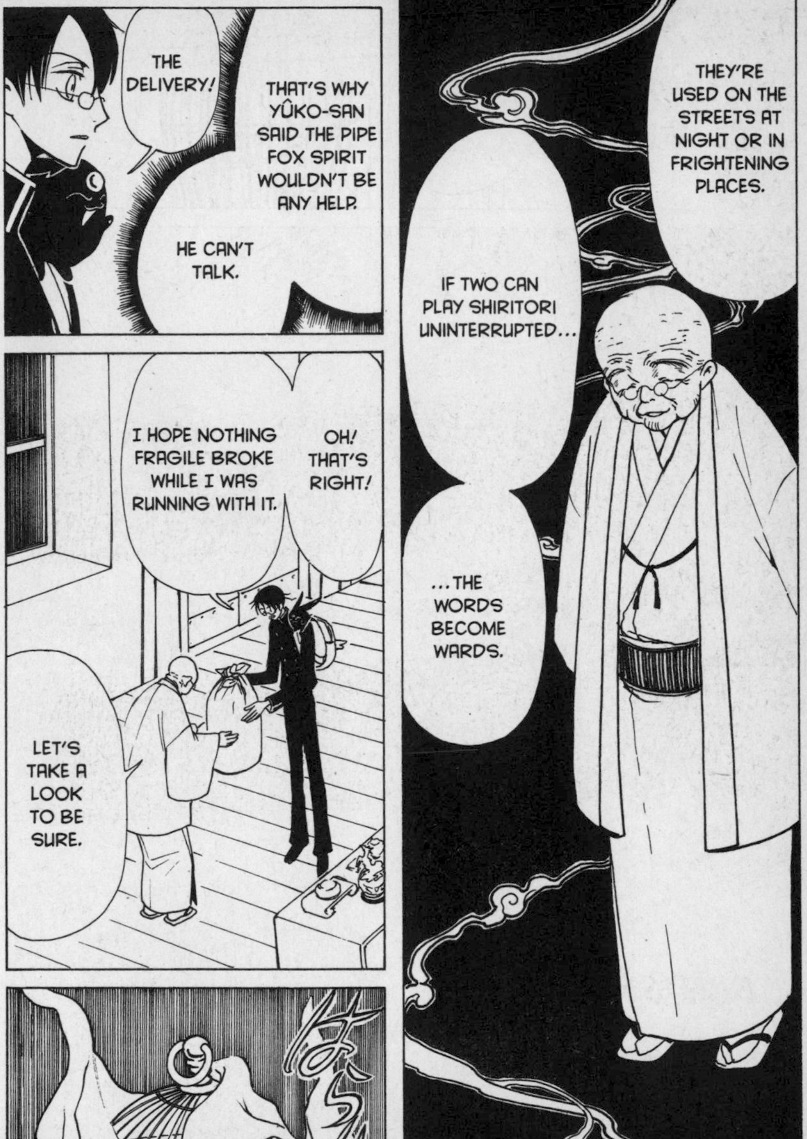
THEY'RE USED ON THE STREETS AT NIGHT OR IN FRIGHTENING PLACES.
IF TWO CAN PLAY SHIRITORI UNINTERRUPTED...
...THE WORDS BECOME WARDS.
THE DELIVERY!
THAT'S WHY YÛKO-SAN SAID THE PIPE FOX SPIRIT WOULDN'T BE ANY HELP.
HE CAN'T TALK.
OH! THAT'S RIGHT!
I HOPE NOTHING FRAGILE BROKE WHILE I WAS RUNNING WITH IT.
LET'S TAKE A LOOK TO BE SURE.
FWUFF

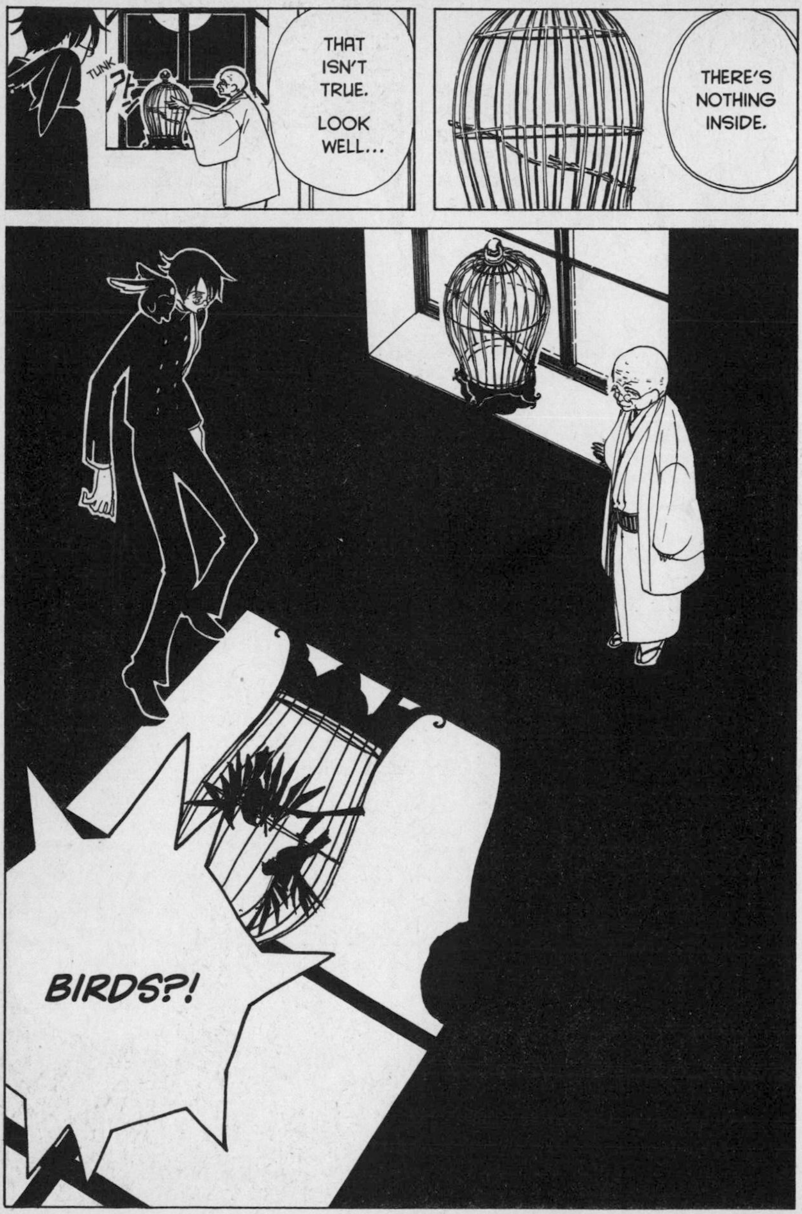
THERE'S NOTHING INSIDE.
TUNK
THAT ISN'T TRUE.
LOOK WELL...
BIRDS?!

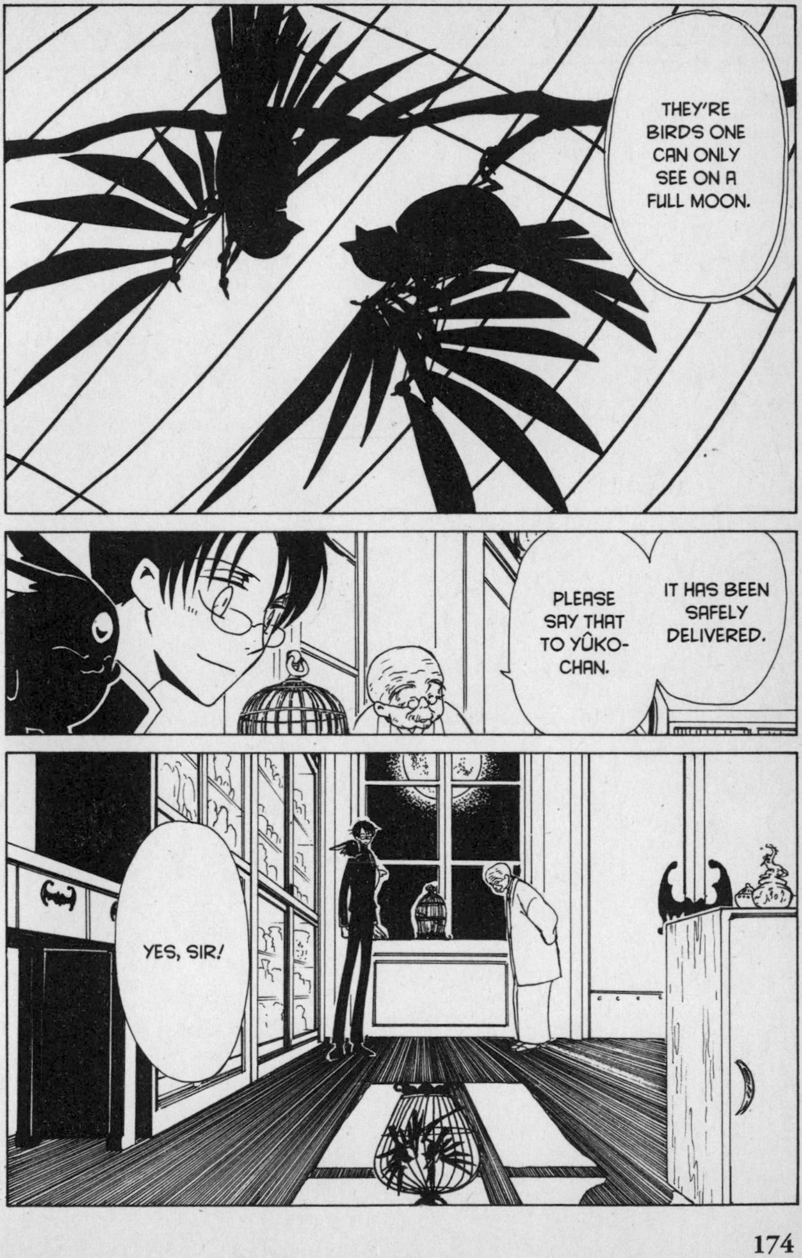
THEY'RE BIRDS ONE CAN ONLY SEE ON A FULL MOON.
IT HAS BEEN SAFELY DELIVERED.
PLEASE SAY THAT TO YÛKO-CHAN.
YES, SIR!

⊰ Continued ⊱

in *xxxHOLiC* Volume 7

About the Creators

CLAMP is a group of four women who have become the most popular manga artists in America—Satsuki Igarashi, Tsubaki Nekoi, Mokona, and Ageha Ohkawa. They started out as *doujinshi* (fan comics) creators, but their skill and craft brought them to the attention of publishers very quickly. Their first work from a major publisher was *RG Veda*, but their first mass success was with *Magic Knight Rayearth*. From there, they went on to write many series, including *Cardcaptor Sakura* and *Chobits*, two of the most popular manga in the United States. Like many Japanese manga artists, they prefer to avoid the spotlight, and little is known about them personally.

CLAMP is currently publishing three series in Japan: *Tsubasa* and *xxxHOLiC* with Kodansha and *Gohou Drug* with Kadokawa.

Honorifics Explained

Throughout the Del Rey Manga books, you will find Japanese honorifics left intact in the translations. For those not familiar with how the Japanese use honorifics and, more important, how they differ from American honorifics, we present this brief overview.

Politeness has always been a critical facet of Japanese culture. Ever since the feudal era, when Japan was a highly stratified society, use of honorifics—which can be defined as polite speech that indicates relationship or status—has played an essential role in the Japanese language. When addressing someone in Japanese, an honorific usually takes the form of a suffix attached to one's name (example: "Asuna-san"), or as a title at the end of one's name or in place of the name itself (example: "Negi-sensei," or simply "Sensei!").

Honorifics can be expressions of respect or endearment. In the context of manga and anime, honorifics give insight into the nature of the relationship between characters. Many translations into English leave out these important honorifics, and therefore distort the "feel" of the original Japanese. Because Japanese honorifics contain nuances that English honorifics lack, it is our policy at Del Rey not to translate them. Here, instead, is a guide to some of the honorifics you may encounter in Del Rey Manga.

-san: This is the most common honorific, and is equivalent to Mr., Miss, Ms., Mrs., etc. It is the all-purpose honorific and can be used in any situation where politeness is required.

-sama: This is one level higher than "-san." It is used to confer great respect.

-dono: This comes from the word "tono," which means "lord." It is an even higher level than "-sama," and confers utmost respect.

-kun: This suffix is used at the end of boys' names to express familiarity or endearment. It is also sometimes used by men among friends, or when addressing someone younger or of a lower station.

-chan: This is used to express endearment, mostly toward girls. It is also used for little boys, pets, and even among lovers. It gives a sense of childish cuteness.

Bozu: This is an informal way to refer to a boy, similar to the English term "kid" or "squirt."

Sempai/Senpai: This title suggests that the addressee is one's senior in a group or organization. It is most often used in a school setting, where underclassmen refer to their upperclassmen as "sempai." It can also be used in the workplace, such as when a newer employee addresses an employee who has seniority in the company.

Kohai: This is the opposite of "sempai," and is used toward underclassmen in school or newcomers in the workplace. It connotes that the addressee is of a lower station.

Sensei: Literally meaning "one who has come before," this title is used for teachers, doctors, or masters of any profession or art.

-[blank]: Usually forgotten in these lists, but perhaps the most significant difference between Japanese and English. The lack of honorific means that the speaker has permission to address the person in a very intimate way. Usually, only family, spouses, or very close friends have this kind of permission. Known as *yobisute*, it can be gratifying when someone who has earned the intimacy starts to call one by one's name without an honorific. But when that intimacy hasn't been earned, it can also be very insulting.

Translation Notes

For your edification and reading pleasure, here are notes to help you understand some of the cultural and story references from our translation of *xxxHOLiC*.

Page 6, *Mirin Boshi*

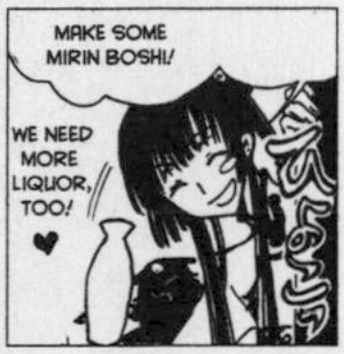
MAKE SOME MIRIN BOSHI!
WE NEED MORE LIQUOR, TOO!

Fish, such as round herring, sardines, small flatfish, or other kinds, are filleted, soaked in seasonings including mirin saké, and finally dried.

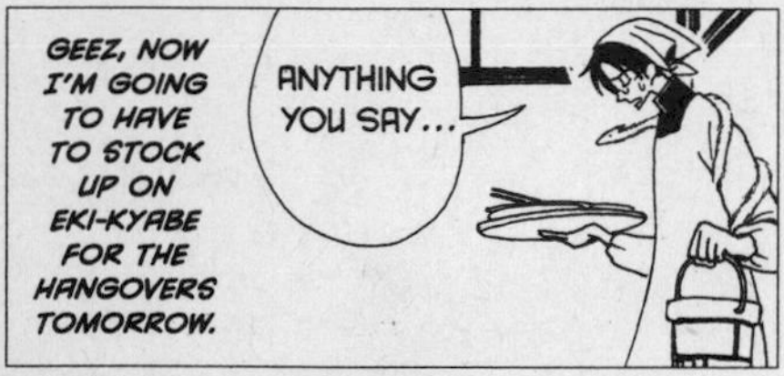
ANYTHING YOU SAY...
GEEZ, NOW I'M GOING TO HAVE TO STOCK UP ON EKI-KYABE FOR THE HANGOVERS TOMORROW.

Page 7, *Eki-kyabe*

A medication for indigestion, commonly used as a cure for hangovers.

Page 12, *Hôzuki*

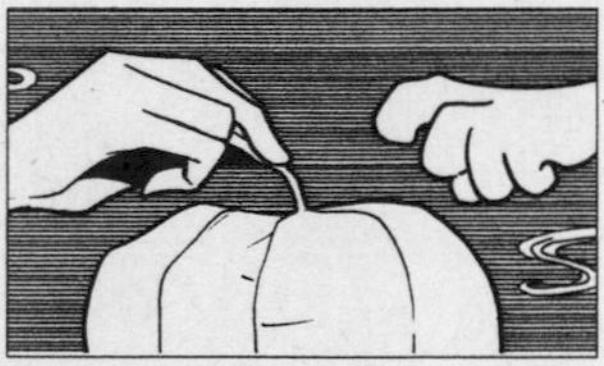

Spelled with the characters for "demon" and "lamp," *Hôzuki* is a vegetable in the eggplant family that is also called the "Chinese Lantern Plant." The fruit looks like tiny lanterns, about an inch long. Of course the *hôzuki* of the spirit world are both larger and give off light.

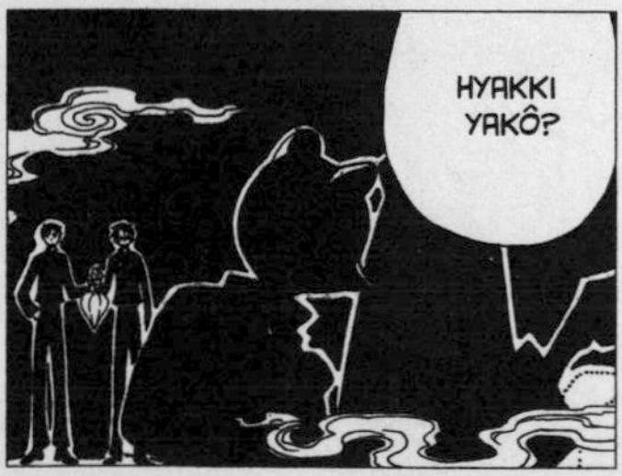
HYAKKI YAKÔ?

Page 23, *Hyakki Yakô*

This is a Japanese phrase meaning pandemonium, but it's made of Chinese characters that mean "a hundred demons moving in the night." There is a series of paintings by the name of *Hyakki Yakô* which illustrates Japanese demons moving under lantern light.

Page 23, Edo Period

Also called the Shogunate or the Tokugawa Shoganate, the Edo period was an era of stability and few technological or social advances between 1603 and 1867.

THEY PAINTED SCENES LIKE THIS DURING THE EDO PERIOD.

Page 36, *Haja-ya*

A destruction-of-the-wicked arrow.

Page 44, *Kampai!*

Every culture has its way of making a toast with a drink, and the standard word in

Japanese is *kampai!* (alternatively spelled, *kanpai*) and pronounced "kahm-pie." *Kampai* is used in every situation that English speakers would use "Cheers," and means simply "empty glass."

I THINK TSUMIRE SOUP WOULD BE GOOD FOR TOMORROW.

Page 53, *Tsumire* Soup

A soup made of dumplings and/or seafood meatballs.

Page 70, Sweet Potato (*Yaki-imo*)

Sweet potatoes originated from Central and South America, and during the age of discovery, they migrated to many points around the world. Around 400 years ago, they were introduced from China to the Ryukyu islands and the southern island of Kyushu as a good crop to plant when more profitable crops like rice and wheat failed. Since they were heavily adopted in the Kyushu province of Satsuma, they are still called *satsuma-imo* in Japanese today. The baked sweet potato, *yaki-imo*, usually baked for about an hour on hot rocks and sold from small wooden carts from venders on the street as warm snacks, are considered a welcome sign of the coming of autumn.

Page 71, Presents

Bringing back presents for the kids after a long trip is a custom even in the west, but in Japan it's even more ritualized. It still has a slightly "childish" feel, but if one goes on a long trip and does not bring home something for a spouse, significant other, mother, or other close friend, relative, or work associate, the delinquent traveler can expect at least a cold shoulder as punishment!

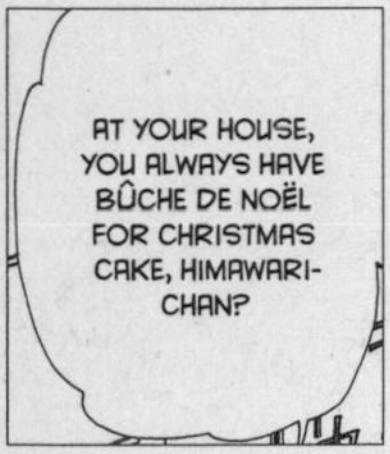
AT YOUR HOUSE, YOU ALWAYS HAVE BÛCHE DE NOËL FOR CHRISTMAS CAKE, HIMAWARI-CHAN?

Page 72, Bûche de Noël

A French cake that is baked flat, then filled, rolled, and decorated to look like a small wooden log. The tradition stems from the pagan custom of decorating a special log and burning it during winter solstice. The Christian religions adopted the tradition, but with the advent of wood-burning stoves the real-wood log tradition died out and the cake tradition was born in France. Christmas Cake (of the very sweet birthday cake variety) is now a solid and honored custom in Japan, so the French Christmas cake tradition fits right in.

Page 75, Go Home Early Club

Students who decide not to join a club in order to leave school as soon as classes let out. Another name would be the "Go Home Right After School Club" which has a more extensive translator's note in Volume 2.

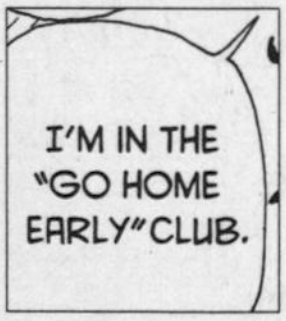
I'M IN THE "GO HOME EARLY" CLUB.

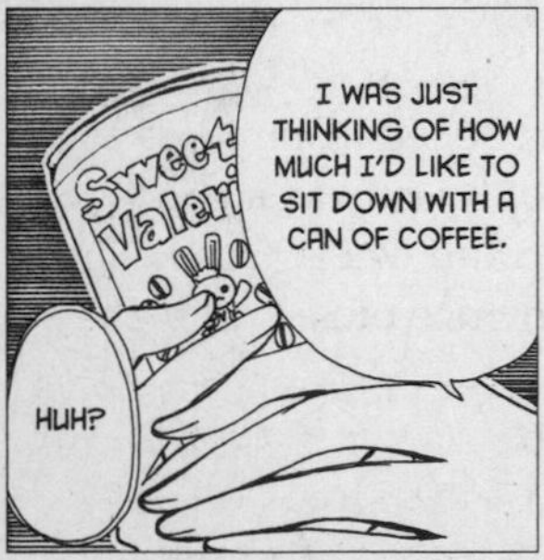
I WAS JUST THINKING OF HOW MUCH I'D LIKE TO SIT DOWN WITH A CAN OF COFFEE.
HUH?
Sweet Valeri

Page 76, Canned Coffee

Canned coffee made an appearance in the United States in cans and bottles under the Starbucks label and other brand names. In Japan canned coffee has been around for decades and can be found hot or cold in nearly any vending machine.

Page 81, Dual Comedy Act (*Manzai*)

Manzai is a traditional two-man comedy act that is very much akin to the tradition of Abbott and Costello and the Smothers Brothers, where one comedian plays a character of very low intelligence (the *boké*) and the other gets mad out of frustration with the nonsensical answers (the *tsukkomi*). It usually ends up in a certain amount of Three Stooges–style slapping.

Page 88, *Gomoku* rice

Boiled rice mixed with vegetables, fish, and other ingredients.

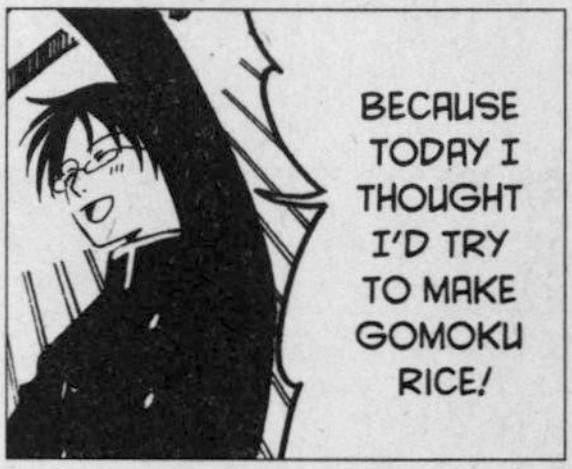
BECAUSE TODAY I THOUGHT I'D TRY TO MAKE GOMOKU RICE!

Page 102, Colds and Fevers

In the West, we usually separate the symptoms of colds and fevers, but the raised body temperature of a fever has been proven to limit the spread of viruses and other cold-causing infections. To Dômeki, the lack of fever indicates a lack of a normal viral infection.

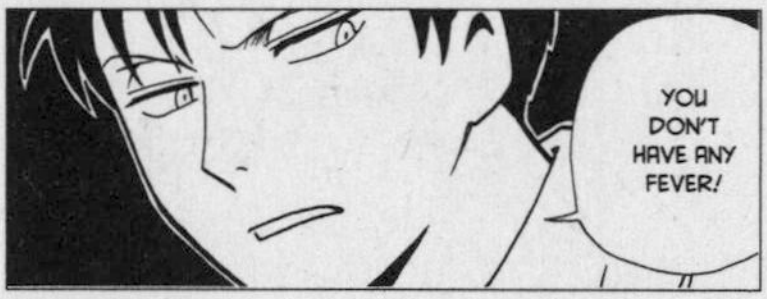
YOU DON'T HAVE ANY FEVER!

Page 160, *Inari* Sushi

Since the Shinto *kami* (god or goddess) Inari uses foxes as messengers, one can only surmise that foxes like this kind of sushi. It consists of tofu pouches stuffed with specially seasoned rice, vegetables, and more tofu.

Page 160, *Sanshoku Onigiri* ("Three-color rice balls")

Basically they are like normal rice balls, but the inside is stuffed with three different flavors, usually the flavors of fish flakes, pickles, and a pickled plum (*umeboshi*).

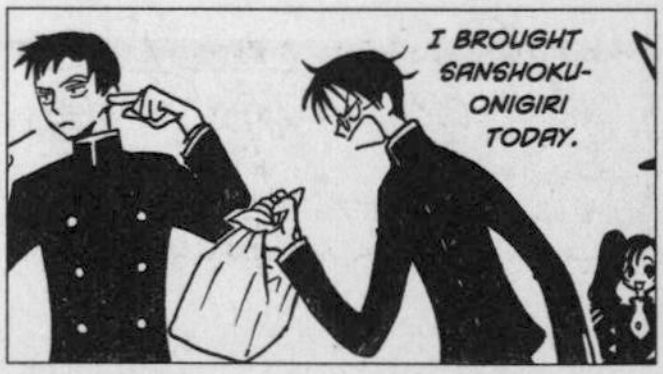
I BROUGHT SANSHOKU-ONIGIRI TODAY.

Page 168, *Shiritori*

A popular Japanese word game where you must take the last letter (syllable) of the word spoken by your opponent, and begin your word with that same letter (syllable). Note: Because the rules of the game demand that you take the last syllable, even of long vowels, for the purpose of the game we spelled our long vowels not as "ô" and "û" like we usually do, but this time as "o" and "u" respectively.

HURRY, U!
"UMI"! ("THE SEA.")
"MIDORI"! NEXT, "RI"! ("GREEN.")
"RINGO"! ("APPLE.")
"GOMA"! ("WOOD OFFERING.")
"MARI"! ("A BALL.")

洋燈堂

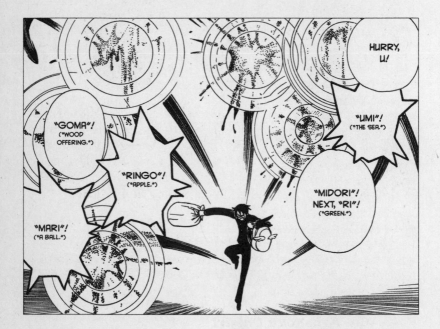

Page 170, The sign

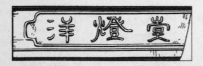

It says "Yôtô-dô," which would probably translate as The Lamp House.

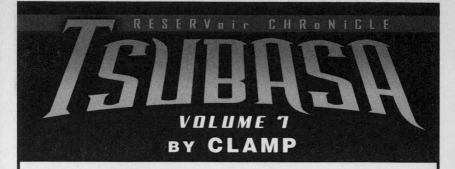

Sugar Sugar Rune

BY MOYOCO ANNO **VOLUME 1**

QUEEN OF HEARTS

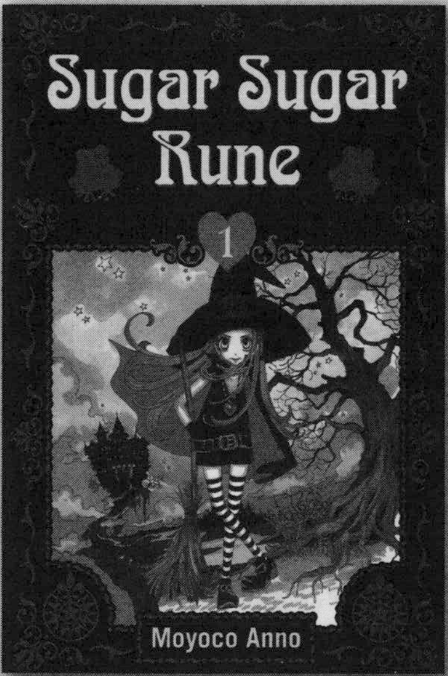
Sugar Sugar Rune
1
Moyoco Anno

Little witch-girls Chocolat and Vanilla are best friends, but only one of them can be Queen of the Magic World. To determine who deserves the title, they must go to the Human World and enter a strange competition. Whoever attracts the most human boys wins!

Here's how it works: When a boy falls for a witch-girl, she utters a few mystic words and the boy's heart will be hers in jewel-like form. It may sound simple, but winning hearts is tricky business. While Chocolat had no problem enticing witch-boys with her forthright personality, human boys seem to be drawn to shy and modest girls like Vanilla. And to make matters worse, Chocolat is finding herself increasingly drawn to the cool and mysterious Pierre—who feels nothing for her! The girls had planned to be best friends forever, but both of them want to be Queen. Will their rivalry ruin their friendship?

Ages: 10+

Includes special extras after the story!

VOLUME 1: On sale September 27, 2005

DEL REY

For more information and to sign up for Del Rey's manga e-newsletter, visit www.delreymanga.com

GUNDAM SEED

ART BY MASATSUGU IWASE
ORIGINAL STORY BY HAJIME YATATE
AND YOSHIYUKI TOMINO

In the world of the Cosmic Era, a war is under way between the genetically enhanced humans known as Coordinators and those who remain unmodified, called Naturals. The Natural-dominated Earth Alliance, struggling to catch up with the Coordinators' superior technology, has secretly developed its own Gundam mobile suits at a neutral space colony. But through a twist of fate, a young Coordinator named Kira Yamato becomes the pilot of the Alliance's prototype Strike Gundam, and finds himself forced to fight his own people in order to protect his friends. Featuring all the best elements of the legendary Gundam saga, this thrilling series reimagines the gripping story of men, women, and magnificent fighting machines in epic conflict.

AS SEEN ON TV!

Art by
MASATSUGU IWASE
Story by
HAJIME YATATE and
YOSHIYUKI TOMINO

Ages: 13 +

Special extras in each volume! Read them all!

TOMARE!

[STOP!]

You're going the wrong way!

Manga is a completely different type of reading experience.

To start at the *beginning*, go to the *end*!

That's right! Authentic manga is read the traditional Japanese way—from right to left. Exactly the *opposite* of how American books are read. It's easy to follow: Just go to the other end of the book, and read each page—and each panel—from right side to left side, starting at the top right. Now you're experiencing manga as it was meant to be!